Performance Management

Praise for this book

'This is a book for bank/finance professionals written by a professional who clearly understands the discipline of HR/performance management and the environment of banking and finance. The book is pragmatic, focused, comprehensive and eminently readable ... a "must read" for leaders in this field.'
Robert M. Fulmer, PhD, Vice-Chair, World Business Academy and co-author of The Leadership Advantage: How the Best Companies Are Developing Their Talent to Pave the Way for Future Success

'*Performance Management* is a straightforward and engaging book that equips HR professionals with the practical advice and systemic insight to make performance management a strategic tool for achieving the business goals of the financial institution, and the human mission of giving women and men access to the financial services they need to move out of poverty.'
Judy Rosenblum, Past President and Advisor to Duke Corporate Education

'This handbook for banks and microfinance institutions provides tools to turn over mountains or oceans of hardships facing any leader dealing with financial services in difficult-to-reach markets, to discover a goldmine of success on the other side.'
Bold Magvan, Chief Executive Officer, TenGer Financial Group LLC

Performance Management

A handbook for small business banks and microfinance institutions

Prinny Anderson

PRACTICAL ACTION
Publishing

Practical Action Publishing Ltd
The Schumacher Centre
Bourton on Dunsmore, Rugby,
Warwickshire CV23 9QZ, UK
www.practicalactionpublishing.org

ISBN 978 1 85339 792 9 Hardback
ISBN 978 1 85339 793 6 Paperback
ISBN 978 1 78044 792 6 Library Ebook
ISBN 978 1 78044 793 3 Ebook

A catalogue record for this book is available from the British Library.

Anderson, Prinny (2013) *Performance Management: A Handbook for Small Business Banks and Microfinance Institutions*, Chicago, IL: CapitalPlus Exchange, and Rugby, UK: Practical Action Publishing.

Since 1974, Practical Action Publishing has published and disseminated books and information in support of international development work throughout the world. Practical Action Publishing is a trading name of Practical Action Publishing Ltd (Company Reg. No. 1159018), the wholly owned publishing company of Practical Action. Practical Action Publishing trades only in support of its parent charity objectives and any profits are covenanted back to Practical Action (Charity Reg. No. 247257, Group VAT Registration No. 880 9924 76).

Typeset by SJI Services
Printed in the United Kingdom

Contents

Acknowledgements

Performance Management grew out of the recognition by Small Business Banking Network (SBBN) of the need among the organizations that it serves for practical reference materials, guides, tools, and templates, and its commitment to draw on its members' experiences to address those needs.

Virginia (Prinny) Anderson is the author of this Handbook. Urmi Sengupta initiated the work and provided ongoing encouragement and support. Lynn Pikholz added insights and ideas from her wide experience.

Kim Pityn and Scott Ruddick of MEDA (Mennonite Economic Development Associates) generously contributed to chapters, free access to MEDA's handbook and training materials, ideas, review comments, and moral support.

Colleagues around the world, from FINA Bank, Southern Credit, Planters Bank, SKS, Reliance, and XacBank, read chapters, gave comments, and offered enthusiastic feedback.

MicroSave India helped collect inputs and experiences from a range of Indian institutions that informed many of the examples here, and we appreciate all the contributions from MicroSave colleagues and clients. Colleagues of the primary writer, Prinny Anderson, have offered ideas, samples, and suggestions over the years before the Handbook was started. Thanks go out to Jay Colker, Amy Harris, Heather Jones, Gail Kelley, Tamara Oros and Lea Wharton.

The work of many authors in the field of performance management, organization development, training, management, and leadership has contributed to the ideas, processes, and tools given in the Handbook. Specific acknowledgement is given below to those whose input can be discerned clearly, and general thanks are owed the others.

- John Whitmore
- The Center for Creative Leadership
- Morgan McCall
- John Kotter
- Personnel Decisions International

The SBBN Team
Small Business Banking Network
CapitalPlus Exchange

Prinny Anderson
SBBN Partner
Consultant/Coach
Design for Learning & Change

About the author

Prinny Anderson is a globally recognized human capital educator, coach, author, and consultant and the principal of Design for Learning & Change in Durham, North Carolina, USA. Prinny is the lead human capital professional for the Small Business Banking Network (SBBN), a CapitalPlus Exchange initiative, which serves financial institutions committed to scaling financial services to underserved entrepreneurs in developing and emerging economies. She has an MBA with a specialization in Organizational Behaviour/Organizational Development from the London Business School, University of London.

The author integrates experience in designing learning programmes, and training and coaching executives and managers, with consulting to managers and HR practitioners and applying systemic principles to business problems and human capital challenges. Her clients come from the public and private sectors, from a variety of industries, and from developing and emerging economies around the globe. Over the past six years, Prinny has focused her work on strengthening human capital systems in microfinance and small business banking institutions, mostly in Africa and Asia, partnering primarily with SBBN.

Introduction

What inspired this Handbook

Performance and the management of people to achieve desired business targets are issues relevant to many types of business, including financial institutions, the primary audience for this Handbook.

Beyond the practicalities, though, all institutions and most endeavours are energized and guided by a larger purpose, be it social responsibility or a 'green' agenda. The larger purposes that inspired the Handbook start with a passion for seeing people rise out of poverty through their own efforts, supported by access to financial institutions with a commitment to offering them the products and services appropriate to their circumstances.

In order for the financial institutions that serve people with limited access to financial services to thrive and to continue achieving their visions and fulfilling their missions, the managers of those banks need to become as effective as they possibly can at managing their people and the performance of those people. The Handbook is intended to help those managers, and thereby help their institutions to be successful.

For managers to be successful at managing people and performance, the human resource (HR) departments that support them also need to become as effective as possible. The Handbook is dedicated to that purpose too.

In short, this Handbook exists to help managers and HR teams be as effective as they can be at managing people and performance so that their banks achieve the vision and mission of giving women and men access to the financial services they need to move out of poverty and into greater prosperity, health, education, and empowerment in their communities.

Overview

As stated, organizations exist to fulfil their social and commercial missions and to satisfy their investors. What makes these outcomes possible are the services and products created and delivered by the employees and the leaders of the organizations. In the process of delivering services and products, the organization makes money – revenue – which satisfies the investors and pays the people and the expenses of doing business, thus sustaining the business.

To sustain the business, its leaders and managers must focus on 'performance'. At the most general level, performance refers to making a profit. But making a profit is complex, so 'performance' covers a number of areas and differs depending on the responsibilities of a given business unit. For example, 'performance' means the following:

http://dx.doi.org/10.3362/9781780447926.001

- for tellers, how efficiently they can handle transactions, how many customers they can serve during business hours, and how accurately they work;
- for customer service associates, how many deposit accounts they open, the amount of assets they take into the bank, and the amount of fees from transmittals and other services they process;
- for credit or loan officers, the number of high-quality loans and the associated interest payments, the on-time loan repayment rate, and the level of repeat lending with reliable borrowers.

What these examples show is that it is the people who provide customers with services and products who deliver the most important types of 'performance'.

'Managing performance' means managing these people and the way they work so that they handle as many transactions as they can, open as many deposit accounts as they can, and process as many high-quality loans and repayments as they can. Managing performance also means doing what is necessary to manage people so that they maintain quality, efficiency, productivity, cost-effectiveness, and ethical business practices. Managing performance is the primary responsibility of managers in every organization; in other words, managers exist to manage the people who 'perform' by serving customers.

To emphasize the fact that people are central to the performance of an organization, they are also referred to as 'human capital' or 'human assets', since some business cultures are more likely to treat anything called 'capital' or 'assets' as valuable. Another way of emphasizing the importance of people to business is conveyed by the term 'talent', which highlights the fact that people's efforts and competencies are what make the business run.

Institutions establish performance management systems to support the management of performance in an effective, consistent, and organized way. These systems may also be referred to as 'human capital management systems', 'human resources management systems', or 'talent management systems'. They exist to make it possible to manage performance in ways that work well for the employees, the managers, and the business as a whole.

Since managers have the primary responsibility for managing people and their performance, it stands to reason that managers are the primary users of the performance management system. Stated very simply, the HR department exists to structure and administer the performance management system on behalf of and in support of managers' performance management needs.

Of course, all employees are involved in and make use of the performance management system; every effort should be made to acknowledge their ownership of it and to build their buy-in.

To give a more complete description, HR's role in performance management consists of the following duties:

- advising senior leaders about the performance management implications of strategic decisions and operational plans;

- designing and adapting the performance management system not only to help managers manage performance in general but also to support the organization's strategic initiatives;
- advising and counselling managers about how to manage performance and how to carry out various performance management responsibilities;
- advising, counselling, and advocating for employees in their relationships with their managers and with the institution;
- helping employees understand their obligations and responsibilities to the organization as well as the rewards, benefits, and other services they receive from it;
- monitoring the implementation of the performance management system to make sure it is used appropriately and managers comply with the requirements of the system;
- collecting, analysing, and reporting data about people and performance so that managers can combine it with business results data to understand the factors that produce the results and the adjustments needed for greater success;
- collecting, analysing, and reporting data about people and performance so that managers and HR professionals can find out more about what employees bring to the business, what matters to them, why they behave as they do, and how to manage them more effectively.

The performance management system includes the following:

- getting the right people in the right positions so they can do the work effectively: job descriptions; recruiting; interviewing, selecting, hiring
- getting new employees off to a good start: on-boarding, initial training; mentors, peer coaches; setting expectations, initial goals; on-the-job training, coaching
- sustaining performance: ongoing feedback, coaching; motivations, rewards, incentives; training, development; job enrichment, employee satisfaction initiatives
- evaluating performance: performance reviews; development planning
- building on performance: career paths, planning, development; advancement, promotions; redeployment
- managing performance problems: performance improvement programmes; disciplinary actions; terminations (voluntary, involuntary)
- retaining the best-performing people: high-potential programmes; succession planning; compensation benchmarking; special incentive schemes.

Executives or senior managers – the leaders of the organization as a whole – have a limited number of primary responsibilities:

- set the direction – vision, mission, strategy;
- structure the organization for sustainability and strategic success;
- create and sustain the internal community – culture, values, cohesiveness;

- create and sustain connections to external communities – the board, investors, regulators, government, partners, competitors, and many others;
- hold direct reports accountable for implementing strategy, managing operations, and achieving targeted results;
- ensuring the care and development of people.

In managing their own direct reports, executives use all the components of the performance management system.

As leaders, they champion the performance management system and its individual components, encouraging staff to use them, and occasionally penalizing staff who do not. They hold HR accountable for providing reports on the effectiveness of the system, and they hold managers accountable for implementing it.

Leaders also think about performance management from the strategic, big-picture, longer-term point of view. For example:

- the hiring and payroll implications of expansion;
- the hiring and training demands associated with new products;
- succession planning, whether for contingencies or for across-the-board manager deployment;
- leadership development for the near and more distant future through high-potential programmes and mentoring;
- talent retention, especially in competitive markets or economic downturns.

Finally, leaders have to think about how performance management activities serve to support the organization's mission, vision, values, and culture.

Essentially, managers have two main responsibilities: to manage the people who report to them; and to achieve their targeted results through the work of those people. They use the performance management system to help themselves manage the performance of their direct reports. They need a system that is relevant to their operations and their people, whose components make sense from a business point of view, and that does not make excessive or arbitrary demands.

Managers need training, advice, and counsel from HR professionals and their own managers as they manage people's performance. The system cannot exist without those support services for managers.

Performance management is only a part – albeit a significant part – of the work of the HR department. The view of the responsibilities of HR taken in this Handbook is outlined below:

- performance management – design, develop, coordinate, administer, monitor, track, collect data, analyse, report, advise, counsel;
- organizational design and development – working closely with senior leaders;

- community, culture, and values – working with and supporting leadership and managers;
- staff welfare or employee satisfaction, including wellness, stress management, and work/life balance;
- compliance with laws and regulations relating to employment, compensation, terminations, documentation, and so forth;
- compensation and benefits administration;
- administration and monitoring of absences, leave, and so forth;
- maintaining files and records relating to employee information, performance management, and payroll.

These responsibilities are interconnected, are not always easy to distinguish from each other, and may be equally well configured in other ways.

What the Handbook is

The Handbook is a guide and reference to the components of the performance management system and its links to strategy and operations. Its purpose is to provide information and direction for everyone involved in managing people's performance. The topics, the point of view, and the level of information are based on experience in the field with microfinance and small and medium enterprise (SME) institutions in developing economies, on the part of practitioners, consultants, and educators. It is intended for ready, practical application, with the understanding that policies, processes, and tools need to be shaped for the circumstance of each user and organization.

Lengthy and detailed books have been written about each aspect and component of performance management, based on comprehensive and thoughtful research and experience. There are different schools of thought and methodologies in many areas, described in journal articles as well as in professional texts.

For the sake of simplicity and practicality, the Handbook does not attempt to summarize that research or provide a range of variations on methodology. Users of the Handbook are strongly encouraged to make use of as much of the body of work relating to performance management as they can, building on, refining, and even moving beyond what they find here.

How to make use of the Handbook

The Handbook is organized into chapters and sections focusing on the components of the system. Some users may go through the Handbook from beginning to end, using it as a guide or checklist for setting up or upgrading their organization's performance management system. Other users will find the section they need and read only that, taking away whatever ideas, guidance, or tools address their needs and questions.

Many of the chapters are, as described, focused on specific components of the performance management system, with practical guidelines and tools. There are a few chapters with a more overarching or strategic perspective. For example, Chapter 1 is a resource for thinking strategically about human resources and performance management. Chapter 10, on promoting diversity and advancing women in the workplace, provides concepts, guidelines, and processes for addressing two specific strategic issues that touch on every performance management system.

Whom the Handbook is written for

The Handbook is written for people with various interests in, and needs to work with, the performance management system.

Leaders and senior managers need to ensure that a comprehensive and effective performance management system is set up and developed over time. The Handbook describes what goes into the system and designates components and features of the system that can be developed somewhat later in the institution's existence.

Managers at all levels manage people's performance and implement the activities of the performance management system. They may use the Handbook to supplement the briefings and advice from their HR colleagues to help them with their performance management responsibilities.

HR professionals design, maintain, modify, and develop the performance management system over time. For them, the Handbook can be a guide, a checklist, and a reference, which they will add to and adapt in response to their organization's needs.

Trainers who need to include some aspect of performance management in induction sessions or management development programmes can use the Handbook as a source of ideas, tools, and examples.

What's in the Handbook

The Handbook presents a point of view for each component, including its context and the involvement of various parts of the organization in implementing performance management. It describes processes and procedures, gives guidelines, offers tips and experiences from practitioners in the field, and contains tools, templates, samples, and examples. In some cases, the Handbook offers alternatives or suggests the kind of policy or procedure that is needed, leaving practitioners in the field to supply the specifics relevant to their organizational, legal, and regulatory environment.

Most chapters are presented in sections that cover a discrete aspect of the system. The features of the chapters include the following:

- introduction giving significance, impact, benefits, and context;

- table of contributions by business managers and HR professionals to one or more key people-management responsibilities;
- connections to other components of the people management system, indicating the interlocking nature of the system.

Each section is likely to contain the following:

- definitions of terms and concepts;
- table of responsibilities of managers and HR professionals;
- roles and responsibilities of stakeholders;
- detailed information for managers and HR professionals;
- overviews for direct reports, leadership, and board members;
- involving the whole organization, covering the structural, cultural, or general organizational stake in an aspect of performance management;
- policies, which touches on the types of policies needed;
- when and how to implement the performance management activity;
- different ways to use that performance management activity, or different kinds of activity to suit different situations;
- developmental or evolutionary stages of the performance management component;
- 'must dos' and basics as well as refinements, advanced stages, and comprehensive versions;
- examples and non-examples;
- benefits;
- risks, pitfalls, and cautions;
- guidelines and tips;
- documentation, including the need for and kinds of documentation;
- research information and experiences from practitioners in the field;
- problems and troubleshooting;
- forms, templates, and samples to be adapted for use in the processes and procedures described in the section.

In addition to the chapters covering each component of the performance management system, the Handbook has chapters with broader perspectives:

- Chapter 1 takes a look at performance management from a strategic point of view.
- Chapter 2 considers the whole performance management system from an operational point of view.
- Chapter 10 addresses two issues of social responsibility that affect all aspects of the performance management system at the operational and strategic levels – the advancement of women into and upward in the workforce, and the promotion of greater diversity within the employee group.
- Chapter 11 offers approaches to determining how well the performance management system is working.

- Chapter 12 returns to the strategic perspective by addressing the need for HR leadership competencies in order to sustain the strength of the performance management system.

What is not in the Handbook

There are some technical and specialized areas of human resource management that are not discussed in detail in the Handbook, such as:

- compensation, salaries, and benefits;
- employment-related taxes and insurance;
- labour relations;
- employment law.

Nonetheless, the general principles relating to equity, diversity, and the advancement of women in the workplace discussed in later chapters must be applied fully to these areas too.

The Handbook is intended for managers and HR professionals around the world. The technical, specialized topics tend to be linked directly to laws and practices of individual countries, and they may vary widely from one country to the next.

We encourage managers and HR professionals to be well informed and up to date with their country's employment-related laws and practices, and to abide by those laws and practices to the fullest extent.

CHAPTER 1

A strategic perspective on performance management

The challenge for every business manager and human resources (HR) professional on every working day is to balance a thoughtful strategic perspective with excellent operational execution. This Handbook consists primarily of operational guidelines, processes, tips, examples, and templates. However, it would be remiss to focus only on the operational level of performance management. For that reason, the opening chapter introduces the Handbook with a brief consideration of the strategic level of performance management.

Who 'does' performance management?

The performance management system exists to help the business achieve its strategic goals – serving customers efficiently, selling reliable, innovative products, and sustaining itself to fulfil its mission. The performance management system's interconnected tools and processes are the ways in which managers manage and improve the performance of people in the organization.

'Managing performance' means defining the work, preparing people to perform, directing, encouraging, and guiding them, and then rewarding them for producing the desired results. The people primarily responsible for managing performance are managers – managers in branches and in other customer-facing locations, and managers of functional groups. For the most part, managers implement the performance management system every day. The role of the HR function is limited to deploying state-of-the-art performance management systems to meet the needs of their colleague managers, along with designing processes and tools that support effective management of people doing the work. Just as the IT group does for technology, HR exists to set up the people management tools, keep them operating, and inform everyone about how to use them well.

Sometimes the managers within an institution need to be reminded about how the performance management system is contributing to their ability to do the work and achieve results. Here's how the system supports business activities:

Where do those talented new people on our teams come from?

- Recruiting brings them in.
- Interviewers recognize their talents.
- They make internal career transitions from one department to another or are promoted up a level.

http://dx.doi.org/10.3362/9781780447926.002

How did all those branches get up and running?

- Managers were promoted and redeployed to new locations.
- Training prepared the new people to serve customers and sell the products.
- The compensation system adjusted to the special requirements of each location.

What caused us to exceed our sales targets?

- Managers set challenging targets and coached their team members on how to achieve them.
- Regular informal feedback and twice-yearly performance reviews kept everyone on track with goals and how to achieve them.
- Incentives, bonuses, and managers' motivational activities provided ongoing positive reinforcement.
- Reassignments and disciplinary activities caught poor performers promptly and kept them from degrading morale.

Each manager needs to see the benefit to him or herself of using the tools and processes of performance management. Senior managers can use a combination of success stories and 'worst cases' to make the case.

For example, job descriptions can seem tedious and time-consuming to prepare, but the payoff comes when a new employee needs to start work while the manager is on sick leave. The manager can count on the basics of the job to be outlined as intended. Or, in a different situation, a manager can discover that, without a complete job description, it can take many months to terminate an employee who always seems to do less than expected but constantly gives the excuse that 'no one told me' when he or she is confronted.

What the performance management system includes

The performance management system is a combination of tools and processes supported by the professional experience and advice of seasoned managers and HR professionals. The components of the system include:

- job descriptions and performance objectives;
- recruiting and interviewing;
- performance reviews and development planning;
- induction and on-boarding;
- high-potential development and succession planning;
- mentoring;
- training and development;
- on-the-job feedback and coaching;
- compensation, incentives, rewards, and motivation;
- promotions, advancement, and redeployment;
- career paths and career planning;
- disciplinary actions and terminations.

When businesses focus on issues such as finding enough appropriate talent, improving retention or decreasing turnover, and improving results or quality, they are making use of several of the performance management system components to address business problems or achieve strategic goals.

The performance management system also generates data, which can be used to detect and address performance problems. For example, increasing rates of turnover can highlight problems with compensation or incentives. Excessive use of incentives or inappropriate promotions can point to favouritism by a manager. An unusual number of requests for transfers or voluntary terminations may indicate an ineffective boss.

Supporting the business mission and culture

The performance management system needs to be set up so that it is aligned with the mission and the culture of the business. The policies, the design of the processes, and the way they are communicated all need to fit the nature of the organization. Maintaining this alignment is key to integrating performance management into everyday business activities and reinforcing the general understanding that performance management is part of every manager's job.

For example, the organization's mission may emphasize bringing high-quality services to underserved communities. In that case, all the processes should be designed and implemented at a high level of quality, and the associated documents should be professional and look clean.

In a different organization, the mission might focus on efficiency and cost management to maximize the funds available for community purposes. In that business, it will be appropriate for the HR staff and the managers to conduct their performance management activities in efficient and cost-effective ways, such as limiting the amount of paper used and making sure to schedule multiple screening interviews on a single day.

Similarly, the performance management system needs to match and express the culture. If the culture is friendly and family-style, then all contacts with recruits and employees should be done in a friendly, more familiar way. Where the culture values teamwork, the performance management system needs to provide team training, team performance scores, and team rewards.

Supporting key business activities

The performance management system also needs to be set up in a way that is aligned with key business activities. Some of the ways to achieve alignment are listed below:

- The performance review cycle needs to be scheduled so that it does not conflict with quarterly closings and the annual audit.
- Training programmes need to be aligned with quarterly and annual deadlines.

- Recruiting, hiring, and induction for entry-level positions may need to be continuous, but, for other positions, the activities may need to correspond to the schedules of training centres and universities.
- Succession planning and retention analyses need to be conducted in conjunction with board meeting dates.

Each organization will have its own requirements. The key point is for business managers and HR professionals to collaborate to maintain alignment.

Creating an HR strategy

A strategy is a statement of how the HR department thinks about its responsibilities, what the general approach to those responsibilities is, and what the one- to three-year goals are. One reason for having a departmental strategy is to help link the departmental action plans to the business mission and strategy, the culture, and the organizational values. Another reason is that a strategy supports alignment by articulating both the ends and the means – the goals and the ways in which they will be achieved.

With a strategy as a reference point for both what to do and how to do it, managers and staff are able to make independent decisions that are likely to be consistent with the intent of the department even if they encounter situations in which there is no existing policy statement, procedure manual, or operating goal.

The HR strategy, also called the human capital or talent management strategy, outlines the approaches the HR department takes to all aspects of human resources. For example, different approaches to recruiting will be suitable for different situations:

- In an environment with a smaller business community and job market, the HR strategy for recruiting might emphasize pre-employment training and internships as ways to start filling the recruitment pipeline.
- For an organization in a more complex and established business environment, the HR strategy might focus on events at academic institutions and online postings to draw in new talent.

The strategy outlines important HR initiatives and the timeframes for achieving them. The details of how the initiatives will be carried out are usually contained in a separate operational plan.

Below are two examples of strategic goals for an HR department:

- *Training and development.* To establish an internal training curriculum, starting with a 'Basics of Business' course to be launched by mid-year, and a series of organizational skills modules, such as presentation skills and business writing, to be launched one each quarter.
- *Succession planning.* To formalize and expand the succession planning process to include executive team members, key technical experts, and

managers of large branches, with a pilot initiative to be held during Q3 and the full process to be ready for launch by the middle of Q4.

Specific strategies for specific performance management components

Over time, the HR department will formulate strategies for several major components of the performance management system. Each of these strategies outlines the major approaches to the activities of that component. The recruitment strategy describes key aspects of how the organization approaches recruiting. The training strategy outlines important points on how the organization goes about providing training to its employees.

These strategy documents may contain some elements of vision or mission, a brief summary of the organization's philosophy about the particular domain, the overall approaches, and statements of specific goals and initiatives for the upcoming one to three years.

For example, a compensation, rewards, and benefits strategy might include the following points, some of which state the approach and some of which describe a specific goal:

- *Our philosophy or approach to compensation.* To support our organizational mission of extending financial services to every corner of our nation, we intend to use our compensation, rewards, and benefits programmes to encourage and reinforce innovation, flexibility, and customer focus within the parameters of ethical management of funds and regulatory requirements.
- *Positioning our compensation plan.* Our compensation plan aims to remain at the mid-range for microfinance institutions (MFIs), and we intend to enhance it through a number of non-financial programmes.
- *Our view of benefits.* Our benefits programmes are intended to allow our employees to provide reasonably for the current and future care of their families, through low-cost education and housing loans, savings schemes, and on-site childcare services.
- *A specific goal.* In acknowledgement of the increasing complexity of our business, we intend to review and re-benchmark salaries for all levels of management during this fiscal year.
- *A specific goal for mid-year.* By mid-year, we will propose a graduated commission scheme that reflects the increasing sales competence of our more experienced loan officers and provides a stable starting point for new officers.

The components of the performance management system that are most likely to have strategies are:

- recruitment – what talent we seek and how we reach them;
- compensation – principles and approaches to paying, incentivizing, and providing benefits for employees;

- training and development – how we approach training and how we think about development;
- talent management – how we develop careers, advance and promote, nurture high-potential staff, and develop succession plans;
- employee relations – how we handle employee concerns and complaints and provide employee assistance or welfare services.

In addition, an institution should consider a retention strategy, which describes all the organizational and management actions that will go into promoting retention, as well as what the retention targets are by position and possibly by region. The retention strategy also describes how the business will measure its success in achieving its retention goals.

Policies, procedures, and action plans

Policy statements are linked to strategy, but they emphasize 'the rules' – what is required and what is prohibited. For example, in the area of hiring, there may be a policy requiring equal consideration for all job applicants and another one prohibiting the hiring of spouses of employees for positions reporting to the other spouse. Policies may reflect organizational culture and values, they may be based on financial or operational requirements, or they may grow out of laws and regulations.

Procedures are typically contained in manuals and outline what the steps are for carrying out each aspect of the performance management system. There are procedures for conducting performance reviews, for creating development plans, for documenting disciplinary problems, and so on.

In addition to routine procedures that are followed daily, weekly, and monthly, the HR department will have a set of *action plans* for its strategic initiatives. These plans lay out roles, responsibilities, tasks, steps, time requirements, resource needs, and deadlines for any non-routine activities that are specified in the strategies mentioned above. For example, if the compensation strategy includes a goal to re-benchmark managers' salaries and benefits, there will be an action plan to outline how that strategy will be carried out.

Aligning HR strategy with the business strategy

The HR strategy is closely linked to the overall business strategy, showing how the performance management system and other HR activities will support the business in achieving its goals. For example, consider the organization with a growth strategy that includes both regional expansion and partnering with other businesses to provide additional products. Most components of the performance management system will need attention if the business is to succeed with its expansion:

- Recruiting will need to be intensified and made as efficient as possible, and the strategy will outline numbers of candidates and turnaround time from first posting to hiring.
- Induction or on-boarding will need to happen more often than it does during steady-state times, and the strategy will state how often. It may also indicate that additional managers will need to be involved in recruitment, and the induction programme may need to be redesigned in order for it to be delivered in multiple or distant locations.
- Job descriptions will need to be reviewed, and the strategy will indicate which areas need attention.
- More people will be stepping into managerial positions, and the HR strategy will state how they will be recruited and prepared, whether through internal promotions, external hiring, or a combination.
- Changes to product training will be required, and the strategy will state when those changes are likely to be ready and which training sessions they will apply to.
- The incentive system may need alteration to cover sales of the new products, and the strategy will state how those changes will be rolled out.

Conclusion

As you read through sections of the Handbook, keep in mind the strategic level to help you establish or refine the operations of your performance management system. Make sure that the system is designed around the needs of the managers who will implement it and that it reflects the strategy, culture, mission, values, and key activities of the business.

CHAPTER 2

Operational overview of performance management

While business managers and human resources professionals need to think strategically about the people side of the organization on a regular basis, most of their time and attention is on daily tasks and decisions – the day-to-day operations.

In a high-performing organization, business managers and HR professionals work closely together on all the issues of managing people. Their interconnected responsibilities make up the performance management system.

People management responsibilities

For an organization to function, the following people management responsibilities must be addressed, and business managers and HR professionals have roles to play in all of them:

- defining the work to be done;
- choosing people to do the work;
- organizing what the people do;
- ensuring people learn how to do the work;
- making sure people do the work;
- making sure people get better at doing the work;
- finding ways for people to do more work – enlarging or enriching jobs;
- creating ways for people to do different types of work and take more responsibility;
- preparing people for leadership;
- measuring the results of work – quantity, quality, efficiency, timeliness;
- maintaining contractual agreements with people;
- maintaining workplace conditions that support people's safety, security, satisfaction, and productivity.

In many of these areas of responsibility, business managers define substance, needs, or requirements; make final decisions; manage and communicate with employees; review or collaborate on proposing processes, procedures, and programmes; contribute content or expertise; and keep supporting records.

The contribution of HR professionals is to:

- propose processes, procedures, and programmes;
- formalize previously ad hoc processes and procedures;
- provide forms or templates;
- review managers' requirements;

http://dx.doi.org/10.3362/9781780447926.003

- monitor compliance with regulatory requirements;
- organize and schedule processes and events;
- interact and communicate with employees;
- create and maintain documentation;
- train, coach, advise, and counsel;
- monitor, record, analyse, and report on people-related data;
- administer 'back-office' HR tasks.

The interconnected responsibilities of HR professionals and managers can be illustrated in the process of filling an open position. When a business manager needs to fill an open position, he or she defines the responsibilities of the position and the competencies needed by the jobholder, documenting the requirements in a form provided by HR. The manager also establishes performance expectations.

After the HR professionals have reviewed the manager's requirements, they go through the recruiting process. Once they have screened the recruits and found several likely candidates, the manager interviews them and makes the final decision about which one to hire. He or she either documents the hiring decision or works with an HR professional to make sure it is documented and to ensure that the job offer, whether by mail or in person, is consistent with the manager's assessment of the new hire. The HR department assembles the job offer pack and the employment contract and makes sure the employment file is opened, payroll is notified, and benefits are initiated for the new employee. HR also updates its data-tracking systems for data such as employee demographics, hiring/firing, and salary levels.

Charting responsibilities

Table 2.1 illustrates the major areas of people-related responsibility typical for a business and shows how business managers and HR professionals contribute to each one. Each party plays a significant role in managing people, and their collaboration is essential. The following chapters provide detailed information about designing and implementing many of these areas of responsibility, with information and tools for managers and HR professionals.

You can use Table 2.1 to make an informal assessment of the alignment of people management responsibilities in your organization:

- Are managers aware of all their people management responsibilities?
- Do they have the capabilities (skills, knowledge, and attitudes) to carry out those responsibilities?
- Does the HR department fully understand managers' needs as they relate to people management?
- Is the HR department positioned – with staff, resources, and capabilities – to be a partner with managers in managing people?
- Are the alignment and partnership between managers and HR professionals effective and satisfactory to both parties? Are they working for employees?

Table 2.1: Checklist – alignment of people management responsibilities

Business manager – typical contributions	*People management – major responsibilities*	*HR professional – typical contributions*
Job specifications	Define the work	Forms and templates Review of job specifications
Selection criteria for jobholders Interview and file reviews Suggest sources of candidates Candidate evaluation and selection Salary level and job offer details	Match the right people to the work	Finalized job description and selection criteria File reviews Recruitment, interviewing, candidate evaluation, and hiring Documentation, files, payroll, benefits, and other 'back-office' procedures
Structures Expectations for team and individuals Documentation – procedures and rules	Organize the work	Forms and templates Counsel, advise, and provide training to managers
Job manual On-boarding Teaching, coaching, and feedback Training needs, training content, and training delivery	Ensure employees learn to do the work	Job manual On-boarding Counsel, advise, and provide training to managers Training curriculum and registration
Performance expectations, standards, goals, and directions Monitoring, feedback, and standards enforcement	Make sure people do the work	Forms and templates Advice
Motivation, coaching, mentoring, and feedback Design of incentive schemes and performance review processes Performance reviews and performance records	Make sure people get better at doing the work	Advice and counsel Incentive scheme tracking Performance review process design, manuals, calendar, monitoring completion, appeals process, and data in files
Job redesigns, enrichment, and enlargement Development options, planning, implementation, and monitoring High-potential employee identification, coaching, and training	Find ways for people to do more work – redesign, enrich, and enlarge	Job redesign Development options, planning process, forms, and templates Tracking development needs and activities High-potential identification process, decisions, and programmes
Development planning and implementation Performance reviews, stretch goals, and high-potential programmes	Find ways for people to do different types of work and take more responsibility	Development planning, performance reviews, and high-potential programmes Leadership training curriculum, resources, enrolments, and delivery

Business manager – typical responsibilities	*People management activities*	*HR professional – typical responsibilities*
Leadership training curriculum and training sessions Promotion criteria, readiness evaluation, and communication with employees Organizational succession planning priorities, planning process, preparing own successor, and communication with employees	Prepare people for leadership	Promotion criteria, processes, review scheduling, readiness tracking, follow-up, and job change and promotion 'back-office' activities Succession planning process, planning documents, and maintaining records
Performance review and documentation Rewards and penalties, and documentation Termination case, decisions, documentation, and communication	Measure people's results	Performance review process Rewards and penalties, and documentation Termination processes, legal compliance, forms, and case review Exit interviews, documentation, and data
Pay and benefit systems, and communication to employees Advocacy and problem-solving for employees	Maintain contractual agreements with people	Pay and benefit systems, regulatory and legal issues, documentation, communication, training, administration, and tracking
Conditions, policies and procedures, monitoring, and enforcement Advocacy for employees	Maintain safe, secure, satisfying, productive workplace conditions for people	Conditions, policies and procedures, documentation, publishing, communication, training, monitoring, and enforcement Legal and regulatory concerns Processes for complaints, appeals, and whistle-blowers Satisfaction surveys and reports

Evolution of performance management systems

Just as a microfinance institution (MFI) evolves from an entrepreneurial group with more expenses than revenue, an informal structure, and a small staff to a larger, revenue-producing, multi-layered, more stable business, its performance management system also evolves. Table 2.2 outlines a series of growth points.

Table 2.2: Checklist – phases of evolution of performance management systems

	Age and organization stage		
System component	*Year 1–2: small, informal start-up organization*	*Year 3–6: growing, dynamic, medium-sized organization*	*Year 7 and beyond: larger, stable, more complex and more sophisticated organization*
Defining the work			
Job descriptions	Simple, informal, not always written	Written, including competencies	Performance standard included
Matching people to work			
Recruitment	Obvious sources Informal process Simple materials	Diversified, more unusual sources Formalized process More comprehensive materials	Recruitment campaigns and incentives Partnerships and integrated programmes
Interviewing	Informal	Planned and formalized Training	Assessments and exercises included in process
Selection	Informal and more personal	Clearer, more objective criteria	
Hiring	Legal compliance	Written letters always used	
Organizing the work			
Process and job design	Oral, in person	Manuals and written expectations	
Learning the work			
On-boarding	Casual, 'walk around', and may meet everyone Job manuals and notes	More structured, with materials and assigned roles May not meet everyone More job manuals	Documented on-boarding process Many job manuals
Training	Technical training May have business management training Much on-the-job learning and in-house expertise	Business management training May have people management training Competencies and training curriculum being defined More classroom learning Combination of internal and external expertise	People management training May have leadership training Competency outlines for all positions Curriculum for all levels and positions Broader range of learning resources internally and externally
Coaching and feedback	Informal, instinctive, and ad hoc	Training for managers may begin Feedback required for performance reviews, which are encouraged more often	Training for managers in place Coaching and feedback considered part of the daily management job
Getting the work done			
Expectations and standards	May have oral standards and goals Personal oversight Informal feedback	May have written standards	Written standards

Goals – individual and team	May have oral goals	Written individual goals May have team goals	Written team goals where teams are permanent
Monitoring performance	Personal oversight and informal feedback	Documented performance results and feedback	May have self-monitoring and self-reporting
Getting better at work			
Motivation and incentives	Idiosyncratic approaches to motivation and incentives	May have training on motivation More formal, consistent incentive schemes documented	Training on motivation Incentive schemes better matched to culture and goals
Performance reviews	Informal, with casual schedule and documentation May have training on doing reviews	Formal, with established schedule and formal documentation	Training on doing reviews More complex process and documentation
Redesign, enrich, enlarge work			
	Ad hoc	More likely in response to business changes	In response to business changes and individual needs
Development and career planning	Ad hoc	Simple development planning Career paths and planning may emerge	Formal development planning and follow-up Includes career planning
High potentials		Informal, with ad hoc development	Formal high potential identification process and development programme
Do different work, take more responsibility, leadership			
Leadership	Ad hoc	May have leadership training and mentoring	Leadership development curriculum and processes
Promotions	Ad hoc	More formal, may be in response to business changes, but little preparation	Formal process and preparation In response to business changes and individual readiness
Succession planning		For CEO, and 1 or 2 other key positions Often informal, but may be dynamic as business changes	For all high-risk positions, and may be others More formal process, with successors informed
Measure people's results			
	Reviews more informal Rewards informal, and limited in amount and type Penalties arbitrary or ignored Terminations difficult or avoided	Reviews more formal Reward schemes more formal and more diverse Penalties may be more defined and better applied Terminations clear for egregious violations, but may be avoided otherwise	Reward schemes more elaborate Penalties may be more defined and better applied Terminations more easily handled

Assessing system evolution – checklist

You can use this table to make sure that your performance management system includes all the components typical of an organization the age and size of yours.

Does your performance management system include all the components of a typical system for the age and organizational stage?

- If not, what has prevented the development of the missing components?
- If you have gone beyond the typical organization, what factors have allowed you to do so?

If your system is current for its age and stage, what will you need to focus on to be current in the next stage?

- Among the components that need further development, which ones are top priorities? Why?
- How will those components support the organization in moving to its next stage of growth and strategic positioning?
- What will you need to do to develop the specific components and ensure that the performance management system as a whole continues to evolve with the organization?

Successes and problems in the performance management system

For a performance management system to be successful, everyone needs to be involved and the effort needs to be continuous. Even when all the components of a mature, stable, and sophisticated system are in place and functioning, managing the performance of people requires ongoing attention.

On the other side of the picture, if a senior leader downplays a component of the system, if an HR professional is not in touch with managers about their people management needs, or if a manager fails to implement routine people management responsibilities, then the whole performance management system is weakened.

Success factors – checklist

You can use the success factors checklist as a 'health check' for the management of people's performance in your organization. If one of the success factors is not in place in your institution, develop a proposal or a strategy for achieving it.

Table 2.3: Checklist – success factors for performance management systems

If the problem is ...	*The suggested direction is ...*
1. Managers have people management needs or problems that HR is not addressing.	A. Individual conversations or small-group dialogues to find out what is preventing HR from meeting the needs. B. Surveys or other written communication to convey the needs and request action. C. Bring the needs to the attention of the leadership team to request support for solutions.
2. HR has proposed, designed, piloted, or rolled out one or more performance management processes that managers do not comply with.	A. Individual or small-group conversations to explore managers' people management needs, to ensure new processes meet those needs. B. Involvement of managers in committees or task forces to identify, design, and pilot performance management processes. C. Develop the business case for and develop alliances with senior managers to gain a champion at a senior level for performance management in general or for a specific initiative.
3. Executives or the leadership team give little attention to performance management problems or proposals brought forward by HR.	A. Frame HR proposals or concerns with direct relevance to strategic goals or operational success (see Chapter 11). B. Present HR proposals or concerns in terms of how they will make the organization successful and/or make one or more leaders appear more effective (see Chapter 11). C. Consider demonstrating how failure to address performance management problems presents financial, competitive, or legal risks to the business (see Chapter 11).
4. Executives or the leadership team give little attention to the people management problems associated with performance challenges or raised directly by managers. Issues other than management of people are consistently given higher priority for decision-making, resource allocation, or communication.	A. Frame people management problems in terms of how they affect the organization's ability to meet goals or succeed in its operations. B. Build alliances with leaders who have political 'weight' and credibility. C. Articulate the financial, competitive, operational, or legal risks caused by continuing failure to address the problem(s).
5. Managers and HR professionals are overwhelmed by operational demands, new strategic initiatives, or changes of direction and are unable to give sufficient attention to performance management.	A. Look for coaching on how to 'work smarter'. B. Point out the risks of prolonged lack of attention to performance management. C. Propose a reprioritization that includes attention to at least one important area of performance management. D. Build an objective business case or work plan around the existing situation demonstrating the need for additional resources, the poor use of existing resources (insufficient return on time or money spent), or the excessive work hours required.

6. There is insufficient funding for the performance management initiatives proposed by HR.	A. Make sure performance management initiatives are presented as business cases and are linked directly to the business strategy and key operations. B. Present the business benefits of a given initiative to explain the funding need. C. Present the strategic or operational risks of failing to carry out the initiative, in terms of costs, legal or regulatory risk, turnover, or poor productivity or quality.
7. Managers do not receive training in the competencies needed to be effective managers of people's performance – e.g. giving feedback, evaluating performance, or on-the-job coaching.	A. Link the competencies to business needs such as quality, productivity, sales volume, revenue, or customer service. B. Link the lack of these competencies to current problems, such as turnover, attracting talent, reputation in the job market, or staff morale. C. Look for alternatives to classroom training for getting concepts, tools, and examples out to managers, such as briefings during branch or team meetings, 'tag-ons' to other gatherings of managers, short online modules, newsletter articles, and so on.

CHAPTER 3

Getting the right people in the right positions at the right time

The very first step in effectively managing people's performance is to define carefully the duties, responsibilities, and performance expectations of each position. Writing job descriptions while an organization is being set up ensures that all the work that needs to be done has been accounted for and assigned. At the same time, written job descriptions allow the founders of the organization to form teams or departments that have a logical focus, bringing together people with associated responsibilities.

Then, as the business begins to hire, job descriptions form the basis on which to search for the right candidates to perform the work. When new employees start work, their managers talk through their job descriptions to establish clear expectations, and then refer to them regularly to give effective feedback and to guide performance. Finally, job descriptions are the basis for each manager to evaluate how well people are doing on the job.

Job descriptions: defining the work

Caution!

Surprisingly, it is not unusual for start-up organizations to launch operations and put people to work with minimal, sketchy job descriptions. In those circumstances, no one should be surprised when jobholders turn out to be ill-suited for the work or when performance is not up to expectations. Experienced HR professionals will testify to the importance of taking the time to prepare descriptions for every job in an organization as early as possible.

Definition

A job description is a short outline of the major role, tasks, and responsibilities of a particular position; it documents the functions of the job – what the jobholder will do. It is used in recruiting for a position, and it is also important for successful on-boarding, for reviewing expectations, for setting goals, and for performance evaluation.

A sample job description and a template for creating a job description are included at the end of the section.

Basic job description. To be functional, job descriptions must include the following:

http://dx.doi.org/10.3362/9781780447926.004

- name of position;
- to whom the position reports;
- positions reporting to this job, if appropriate;
- significant tasks and responsibilities, representing 85 to 95 per cent of the time committed to the position;
- special requirements for the position, such as a licence or certificate, or knowledge of languages;
- special conditions of the position, such as frequent travel, working alone, or a high level of interruptions;
- significant results to be achieved by this position, such as the number of transactions or size of loan portfolio;
- performance standards, such as level of accuracy, or allowable late payment or default rates.

Note: The last two items, significant results and performance standards, can be included in the basic job description if they are likely to remain stable over a period of years. Or they may be included in an addendum, to make updating easier. Finally, if it suits the operating procedures of the institution, they may be included in the employee goals forms, to allow for frequent updating and to build a tight link between goals and expectations and actual performance. The important point is that **results and performance standards must be spelled out** in one of the basic and widely used performance management documents, for all managers and employees to read and apply.

Comprehensive job description. To be comprehensive, job descriptions will also include the following:

- where the job fits in the organization;
- competencies – required skills, knowledge, and attitudes;
- key characteristics or qualities of the jobholder.

Table 3.1: Alignment of people management responsibilities

Business manager – typical contributions	*People management responsibilities*	*HR professional – typical contributions*
Job description specifications	Define the work	Job description form Reviewing description specifications

Table 3.2: Job descriptions through the stages of organizational growth

Getting established	*Established and growing*	*Settled and mature*
Develop basic job descriptions – tasks, responsibilities, and key performance targets	Convert basic job descriptions to comprehensive job descriptions May add interdependencies – significant inputs from outputs to other parts of the organization, and scale of standards (meets, exceeds, below)	May develop 'bands' of competency for novice, accomplished, and master levels

Connections to other components of the performance management system

Job descriptions affect several other aspects of the performance management system.

Recruiting depends on accurate and comprehensive job descriptions as the basis for advertising openings and then determining whether applicants are appropriate for the position. Job descriptions are one of the most critical sources of information that candidates rely on when deciding to apply for a job, so they need to give applicants a clear and complete picture of the duties and tasks of the position.

Setting expectations for someone new to a position or as part of the annual review and goal-setting activities also depends on the accuracy and completeness of job descriptions.

The backbone of the *performance review* is the outline of the responsibilities and targets of the job, coming out of the job description.

A *training needs analysis* often begins with the information about tasks and responsibilities in job descriptions.

Job descriptions are also useful to *career path* outlines and *career development*.

Table 3.3: Responsibilities for developing the job description

Business manager	*HR professional*
Must • Coordinate with the HR professional about who writes the description and when it is to be completed • Provide the content (the 'specifications') • Review the description if it is written by someone else • Keep the description updated **May** • Write the description	**Must** • Provide information and a template for preparing the description • Remind the manager of the need to have the description • Establish with the manager who will write the description • Have the description reviewed by the manager if it is written by someone else • Support the manager in keeping the description updated **May** • Write the description

From the field

In an Asian MFI, reporting managers prepare the first draft of the job description, as they know the job requirements for their direct reports. Then they consult with HR to make sure that the description is complete and appropriate.

Involving the whole organization

To sustain effective collaboration in all the activities of defining the work, the whole organization needs to expect to be involved.

When preparing job descriptions is left to the business manager or the HR professional alone, they may begin to believe that this component of designing the organization, defining the work, and managing people is unimportant to more senior leaders or to the organization as a whole. They may become discouraged, or they may develop policies and procedures that are not effective or not in the interest of the whole organization.

Ways to involve the whole organization include: creating an advisory group or HR council that reviews and advises on a range of people management activities, starting with job descriptions; and involving the leadership team, and even the board at times, in reviewing job descriptions in the context of organizational design.

The job analysis

The job analysis is the process for developing a job description. Some steps in the process are necessary for a basic job description; others are used to add the components of a comprehensive job description. (See labels in the outline of steps below.)

A job analysis can be undertaken by the manager of the position being analysed and/or by an HR professional. The best outcome results from the two collaborating. In addition, managers, co-workers, and direct reports to the position can provide useful insight into the role, tasks, and requirements. A key person to include in the analysis is a current jobholder, if possible. Others in the business can describe how the position interacts with other positions, especially in terms of its most important outputs.

There are two approaches to doing a job analysis:

1. *Ground-up.* Appropriate for a new position or a position in which many previous jobholders have been less than fully successful.
2. *Role model.* Appropriate when there has been at least one successful jobholder and the people doing the analysis are objective enough to separate the jobholder from the responsibilities and essential qualities needed for the job. This approach can also be used if there are appropriate role models in another organization.

For either approach, use the steps of the analysis given below to guide the process.

Note: The *comprehensive job description* contains information required for successful recruiting. If this is not included in the original job description, it should be included in the recruiting materials.

Steps of the job analysis

1. For a **basic** job description, outline the reason for the job (why it exists) and the major goals of the job – the significant results to be achieved by this position (e.g. number of transactions, size of loan portfolio).

For a **comprehensive** job description, include the context for the job – how it fits into the organizational structure.

2. For a **basic** job description, list the major functional responsibilities of the position, in order of importance: the activities necessary to achieve the major goals; and the key tasks – those tasks that take up the majority of the jobholder's time.
3. For a **basic** job description, list any unique requirements for the job, such as an accounting licence or fluency in a local language.

   For a **comprehensive** job description, also list the essential skills and knowledge required.

   Note: If the job description is being written in conjunction with a recruiting campaign, be sure to include the educational preparation required, both in terms of level (secondary school, technical training, university) and key subject areas (reading, writing, presenting, maths, analysis).

   Also for recruiting purposes, include the amount and type of work experience required, both in terms of job level (technician, supervisor, manager) and in terms of area of work (finance, marketing, sales, accounting).

   While education and experience information is not typical for a job description, it is mandatory for recruiting appropriate job candidates.
4. For a **basic** job description, research and describe special conditions of the position, such as frequent travel, working alone, or a high level of interruptions.
5. For a **basic** job description, determine performance standards, such as level of accuracy, or allowable late payment or default rates.
6. For a **comprehensive** job description, list the personal qualities that will be important in performing the job.

   Consider the personal qualities needed for:
   - interacting with customers (sociability and articulateness);
   - performing in the work environment (comfortable in an open work environment, or with changing work locations);
   - the demands and pressure of the duties (accuracy, detail, fast response times, or the ability to handle multiple tasks);
   - the culture of the organization (social, independent, urban, easy-going, or constantly changing).
7. The **basic** job description will consist of the information from steps 1 to 5.

   Note: If the job description is being prepared for a recruiting campaign in a challenging job market with a limited talent pool, determine which components of the basic job description an applicant **must have** and which are **nice to have**.

   'Must-have' items are the absolute minimum requirements that an applicant must have to do the job. 'Nice-to-have' items are ones that would enhance performance and fit, but could be developed on the job if necessary.

Table 3.4: Elements of the job description

Basic job description	*Comprehensive job description*
Reason for the job	Reason for the job
Major goals of the job	How it fits into the organizational structure
Activities and tasks	Major goals of the job
Unique requirements	Activities and tasks
Special conditions	Essential skills and knowledge required
Performance standards	Amount and type of prior work experience
	Unique requirements
	Special conditions
	Performance standards
	Personal qualities relevant to the job requirements

Caution! Job descriptions alone do not ensure a clear reporting structure

From its earliest days, the MFI Mooldhan developed job descriptions for all levels of staff in an effort to clarify responsibilities and reporting structures. However, the job descriptions were not cross-referenced, and it turns out that there are overlaps of responsibility among positions. Furthermore, management supervision is not sufficient to ensure that individuals remember their assigned responsibilities and stay within their reporting protocols. Without management involvement, the job descriptions alone are not providing the desired level of clarity.

Template 3.1: Job analysis form

1. Goal of the position

Describe the principal purpose of the position – the reason it exists. (Focus on the overall objective rather than specific responsibilities.)

2. Supervisory accountability (if appropriate)

List the job titles and numbers of people supervised by the person in the position (if any).

A. Direct (i.e. report directly to this position)

B. Indirect (i.e. supervised by the people reporting to this position)

3. Financial impact (if appropriate)

Describe this position's accountability for budgets, revenue generation, expenditures, equipment, etc., to demonstrate the size or impact of this position.

A. Revenue

B. Expenditures

C. Materials/equipment

4. Major responsibilities

List the major responsibilities of this job. Indicate the percentage of time spent on these activities. The last statement on all job descriptions should normally be: 'Perform any other related duties as required.'

Responsibility	Percentage of time spent on it
1.	
2.	
3.	
4.	
5.	
6.	
7.	
8.	
9.	
10.	

5. Required knowledge and skills

A. Knowledge (e.g. accounting, typing, use of equipment)

B. Mental skills (e.g. communication, presentation, leadership, negotiation, language(s))

C. Physical skills (e.g. manual dexterity skills for typing, strength for lifting heavy boxes, driving)

D. Education/experience (specify the formal education and/or work experience required for preparation for and/or performance of the job)

6. How often a person in this position works under the following conditions

Circle the rating that best applies to this position, and, if necessary, describe the specific situation in the space beneath each statement.

		Never	Occasionally	Frequently	Mostly
1.	Meeting tight deadlines Describe:	1	2	3	4
2.	Performing work outside normal work schedule (i.e. overtime, unusual shifts) Describe:	1	2	3	4
3.	Travelling during the day (e.g. meetings, deliveries) Describe:	1	2	3	4
4.	Travelling overnight (e.g. meetings, conferences) Describe:	1	2	3	4
5.	Dealing directly with upset or impatient people who create stress for an individual in this position Describe:	1	2	3	4
6.	Giving information or discussing subjects with staff or clients that can create stress for these people Describe:	1	2	3	4
7.	Working for extended periods looking at a computer screen Describe:	1	2	3	4
8.	Working standing up for more than 15 minutes at a stretch Describe:	1	2	3	4
9.	Working in an unusual or challenging environment (e.g. crowded area, urban kiosk) Describe:	1	2	3	4
10.	Other:	1	2	3	4

Template 3.2: Job description for human resources manager

Position summary

The human resources manager is responsible for the overall success of the human resource management (HRM) systems and for providing strategic planning and guidance to senior management.

Duties

Determine the organization's current and future staffing needs.
- Communicate with staff managers on staffing requirements, and help to identify potential internal candidates for promotion.
- Lead senior management in succession planning.

Manage the administration of HRM and corporate policies.
- Ensure that the organization has current and appropriate HRM policies in place and is in compliance with all applicable human rights and labour laws.
- Distribute HRM policies and train staff on policies and procedures.
- Provide guidance and support for staff managers' decisions in applying HRM policies.
- Ensure that current and accurate records for each employee are kept on file.

Manage the MFI's compensation strategy and processes.
- Ensure that appropriate systems and tools are in place, including a salary administration system, benefits, and an incentive scheme.
- Oversee and coordinate the annual salary increases, and support managers in salary decisions; review all salaries to ensure equity and fairness.

Oversee recruitment and selection.
- Ensure that an appropriate recruitment and selection process is implemented, and, where necessary, make sure staff and managers are trained on the processes.
- Maintain a candidate database of new résumés, purging old files, to be used to search for qualified candidates for employment openings.
- Plan and coordinate terminations with staff managers, as necessary.

Oversee the performance management process.
- Develop and implement a staff performance appraisal system, and support staff and managers in using it.
- Review year-end appraisals to monitor overall performance and trends, as well as managers' ability to give feedback and provide development.

Oversee the training and development programmes.
- Develop institution-wide training and development initiatives as appropriate.
- Support managers and staff in preparing personal development plans, and provide strategies to reach their development goals.
- Support each staff manager with the necessary skills for effective staff management.
- Create a plan for new staff orientation, including content and a schedule. Ensure that staff receive introductions to the organization's history, philosophy, policies, and structure. Support managers in training new staff on job details.

Qualifications

- University degree or certificate in HR and/or business administration.
- Minimum three years of work experience in HR.
- Demonstrated interpersonal and communication skills and experience of dealing with issues of a confidential and sensitive nature.
- Ability to efficiently and effectively organize and prioritize several tasks at once.

Supervisor: Executive Director **Location:** Head Office

Date:

Template 3.3: Job description for credit officer

Position summary

To develop and manage a viable loan portfolio for micro-entrepreneurs, providing them with basic business training and advisory support.

Duties

Manage the client-level portfolio lending process.

- Recruit and select new clients and orient them to the lending programme, policies, and procedures.
- Assist potential clients in preparing loan applications and business plans.
- Analyse loan proposals and make recommendations to the loan committee.
- Document and report client feedback regarding the lending process.
- Promote the organization's credit services in the community.

Maintain client-level portfolio quality and control.

- Monitor loan repayments.
- Follow up loans.
- Make recommendations to the loan committee regarding repeat loans.
- Submit regular status reports to the branch manager.

Provide basic on-site businesses advisory support to clients.

- Visit client businesses regularly.
- Carry out quarterly basic business assessments and convey results to the client.

Participate as an active member of the overall branch team.

- Attend weekly staff meetings.
- Participate in quarterly and annual branch planning workshops.
- Provide back-up support to other team members as needed.
- Organize training schedules, venues, and materials.
- Train participants.

Assist in the delivery of business basics training courses to new employees.

Qualifications

- Completion of high school education.
- Strong mathematical and organizational skills.
- Excellent interpersonal skills, and effective written and oral verbal communication skills.
- Team player.
- Knowledge of the local community.

Supervisor: Branch Manager **Location:** Branch Office

Date:

Template 3.4: Job description for executive director

Position summary

The executive director is responsible for the overall success of the institution. The position exists to provide leadership to the institution, enabling the facility to sustainably provide credit and training to the poorest of the economically active. The primary areas of responsibility for the executive director are programme management, financial planning and monitoring, HR management, and relations with the board, other development organizations, and the business community.

Duties

Provide direction for overall institutional development and management.

- Develop strategies for the institution's business activities and growth, ensuring that the environmental business factors within [the country] are monitored and incorporated in the institution's plans.
- Ensure that revenue targets and strategic plans are achieved, and all the institution's activities are conducted with a high commitment to business orientation, legal requirements, and the institution's values.
- Oversee compliance with the pattern of planning, monitoring, evaluation, and reporting as established by the institution and as defined by the board of directors, contracts, and donors.
- Effectively coordinate the institution's senior management team.

Ensure that appropriate HR management practices are implemented.

- As necessary provide support and approval on staffing decisions (hiring/terminating), salary increases, and other executive-level decisions.
- Provide supervision to direct reports.
- Place a high priority on staff development and their understanding of the institution's vision.

Ensure proper management of financial planning, internal controls, and monitoring.

- Secure capital as required, and ensure appropriate use and availability of financial resources.
- Ensure that financial, internal control, and administrative policies are established and followed.
- Coordinate budgetary planning and ensure that timely and accurate financial reports are provided by the director of finance and administration.

Act as the most senior representative of the institution.

- Represent the institution in negotiations and other affairs with donors and state and private organizations.
- Ensure that relations with donors are maintained, as well as relations with other development organizations, and the business community.

Qualifications

- University degree in business administration or economics, with studies in finance or banking.
- Minimum 10 years of experience as senior manager in state or private companies.
- Demonstrated experience in personnel management, financial planning, banking, and credit.
- Excellent interpersonal skills.
- Computer literacy.
- Commitment to the institution's mission, values, and goals.

Supervisor: Chairman of the Board **Location:** Head Office

Date:

Template 3.5: Key qualities and characteristics of a credit officer

The effective credit officer demonstrates:

A professional commitment to the job and a desire to help

- Takes the responsibilities seriously and completes the work to a high standard without excessive concern about work hours.
- Keeps the focus on work while working.
- Pays attention to borrowers, other clients, colleagues, and superiors in a respectful way and takes the initiative to help when needed.

The necessary technical background and skills

- Has work experience in lending, working with customers, and making presentations to groups.
- Has the appropriate level of education.
- Has experience applying mathematical and analytical skills.

Interpersonal skills

- Shows an interest in, attentiveness to, and respect for others.
- Is able and willing to get along well with others of various social levels; is a team player.
- Shows a warm, friendly, and open manner; is a good listener and communicator.

Presentation skills

- Demonstrates confidence and a professional manner when speaking to groups.
- Understands how to design and use flip charts.
- Can communicate a process or a method in clear, simple, understandable language, appropriate to the audience.

Action orientation

- Takes the initiative; is one of the first to act or propose a plan of action.
- Demonstrates self-confidence with regard to personal goals, and judgement without arrogance or disregard of others' input.

Honesty and integrity

- Is frank, direct, and open in dealing with others.
- Is dependable and reliable.

Template 3.6: Blank job description	
Job title	
Position summary	
Duties – key areas of responsibility and tasks	
Qualifications – educational level	
Work experience/level	
Key skills	
Key areas of knowledge	
Characteristics, qualities, and attitudes	
Supervisor	
Location	
Date	

Recruiting

This section on recruiting covers who is involved, how recruiting supports the overall strategy, what goes into doing it, and the tools necessary for the tasks.

Effective recruiting – getting the right people in the right positions at the right time – is the starting point for managing people's performance and for the systems that support that responsibility. Recruiting includes preparing job descriptions, interviewing, selection, and hiring.

The process that results in putting the right people in the right positions at the right time gets started when the business has any of the following:

- a vacant position that needs to be filled;
- a new position created in response to a new need in the business;
- one or more new positions as a result of growth – new branches or kiosk locations or expansion of a head office function.

Most recruitment and hiring is reactive, in response to a vacated position or a newly created one, as a need arises. Some recruitment is conducted on a scheduled basis, as part of the recruitment strategy, to allow the bank to become familiar with new groups of possible job candidates or to maintain contact with promising individuals or sources of talent. Of course, some hiring happens without recruitment but as a result of proactive applications or referrals.

Regardless of what starts off the recruitment effort, good performance comes from how well recruitment is carried out – creating a good match between the job and the person who fills the job, and the activities that bring about the good match. The more often a business can make a good match with its first effort, the lower the overall costs to the organization in terms of budget and people's time, and the more often new employees rapidly become productive, loyal, satisfied, high-performing members of the organization.

Making good matches is an important first step in effective performance management, and it is a good operating standard. Successful recruiting means lower costs in the hiring process, fewer performance or discipline problems, less rework, fewer customer complaints, and lower costs for replacement hiring and replacement training.

To make good matches, the performance management system needs to include solid job descriptions; procedures for recruiting, interviewing, evaluating, and hiring candidates; and policies to guide the managers and HR professionals involved in using the system.

Table 3.5: Alignment of people management responsibilities

Business manager – typical contributions	*People management responsibilities*	*HR professional – typical contributions*
Setting/reviewing selection criteria Participating in the search team Suggesting sources of talent Reviewing applications and files Interviewing Evaluating candidates Selecting finalist Determining salary level, based on pay scale Making or reviewing job offer documents, or making the offer in person	Match the right people to the work	Setting/reviewing selection criteria Forming and coordinating the search team Publishing the job description and selection criteria Conducting recruiting activities Coordinating interviews Interviewing Contributing to the evaluation and selection Advising on salary level, based on pay scale Preparing and making the job offer Maintaining documentation and files Administering payroll, benefits, and other 'back-office' procedures

The activities involved in getting the right people into the right positions include the following steps:

1. defining the job and the requirements for appropriate candidates;
2. setting up a search team;
3. recruiting candidates;
4. screening applications;
5. assessing, interviewing, and checking references;
6. selecting the finalist;
7. making a job offer.

Connections to other components of the performance management system

Recruiting and hiring are related to other people management responsibilities.

Succession planning may reveal a lack of people ready to succeed a person in a key position. The organization might begin to look for people with strong potential and track their careers; in other words, begin building the talent pool. Or it may initiate active recruitment.

High-potential candidates may be noticed in the recruiting and hiring activities and considered for more rapid development towards leadership positions.

Development planning can begin during interviewing and on-boarding, to make sure the newly hired employee receives appropriate training and some attention to his or her future interests.

Information about *career paths* can be an incentive for someone to apply for a job or to take an offer from the institution.

Career planning may be another inducement to persuade a particularly attractive candidate to apply or to take up an offer.

Table 3.6: Recruitment through the stages of organizational growth

Getting established	*Established and growing*	*Settled and mature*
HR and job manager do most recruiting tasks Need for imaginative, high-impact communication activities to establish the organization's 'brand' in the job market Assessments are basic, if any	HR and more than one level of management are involved in final screening and hiring High-volume recruiting leads to standardized methods and documents Consider incentives to involve staff in recruiting	May use more sophisticated assessment tools More complex outreach programmes to develop larger, deeper talent pool Regular reviews of recruitment strategy, policies, and hiring practices

A recruitment strategy

A recruitment strategy expresses the organization's intentions, plans, and key policies related to finding the right people for the right positions. It is adjusted from time to time to reflect changes in the overall business strategy.

Tip

Younger organizations tend to handle recruitment in an ad hoc manner, appropriate to their size and organic formation. However, as a business moves towards its first serious growth spurt, it is very valuable to write a recruitment strategy and standardize recruitment practices. Written, standardized information makes it much easier to involve more managers in recruiting and handling a large volume of applicants.

Sample recruitment strategy statement

We are always on the watch for individuals who have the right skills, experience, and attitude to be able to learn to perform at a high level of quality, productivity, and creativity, and who will fit well with our culture. Everyone in the bank helps build the talent pool and seek candidates for specific positions. We go to many sources for job candidates, both traditional and non-traditional, and we involve a number of people in our organization in the recruiting, interviewing, and hiring process.

We use carefully prepared job and candidate profiles to ensure an objective and efficient match of applicants to positions.

At a minimum, the hiring manager, the supervisor of the hiring manager, and an HR professional work together on all aspects of finding the right people for open positions.

Our primary traditional sources for candidates are:

- business training schools;
- university accounting programmes;
- post-secondary technical programmes;
- businesses located near our head office and branches.

Our non-traditional sources are identified by thinking creatively about the primary qualities and attitudes needed for positions that are harder to fill or in locations with more challenging job markets.

To avoid conflicts of interest, we do not hire close family members of current employees to work in the same office or branch as their family member. We do not allow family members or close associates to participate in any aspect of recruiting, interviewing, and hiring their relative or colleague.

We use objective and publicized criteria for selecting people for positions.

We follow all national and local laws and regulations that apply to hiring and employment.

We keep personal information about all applicants obtained through application forms, letters, and interviews completely private and confidential. We take measures to protect sensitive information such as identity numbers or bank account information.

The bank's goal is to establish eight new branches during the first two quarters of the next fiscal year, and 12 in the second two quarters. Our strategy is to define the hiring needs for each location at least six months in advance, including job descriptions and candidate profiles. Three to six months before the opening of each location, we will research the job market and make location-specific plans for locating potential job candidates and publicizing job openings for tellers, cleaning crew, drivers, and support staff. In addition to researching the prospects for hiring credit officers locally, we will prepare to recruit them elsewhere and plan for relocation.

At least six months before opening the new branches, we will recruit internally for branch managers who will transfer to a new location. We will also recruit internally for candidates to replace any branch managers who transfer, and we will begin to recruit externally for additional replacements for individuals who transfer or are promoted.

> **Caution!**
>
> It is easy to underestimate the amount of lead time required to prepare to recruit staff for new branches. There are considerations that relate to the locations of the new branches and the possible need for incentive, salary, or relocation schemes. It is also critical to have enough managers prepared to supervise the new staff. Finally, the business needs to have the capacity to hold inductions for a higher volume of new hires – trainer time, meeting locations, executive availability, and so forth.

Involving the whole organization

To sustain effective collaboration for finding the right people for the right positions, the whole organization needs to expect to be involved.

When recruitment, interviewing, and selection are left to the business manager or the HR professional alone, they may begin to believe that these components of managing people are unimportant to more senior leaders or to the organization as a whole. Also, they may make poor choices or ones that are not in the interest of the whole organization.

Activities essential to involving the whole organization in recruiting are:

- creating an advisory group or an HR council – a cross-functional group of managers – that reviews and advises on a range of people management activities;
- involving the leadership team, and even the board, in reviewing policies relating to recruitment, selection, and hiring;
- reporting regularly to the leadership team or management committee about recent recruiting efforts and hiring data.

Refinements include:

- using communication and incentive programmes to generate enthusiasm among staff about participating in finding and attracting good job candidates;
- reviewing with the leadership team or the management committee on a regular basis the recruitment strategy, policies, hiring practices, and legal and regulatory changes;
- assembling a search committee to help ensure that all aspects of finding the right people for the right positions take advantage of the knowledge and contacts of several individuals across the organization. (See below for more detail.)

Purposes of recruiting

Recruiting is the search for qualified applicants for an open position and is an integral part of building and sustaining a successful organization. For that reason, business managers need to think about recruitment when they make strategic decisions, and HR professionals need to be fully informed about business strategy as they develop or conduct the recruitment processes.

Properly planned and implemented, recruitment ensures that the organization brings on board the people who have the knowledge, skills, and attitudes to achieve the organization's strategic goals. Effective recruitment also has a significant impact on long-term employment stability and retention.

Did you know?

The HR consulting firm Mercer has periodically conducted studies of the cost of staff turnover in businesses around the world. Its 2004 study found that the cost of turnover is between 50 per cent and 150 per cent of the person's annual salary, and it went on to say that these amounts are only the direct costs. Numerous indirect costs, such as lost productivity or opportunity costs of sales, add to the true cost of turnover.

Recruiting is also an opportunity for letting general or selected groups of people know about the organization and about job opportunities. This means that recruiting has a marketing component that involves projecting the aspects of the institution that would be attractive to the right kinds of job candidates. In addition, it has a review and evaluation component in the initial applicant screening process that determines whether people's past performance warrants getting to know them in greater depth.

Recruiting has several important purposes:

- *For current hiring needs.* With a well thought-out recruitment strategy, good contacts, interesting recruiting materials, and plenty of energy, recruiters can bring in the right people for current job openings as quickly as possible.
- *For the business.* Finding the right people for open positions in an efficient, cost-effective way supports the goals of the institution as they relate to ongoing operations, sustaining productivity, maintaining quality work, ensuring a positive workplace culture, and managing costs well.
- *For future hiring needs.* The size of the pool of available talent to bring into the organization, whether for entry-, mid-, or higher-level positions, is largely determined by the extent and creativity of the recruitment effort. A diligent and ongoing recruitment effort means that the organization will have current contacts with various sources of talent when it needs it.
- *For holding down recruitment costs.* Recruitment based on a sound understanding of the workplace culture and the job requirements of any given position is more likely to bring in applicants who could reasonably become employees. Less time and money need to be spent for the later steps of screening and assessing job candidates when the initial recruitment steps are done well.
- *For public relations.* The people who recruit for the organization, the materials they publish or send out, and the way in which they interact with people outside the organization are other means of positively representing the organization to the public.

Tip: recruiting and organizational culture

The organization's approach to recruitment reflects its values and is an important tool for helping to shape its culture. At the time of recruitment, prospective employees receive signals about the institution they are considering – its values, its norms, and its expectations. By the time these recruits accept a job offer, an implicit psychological contract has taken shape. For that reason, it is critical to ensure that recruitment practices accurately reflect the organization's culture, to ensure that job candidates will fit well with the organization.

The recruiting process

There are two types of recruitment activity, which have different purposes and levels of intensity:

1. A low- to moderate-intensity programme of awareness: this includes activities that keep the business informed about the available talent and keep the organization's name in the minds of sources of talent, such as universities, secondary schools, employment agencies, and even other banks.
2. A moderate- to high-intensity programme of recruiting related to one or more specific positions: this involves finding specific people to fill specific jobs.

Essential elements of recruiting include:

- developing a recruitment strategy that includes ways to ensure full representation of women in the workforce, at all levels in the organization;
- writing recruiting policies;
- developing a recruiting process and forms;
- using existing marketing materials in information packs for applicants;
- involving the hiring manager and the HR professional in recruiting.

The following basic steps of the process should be followed:

1. Make sure there is a current and complete job description to use as the basis for recruitment announcements and screening criteria.
2. Identify sources for candidates, including internal candidates and previously submitted applications.
3. Prepare, review, and distribute materials to bring in applicants, both internally (postings, announcements to all employees) and externally (ads, bulletins or newsletters, flyers, phone calls, website announcements, emails to publications or organizations).
4. Receive and respond to enquiries, and send out information and applications.
5. Screen applicants: receive applications, then organize, distribute, and review them; and apply criteria to identify the best candidates for interviews.
6. Agree among decision-makers on the final selections for interviewing and possible testing.

Refinements to the process include:

- making sure that everyone in the organization is aware of the roles they can play in recruiting talent;
- building relationships with sources of recruits at all levels – entry, middle, and senior;
- preparing recruitment publicity materials;
- establishing search committees for specific positions, especially more specialized or more senior-level ones;
- reviewing and adapting the processes for finding talent, reviewing applications, interviewing, and selection on a regular basis;
- holding an event for external recruitment if several openings need to be filled; for example, a new branch opening or a department expansion.

From the field

A bank in central Asia had been announcing job openings primarily by placing ads. After reviewing the return on this approach, the managers realized that, in an ordinary classified ad, nothing distinguished their position and their institution from many other job openings of all kinds. They decided to try placing an ad for the bank itself, featuring qualities attractive to both customers and employees, and running it in a different part of the paper. They took care to make the web address prominent, and listed job openings only online. The number and quality of job applicants improved noticeably.

General-level recruitment activities. Recruitment strategy, policy, processes, and forms are created, maintained, and updated on an ongoing basis, regardless of how much position-specific recruiting is taking place.

Job descriptions and company marketing and information materials are also developed and kept up to date regardless of recruitment activity.

Position-specific recruitment activities. The first important decision to be made, once the need to fill a specific position is identified, is where to recruit: only internally; only externally; or both internally and externally.

Internal recruitment. For internal recruitment, follow the following steps:

1. Obtain a current and complete job description to use as the basis of job postings, screening, interviewing, and selection criteria.
2. Post the position-opening information in multiple locations, such as in the company newsletter, on bulletin boards, in hand-outs, and on the internal website.
   - Include the duties and responsibilities, requirements for eligibility (experience, education, special skills), salary grade or range, and starting date.
   - Give the timeframe for the posting – when the application period starts and stops, the time period for interviews, and the time period in which a decision will be made.

- Post the process for making an internal application.
- Give contact information for the person who will be receiving applications.
- State any restrictions, such as 'no phone calls to HR', or 'no external applicants'.

3. Receive and respond to enquiries; use a form letter or email to acknowledge receipt of applications.
4. Screen applicants and notify all of them whether they will be interviewed or not.
5. Interview, and test if appropriate. Testing would be appropriate if skills for the position are markedly different from skills used in existing positions. For example, a market analyst might need to know about statistics, which is beyond the mathematical knowledge required for a typical loan officer or customer service associate.
6. Select the candidate and offer him or her the position. Once there is a definite acceptance, notify all the other candidates that they were not selected. Be prepared to explain what made the person selected the most suitable choice, and be sure that HR, the hiring manager, and the candidate's managers are aligned as to why the successful candidate was chosen and others were not.

Tip: managing internal recruitment

These tips apply equally to business managers and HR. Internal recruitment is a situation in which **collaboration** is imperative for success and good morale.

Remember the rumour mill! Whatever is communicated to one internal applicant will be shared throughout the organization with the click of a mouse or the ring of a mobile phone. Be thoughtful about what is said and how it is said, whether in conversation or in writing.

Act promptly to screen, interview, and select. Employees are likely to be more aware of delays than external applicants, and they are more easily able to drop by, send emails, or leave phone messages. They are also more likely to misinterpret delays in the recruiting process and take them personally, worrying that there is a problem with the organization, a problem among the senior managers, or a personal dislike for them as individuals.

All applicants are company employees! Treat them respectfully and considerately, regardless of how well they are qualified for internal positions they apply for. You want them to stay with the organization, and you want them to continue as productive, loyal, supportive employees. Communicate fully and regularly, with acknowledgements and information, so they know the recruiting and hiring process is fair and transparent and so you can avoid, as much as possible, discontent among the employees who do not get the new position.

External recruitment. For external recruitment, follow these steps:

1. Obtain a current and complete job description to use as the basis of job announcements, screening, interviewing, and selection criteria.
2. Identify typical sources for typical candidates and non-traditional sources for recruiting women and candidates from more diverse backgrounds, including previously submitted job applications.

3. Plan a strategy for reaching those candidates, and prepare and distribute the appropriate materials. Make sure that announcements contain all the necessary information:
   - Include the duties and responsibilities, requirements for eligibility (experience, education, special skills), salary grade or range, and starting date.
   - Give the timeframe for the posting – when the application period starts and stops, the time period for interviews, and the time period in which a decision will be made.
   - Post the process for making an external application.
   - Give contact information for the person who should receive the application.
   - State any restrictions, such as 'no phone calls to HR'.

   Website announcements, advertisements, and employee word of mouth are standard methods of advertising an opening in a basic recruitment process.

   For a more comprehensive process – and depending on the current job market, the available talent pool, and the nature of the position – other recruiting methods may be more effective; for example, mailings, phone calls, news stories, events and job fairs, email or text campaigns, and/or postings in professional publications or at academic institutions.
4. Receive and respond to enquiries and send out information and applications. Streamline this step by using standard cards, letters, emails, or text messages to acknowledge receipt of applications or the closing of the recruitment period.
5. Screen applicants: receive, organize, distribute, and review applications, and then apply criteria to identify the best candidates for interview.
6. Agree among decision-makers on final selections for interviewing and possible testing, and notify candidates. Come up with an effective and inexpensive method of notifying all applicants who are not candidates for interview, while thanking them for their interest and informing them of the organization's policy about keeping applications and résumés for future consideration.
7. Interview, and test if appropriate. Testing would be appropriate if the skills for the position are not widely held even among otherwise appropriate candidates or if there is a risk that candidates have inflated the extent of their qualifications.
8. Select the candidate and offer him or her the position. Once there is a definite acceptance, notify all the other candidates that they were not selected. Be prepared to explain what made the person selected the most suitable choice, if other candidates enquire. HR professionals are best placed to have these conversations.

From the field: creating a pool of agents for stable recruiting of credit officers

To reduce the risk of being unable to fill openings, especially in a period of rapid growth, Sonata, an Indian MFI, has created a 'pool' of potential credit officers.

The chief executive officer always wants a cushion against vacancies in frontline positions and a level of certainty that qualified candidates will be available for consideration. To that end, Sonata developed the concept of business development associates (BDAs). These are not employees of Sonata, but are brought in as part-time agents who form joint liability groups. BDAs are recommended by credit officers (COs) for recruitment to a middle or lower management panel. A CO can train up to four BDAs at a time. Typically, BDAs are unemployed local youth. Sonata pays them for each group they form that meets Sonata's specifications. At the same time, Sonata branch managers are able to observe the BDAs' commitment, communication and people skills, and ability to follow procedures. When Sonata requires additional full-time COs, it turns to the pool of BDAs, who already have experience and knowledge of the organization.

Roles and responsibilities

At the general level, recruitment is an activity that everyone in the institution should be involved in. Recruiting for specific positions also requires the participation of a wide cross-section of people within the organization.

Individuals' involvement in recruiting

Board members have an important role in developing the talent pool of potential executive and senior manager candidates. They should also be promoting the desirability of a career with the organization among their peers and colleagues. Board members expect to hear periodically about the organization's recruitment strategy and recruitment successes or challenges.

Executives or senior managers have a role at the basic level of recruiting, to make sure that the MFI has a recruitment strategy and a sound and thoughtful process in place for recruiting, interviewing, and hiring. As with board members, senior managers take every opportunity to promote the advantages of working in their MFI to public groups and colleagues. They are also alert to sources of talent in traditional and non-traditional situations. When it comes to recruiting and hiring direct reports and managers in the departments or regions they lead, they participate directly in the process. They also review the recruitment statistics on a regular basis.

HR professionals are closely involved in both the general and position-specific levels of recruitment, interviewing, and selection. Their unique contributions are to take the lead in designing processes and tools, organizing and scheduling many activities, maintaining policies and other documentation, providing forms and other materials, compiling and analysing data, and supporting the new employees' transition into the organization.

In a more comprehensive recruiting process, managers collaborate with HR professionals to propose a recruitment strategy for review by senior managers, sometimes by participating in a recruiting, talent management, or HR advisory council. Managers also take advantage of the many opportunities to talk about their institution with neighbours, colleagues, and groups in the community. For all positions that report to them, managers are full participants in recruiting, interviewing, and selection activities.

Functional managers and branch managers' involvement in recruiting

Functional and branch staff members should be encouraged to give positive reviews of their MFI and their work to people they know. For specific positions, they may be included in establishing job requirements and meeting with already screened job candidates. Having staff meet with job candidates can be particularly important if the team the candidate will join is small and works together closely – for such teams, a poor match can be disastrous.

Tip: staffing large, growth-based recruiting campaigns

When your organization goes through a period of intensive growth, the number of applications to be screened, acknowledgements to be sent, and candidates to be interviewed – all in a timely and efficient way – is likely to run beyond the capacity of the HR department. To cope with these situations, consider the following strategies:

- Bring in temporary staff, interns, university students, or part-time staff to process applications, take phone calls, see drop-ins, and send out communications. Balance the expense against the gains to come by having well-matched employees on board and working sooner rather than later.
- Use middle managers – whether from branches or head office departments – to conduct interviews. They will need training, coaching, and initial supervision, but there will undoubtedly be a core group who are good interviewers.

Group involvement in recruiting

A general committee or council needs to provide cross-functional oversight of recruitment. This group may be charged only with supporting the recruiting, interviewing, and selection process, or it may be charged with a wider responsibility for talent management (recruiting and retaining talent) or for serving as advisers across the board to the HR department. Regardless of the scope of the group's responsibility, it plays an important role in keeping the HR department, which may be confined to the head office and consist of non-banking specialists, in regular, fully informed contact with the daily operations of the business. Include women and employees of diverse backgrounds as much as possible on the recruitment committee (as well as on job-specific search committees).

The *search committee* is a group assembled to assist with recruitment, interviewing, and selection. It is formed on a position-specific basis and is intended to augment the regular recruitment process by bringing in people with unique knowledge or special contacts relating to the position.

Depending on the position being filled, the search might be done by the position's manager and an HR professional. Or there might be a search committee that includes board members, key co-workers, or employees with the specialist skills required for the position.

The value of the search committee is that it performs the following functions:

- It brings in the opinions of additional people.
- It helps to reduce subjectivity in the selection decision and promotes objective hiring based on the job requirements.
- It serves as a sounding board for discussing the relative merits of several potentially viable candidates.
- It reduces the pressure to hire a family member or close personal associate of an influential senior manager by sharing the responsibility.
- It promotes a sense of responsibility for new employees among the teams or departments represented in their hiring.

A search committee can be a valuable resource in recruiting, especially for highly specialized positions, but a large committee can be expensive and time-consuming to work with. To decide whether there is sufficient benefit to justify using a search committee, the following questions should be considered:

1. Do the level of responsibility, the scope, and the impact of the position justify the cost of a committee?
2. Will the professional contacts of the proposed members of the committee be useful resources for finding qualified job candidates?
3. Is there another, less resource-intensive way of finding recruitment sources and selection evaluations for the position?
4. Is there an existing group – a committee or professional association, for example – that could provide assistance in recruiting and hiring?

If the answers to questions 1 or 2 are 'no' or the answers to questions 3 or 4 are 'yes', then a large search committee may not be the most effective resource, and a small committee may be sufficient.

Involvement of the head office in recruiting

Once an institution has expanded into branch offices at a distance from the head office, the question arises as to how the head office should be involved in recruiting, interviewing, and selecting new employees.

It is recommended that the recruitment process continue as a solid collaborative effort between the head office and the branch, supported by clear policies and comprehensive minimum expectations for recruitment and hiring decisions, standardized and documented processes, and training for branch managers. The overall process needs to include clearly designated required steps, such as reference checks and approval by a senior manager or an HR professional, before a job offer can be extended.

When the recruitment and hiring process is conducted for a senior position, final interviews should be conducted at the head office. At that juncture, the candidate can meet potential peers – existing senior managers – and the leadership team can demonstrate the institutional culture. Key head office leaders can provide their input on the candidate's apparent 'fit' with their team and with the organization as a whole.

Review and adapt the process

If the upcoming recruitment, review, interview, and selection process is routine, the search committee will need only a short time to review the steps and set up a timeline.

Sometimes, however, recruitment is not routine; for example:

- recruiting for a new type of position;
- drawing on new sources of job candidates;
- looking for unusual qualifications;
- recruiting within an unusually compressed timeframe;
- depending on key interviewers with limited availability;
- hiring for a senior-level position.

In those cases, the routine recruitment process may need to be adapted in one or more of the following ways:

- change from holding a single interview with the hiring manager and the HR professional to holding two or more interviews with a series of individual interviewers (members of the search committee and others);
- change from having a series of interviews and informal visits to a single, possibly panel-style interview;
- include visits to both the head office and branches or social events to meet board members or other key stakeholders.

Another adaptation of the process can result from the decision to introduce some kind of assessment activity or to change the type of assessment activity.

The important point is to plan adaptations in advance so that the process runs smoothly once it starts and the people who need to be involved are prepared to participate.

Create a job posting

Using the job description, outline of qualifications, and candidate profile, create a brief description of the job and its requirements that can be used for internal posting and in external communications. Make sure the must-have elements of the job description are fully and clearly explained. Include any important working conditions, such as extensive travel, part-time hours, unusual shifts, or office location, so that candidates know whether it is appropriate for them to apply.

The job posting may be the first impression that applicants, the organizations they are associated with, and their friends and colleagues have of the institution. It is a chance to communicate what the organization stands for, how it views the future, what it has to offer employees, and what working there is like. Pay close attention to how the position and the organization are described – the specific choice of words and the priority of the points in the posting.

Provide all contact information and the website address so applicants can learn even more about the organization.

Prepare application packs for distribution

An application pack consists of a cover letter, an application form, information about the opening (if the enquiry is connected to a posted opening), and information about the institution. Do not assume that people who request an application for a specific position remember what they have previously read about the organization or the job.

You may wish to have a list of current vacancies or directions to the website (if it is kept up to date) that you can include when replying to general enquiries about employment with the organization. It can be helpful to include short descriptions of the most frequently hired positions or those most frequently filled during expansion, to help enquirers position their applications.

The application form. The application form gives applicants guidance regarding the information they should provide about themselves. It may offer the option to either fill in the form or attach an already prepared résumé, if the applicant has one.

The form should be checked carefully to ensure that it meets two key criteria. It should include directions and space for all necessary information to determine whether the applicant has the must-have requirements for the position. It must also must comply with the requirements of law, regulation, organizational policy, and local custom.

The application form may or may not include a statement of the institution's code of conduct.

A sample application form is included at the end of this section, and it may be used as a template, provided that it meets the two criteria above.

Identify sources of job candidates

Finding an adequate pool of qualified candidates for a position can be one of the most difficult parts of the recruiting, interviewing, and hiring process. The time to look for good candidates is not right after someone quits or a new position is created. Every day is the time to look for good possible candidates.

Building and maintaining talent pools requires a steady commitment and organizational discipline. It depends on networking, public relations, communication, and regular contacts. Furthermore, hiring needs should be anticipated, based on the institution's strategic plans and succession planning.

Internal candidates. One of the first places to look for job candidates is within the organization. Do not assume anything about current staff – keep an open mind. Ask questions about staff members' interests, accomplishments, and qualifications. Circulate the job posting. Talk to everyone. If a current staff member believes he or she is qualified and is not considered, morale can be damaged.

Résumés on file. If recruitment has been ongoing, there will be applications and résumés already on file. Review them, and contact anyone who looks appropriate.

Networking. Networking, word of mouth, and referrals are the best sources for candidates. All colleagues and acquaintances whose judgement you respect should be regularly asked if they know of suitable candidates for your institution. Your network can come from a variety of areas:

- personal contacts;
- conventions;
- workshops or courses;
- family and friends;
- similar organizations;
- community organizations;
- schools or universities;
- religious organizations;
- professional associations;
- past employers;
- clubs and associations;
- past employees.

Contacts, publicity material and events. In every location, there are traditional sources for job candidates. Recruiting requires regular contact with those sources as well as job-specific communication with them. When an opening is anticipated or occurs, act promptly.

- Call or email contacts at those traditional sources – academic institutions, professional organizations, employment centres, and individuals such as past employees, board members, and colleagues in other organizations.

- Prepare packs of publicity materials – job postings and brochures about the institution – to distribute to the traditional sources and new possibilities.
- Consider holding an event at an academic institution, a convention, or a meeting of a professional organization. It might be purely social – a coffee morning or an evening reception. You might have a table or a booth at a sporting event, at a cultural event the organization contributes to, or in a shopping area.
- Having someone from the organization speak at a school or association meeting is another kind of event that you could consider.

Publicity and advertising. Postings on the organization's website are a modern and no-cost way of letting a wide audience know about a job opening.

Bulletin boards in organizations that are traditional sources of candidates are another no-cost avenue for publicizing an opening.

Notices and ads in specialist journals or association newsletters can be reasonably priced and somewhat targeted.

Advertising in local papers or magazines is a way of broadly dispersing information about an opening and the organization. It should be carefully considered for cost and effectiveness as well as for the impression it might give of the organization.

In general, remember that the placement of publicity and advertising affects who might apply and what readers will think of your organization.

Outreach events. Some organizations use learning events for recruiting. This is a proactive, longer-term approach. Organizations may:

- offer a pre-job course at a local institution;
- participate in an education programme run by a local institution;
- sponsor and participate in ongoing community projects that attract numbers of people who might be job candidates, such as a youth or 'green' organization;
- bring young people into the organization for pre-job education;
- offer internships to secondary school or university students;
- offer or collaborate on business or general leadership programmes for young people.

Table 3.7: Advantages and disadvantages of recruitment methods

Method	*Advantages*	*Disadvantages*
Media job postings	Large audience Targeting specific groups	Expensive Short duration Relatively little information for prospective applicants
Employee referrals	Well targeted Good first screening for cultural fit Whole organization involved in recruiting	Pressure to hire poorly qualified, poor-fit applicants Limited talent pool
Job fairs	Useful for multiple positions Relatively inexpensive Larger talent pool	Time-consuming Often limited to applicants with little job experience
Recruiting at schools	Known talent pool Pre-trained applicants	Time-consuming Possibly limited to less experienced applicants
Walk-ins or mail-ins	Inexpensive	Random Time-consuming Limited talent pool
Government employment centres	Inexpensive Potentially good knowledge and skill fit	Limited to certain categories and jobs Limited control over screening

Receive and process applications

Once the position is published, enquiries and applications will begin to arrive. Typically, the HR professional sets up or follows existing procedures for routing and filing the documents. Sending out cards or email messages – whichever is appropriate – to let applicants know that their documents have been received and to give them a sense of the timeline for review and scheduling interviews, makes a strong positive statement about the organization. This communication may also include space to indicate if any information is missing from their application and to provide a contact number or email address.

Review résumés and applications

At this point in the process, the members of the search committee read the application forms and résumés that have accumulated. As a result of their review, they will decide on a designated number of applicants to bring in for interviewing and assessment.

Although it can be tedious, time-consuming, and sometimes even frustrating to review a large number of applications and résumés, it is important to take the task seriously and allocate the time to review every application, to accomplish the following goals:

- Ensure that every good candidate is identified, even though résumés may all differ widely.
- Avoid any appearance of favouritism towards certain applicants or discrimination against others.
- Convey to all managers and co-workers that the committee takes seriously its responsibility for filling the position.
- Respond to any enquiries from applicants or influential people in applicants' networks.
- Write thank-you letters to all applicants, whether they come in for interview or not.

Sorting criteria. Sort résumé and applications into three categories, as shown in Table 3.8.

Table 3.8: The three application categories

Yes	Has all the must-have requirements
No	Does not have the must-have requirements
Maybe	Unclear whether the candidate has all the must-have requirements, but has enough of them to warrant investigating further *or* Has some must-have requirements and some additional requirements that might be assets – sufficient to merit further investigation

Tips for reviewing résumés. When setting up the review process:

- review the sorting criteria to ensure that all members of the committee are aligned;
- schedule time for the activity;
- schedule search committee check-in meetings to promote accountability among members;
- batch résumés and applications, and review several files in one sitting;
- consider reviewing in two phases. In the first phase, each file is reviewed by only two people, who identify the 'yes' and 'maybe' files, for review by all members of the committee in the second phase.

During the review:

- remember that sorting is only about deciding whether to interview the applicants, not whether to hire them;
- search each applicant's résumé for must-have qualifications;
- exercise discipline and put résumés with strong qualifications that are irrelevant to the position and would not be a good match in the 'maybe' group;
- focus on the content of the résumé; avoid being overly impressed by appearance unless presentation style is an important characteristic for the position;

- look for missing or unusual information – check start and end dates for schooling and jobs, and look for gaps;
- if there are gaps, make notes for follow-up – do not make assumptions about what they mean;
- look for achievements, growth, and progress in studies, non-academic activities, work activities, and activities outside work (such as leadership in professional or community organizations).

Selecting candidates for interviews

The search committee meets one or more times to discuss the applications they have reviewed and the candidates they have selected for the interview process. When they have their complete list (sometimes called the 'shortlist'), they move into preparing for interviews.

1. They prepare an interview schedule or list of times that search committee members are available to participate in interviews and finalize any non-routine aspects of the interview process.
2. They ensure that communications to candidates for interviews are prepared, reviewed, and sent promptly.
3. They ensure that communications to applicants who will not be interviewed are prepared, reviewed, and sent promptly.

Template 3.7: Application form

Your responses on this application form are confidential.

Please print your answers and complete each item fully. You may attach a résumé to the application. If you need more space to provide the requested information, attach additional sheets to the form.

General information

Family name	Given name
Permanent address	Primary phone number
Current address (if different from permanent address) Position applying for	Other phone number/email address Date available

Education

Degree or certificate	Specialization	Institution	Year received

Employment background

Please indicate any employers we CANNOT contact for references.

1. Employer/organization	Position held	
Address	Start date	End date
Name and title of supervisor	Phone number (including area code)	
Reason for change	Annual salary	

2. Employer/organization	Position held	
Address	Start date	End date
Name and title of supervisor	Phone number (including area code)	
Reason for change	Annual salary	

3. Employer/organization	Position held	
Address	Start date	End date
Name and title of supervisor	Phone number (including area code)	
Reason for change	Annual salary	

Languages

Please indicate proficiency: fluent, conversational, basic.

Language	Speaking	Writing	Reading

Skills/qualifications

Please list any special skills, background, or experience that qualify you for this position.

Template 3.8: Sample mission and code of conduct

[The mission and code of conduct or statement of institutional values are included with the job application so that there is no doubt in the minds of potential employees about what will be expected of them should they be hired.]

Organization mission

The mission of the MFI is that every family and microbusiness can have access to affordable and readily available financial services, enabling clients to make a positive impact on their economic, social, and natural environments.

Code of conduct

The MFI recognizes certain values as important to corporate ethics and operational success. These values pervade all levels of the organization and are particularly important in staff dealings with the public. The following code of conduct outlines the values the MFI expects staff to uphold.

- We will always be honest, cordial, and straightforward with our clients, fellow employees, suppliers, and supporting institutions. We will also maintain all client and organization information in the strictest of confidence.
- We will act with integrity and trustworthiness. We will observe the highest ethical principles to ensure that no company policies, procedures, or positions are abused for any personal or family gain or benefit.
- We will maintain clean and neat personal appearances whether in the office, visiting clients, or attending to suppliers or support agencies, or wherever else we may represent the organization.
- We will maintain proper cleanliness, security, and organization of all office equipment, materials, working space, records, vehicles, and buildings.
- We will be diligent, hardworking, efficient, and effective in our working styles. We will not use company time or privileges to conduct personal business.
- We will act creatively, confidently, and courageously to share the best values and ideals we bring to every interaction, whether with clients, staff, or other persons. We will seek positive solutions and outcomes for all concerned, in any relationship or interaction we undertake.

The mission and the code of conduct will be discussed in the pre-employment interview.

All individuals who accept a job offer with the MFI are expected to sign a statement of agreement to follow the code of conduct and uphold the mission. They will do this during the on-boarding process, when they will have the opportunity to learn more about the organization and have questions answered.

Problems and risks in recruiting and selection

The major risk in recruiting is that the wrong people apply for positions and then get hired. Several problems result from this mistake, most of which can be discussed in terms of separation and replacement costs – the resulting direct and indirect costs to the organization – both of which can be high. The indirect costs are more insidious – they take longer to become evident, and they may be hard to detect.

As mentioned earlier, the cost of staff turnover ranges from 50 per cent to 150 per cent of annual salary, with higher costs associated with more experienced and more senior staff. Separation costs are associated with processing a resignation or termination and, in some cases, severance payments. Replacement costs are associated with hiring, such as time spent on the search, screening, and interviewing process; advertising costs; and signing bonuses or relocation costs, if applicable.

Direct costs can include:

- the salary for the badly matched new hire;
- severance pay associated with terminating the mismatched employee;
- legal fees, if necessary;
- security fees associated with changing locks or changing computer access codes;
- advertising and other recruiting costs for the replacement hire;
- orientation and training costs for the replacement hire.

Indirect costs can include:

- reduced productivity while the mismatched employee is brought on board, and further reduced productivity while the replacement employee is oriented and trained;
- the time of the HR professional and the manager spent on-boarding, monitoring performance, and finally, processing the termination;
- quality of work or quality of decision-making, depending on the employee's level;
- decline in morale resulting either from frustration at the poorly performing employee or from poor management or leadership from the poorly performing executive.

Ethical issues in recruiting

Several years ago, an MFI undertook an investment campaign to raise a new infusion of equity. Believing that a team of highly professional senior managers would give the organization a competitive edge, the MFI recruited graduates from a top business school with a good salary package and attractive promises. Once the investment was completed, these business school graduates, who had never fitted well into the institution's culture, were sidelined and pressured to leave their positions.

Reasons for poor selection decisions can include the following:

- *Information.* Decisions have to be made without all details being available.
- *Subjectivity.* Decisions are based on likes/dislikes and not on applicants' skills and suitability for the position or organization.
- *Budget.* Recruitment budget is insufficient to cover all direct and indirect costs of recruiting.
- *Time.* Managers are overworked and not able to give time and attention to recruiting, interviewing, and evaluating, resulting in quick, poorly considered decisions.
- *Tools.* The processes, tools, skills, and knowledge needed for sound recruiting, interviewing, and selection are inadequate or missing.

Legal and cultural considerations. Legal aspects of recruitment have become more and more complex – many decisions about people in an organization are now governed by regulation. It is critical that managers and HR professionals be informed about and comply with the laws and regulations of their region. These legal aspects can include anti-discrimination and equal opportunity provisions to ensure that decisions are based on a person's ability to do the job, not on unrelated factors such as gender, race, or nationality.

Culturally based considerations can lead to complex situations requiring creativity and courage to resolve. For example, in Afghanistan, it is more appropriate to hire women credit officers because most micro-lending clients are women, but it can be difficult for women to go to strangers' homes when they need to follow up in the field.

Policies: hiring family and friends

Another risky issue is recruiting and hiring close friends and relatives of current employees. This risk is significant if no steps are taken to make sure the applicants meet the job requirements. The risks are that managers will feel pressure to overlook poor performance, offer higher levels of pay, give only positive feedback, and avoid terminating unsuitable employees. In addition, managers may feel that their authority is undermined or non-existent. Co-workers will resent favouritism and freeloading, and morale will decline.

There are two possible ways to address the risks inherent in hiring family members. One approach is to adopt an organizational policy against hiring family members. The policy provides guidance for managers and HR professionals in recruiting. It also serves as an objective, face-saving explanation to family members about why they cannot be hired. Another approach is to allow the hiring of family members but restrict them from working in the same department or from reporting to each other or to the same supervisor. In adopting this approach, it is critical to use the recruitment, interviewing, and selection process rigorously to ensure that such applicants are hired only if they are appropriate for the open position.

Interviewing and selection: testing, interviewing, checking references

Interviewing is an integral component of the recruiting process. The interview is the moment when the job candidate 'comes to life' or new aspects of a current employee emerge. As interviewees meet with prospective employers, relationships begin to form, 'chemistry' and 'fit' can be assessed, and all parties are better able to share more in-depth and nuanced information.

Interviewing is the heart of the process. It can be the most satisfying period of finding exciting new members of the organization's team, and it can also be the most vulnerable point for making mistakes.

In every case, candidates for employment go through one or more interviews. In some cases, they may also go through an assessment of some kind. For all candidates who 'pass' the interviews and assessments (if used), the final activity is checking references. The final selection and the decision to make a job offer come after those three steps.

Typically, the interview is the strongest factor in determining whether an organization wants to select a candidate for employment, and in influencing that candidate's decision to join a business.

Although most managers and HR professionals conduct interviews only when they are hiring, the basic skills of interviewing are important communication skills that are useful in other managerial and workplace activities. Preparing for and running a meeting, asking effective questions in a skilful way, listening thoughtfully, and being able to probe and follow up for more information and insight are valuable for teamwork, coaching, giving feedback, holding performance review meetings, running business meetings, and doing research. For those reasons, as many managers as possible should be trained to interview and be involved in the process.

Table 3.9: Alignment of people management responsibilities

Business manager – typical contributions	*People management responsibilities*	*HR professional – typical contributions*
Interviewing Evaluating candidates Selecting the finalist Determining salary level, based on pay scale Making or reviewing job offer documents or making offer in person	Match the right people to the work	Coordinating interviews Interviewing Contributing to evaluation and selection Advising on salary level, based on pay scale Preparing and making the job offer Maintaining documentation and files Administering payroll, benefits, and other 'back-office' procedures

Connections to other components of the performance management system

Interviewing and selection are linked to the same elements of the performance management system as recruiting. As indicated in the introduction to this section, interviewing is also an important competency used in various performance management activities:

Giving *feedback* and *coaching* on a daily basis on the job and during more formal meetings to set expectations and targets, and to review progress.

Effective *performance review* conversations and *goal setting* also require the same competencies as interviewing.

During the *succession planning* process, successors need to be reviewed and selected as if they were job candidates.

High-potential candidates also need to be reviewed and selected for the high-potential programme. In some cases, they are interviewed before being admitted into a formal 'fast-track' programme, to assess their readiness, potential, and commitment.

Development planning can begin during interviewing and on-boarding, to make sure the newly hired employee receives appropriate training and some attention to his or her future interests.

Table 3.10: Interviewing and selection activities through the stages of organizational growth

Getting established	*Established and growing*	*Settled and mature*
HR and job manager interview job candidates Screening interviews are conducted only for high-volume recruitment efforts Assessments are basic, if any References are always checked	More than one level of management is involved in interviewing, especially for managerial positions High-volume recruitment requires the use of many managers to supplement HR staff Consider incentives to involve staff in recruiting	All managers are expected to learn basic interviewing skills More varied forms of interviewing, including assessment centres, may be used May use more sophisticated assessment tools

Involving the whole organization

As indicated in the section on recruiting in this chapter, a broad group of people in the organization need to be involved in interviewing and selection, over time and across various positions.

HR professionals and business managers have a formal role in interviewing and selection.

Potential co-workers of job candidates may have informal conversations, which supplement formal interviews.

Senior management is involved in interviewing candidates for managerial positions, especially at the middle level.

Interviewing and selection policies

Because interviewing, assessment, and reference checks are so important to making a good final selection, the organization needs policies to guide the staff involved in the process. There must be policies covering the following items:

- relevant laws, regulations, organizational policies and procedures, and national or local customs, and a statement of intention to comply fully;
- conditions under which interviews and assessments may be conducted – for example, no undue physical stress, breaks and refreshments during day-long interviews;
- who may participate in interviews and assessments, to avoid the appearance of conflict of interest or violations of local custom;

- as far as possible, interviewing and selection panels need to include at least one woman employee;
- behaviour during interviews and assessments – for example, to avoid stress and to avoid harassment or the appearance of harassment;
- what may be discussed during interviews, to be in compliance with laws and human rights policies – for example, avoiding questions about religion or plans for starting a family;
- the privacy and confidentiality of the candidate's identity and the results of the interviewing and assessment process, especially the safekeeping and security of sensitive information.

Risks in the interviewing and assessment process

Be aware of the most significant risks in interviewing and assessment:

- inappropriate behaviour or conversation, even when unintentional, such as asking about ethnic affiliation if that is a prohibited topic, or having a man interview a woman alone when cultural norms disapprove of such interactions;
- unfairness or subjectivity, whether real or only in appearance, such as allowing someone to interview a close friend.

The kinds of policies outlined in this section are mainly intended to avoid these risks as well as to ensure a sound interviewing and selection process.

Interviewing process

The process must include:

1. Contacting candidates for interviews and assessments to explain procedures and schedule activities.
2. Scheduling people and facilities for interviews and assessments. When the recruiting process is well established, consider scheduling multiple interviews – either single interviews with several people (members of the search committee and others, if necessary) or two or more interviews with the hiring manager and the HR professional, perhaps before and after the assessment activities (if used). If the candidate pool is large, schedule two rounds of interviews, the second round for candidates who are successful in the first round.
3. Conducting interviews and assessments.
4. Agreeing on the candidates who have been successful in the interviews and assessments, and whose references will be checked. Be sure that candidates who are successful in the interviews and assessments know that the final step will be a reference check. Finalize the list of referees to be contacted for each candidate; it may have changed since they first submitted their application.
5. Checking references.
6. Making the final selection, and agreeing on the terms of the offer and the room for negotiation (if appropriate).

Table 3.11: Responsibilities for interviewing, assessment, reference checks

Business manager	*HR professional*
Must • Participate in agreeing on candidates to be interviewed • Help with or become familiar with standard interview questions and the post-interview evaluation form • Prepare for interviews • Conduct interviews (or co-conduct them with an HR professional) • Take the lead in designating candidates who have succeeded in the interviews and assessments • Review the results of reference checking • Prepare for the final selection decision **May** • Participate in contacting candidates for interviews and assessments • Participate in assessment activities or observation, depending on the assessment • Participate in reference checking	**Must** • Coordinate steps and the schedule • Participate in selecting candidates to be interviewed • Take the lead in contacting candidates for interviews and assessments • Take the lead in or coordinate preparation of standard interview questions and the post-interview evaluation form • Prepare for and participate in interviews • Conduct or participate in assessment activities or observation • Participate in the hiring decision • Coordinate reference checking, including the process and protocol to follow • Ensure results of reference checking are reviewed • Prepare for the final selection decision **May** • Propose candidates who have 'passed' the interviews and assessments • Take the lead in or do all the reference checking

Who is involved in interviewing and assessment

The recommended approach is for all members of the search team or search committee to participate in interviewing; they may not all be involved in the assessment activities. At a minimum, the hiring manager and the HR professional conduct interviews and assessments.

Sometimes, other members of the organization should be involved:

- As many board members as possible are involved in meeting candidates for the CEO position, and possibly also for other senior executive posts.
- As many senior managers or executives as possible meet candidates for division or department head or regional director positions.
- Peers and co-workers may be involved, especially if they will be working in a new area of the business together, in a remote location, or under especially challenging conditions.
- Direct reports may at least meet the candidates for the position of their supervisor, especially if there have been problems with the previous supervisor.
- Specialists or experts may meet with candidates for specialized technical positions to assess their qualifications.

The goal is to achieve diverse input, sufficient input, and expert input without overloading the organization or the candidates.

Conduct interviews

An interview is usually an in-person meeting between a candidate and at least one person from the organization. Occasionally, interviews are held by telephone, but this is suggested only for the most unusual circumstances.

Certain aspects of interviewing job candidates come up in more mature HR groups, such as the question of holding multi-party interviews. Interviews with two people can be somewhat stressful for the candidate, and there should be a good reason for holding them. The candidate should have the reason explained to him or her. The two interviewers should carefully orchestrate their questions and comments, avoiding ganging up on the candidate, interrupting each other, or confusing him or her with simultaneous or divergent questions. If the interview is held with one person talking to the candidate and another person observing or taking notes, the reason for this arrangement should also be explained, since it is often unsettling and not conducive to a relaxed, open dialogue.

Multi-person interviews should be reserved for unusual circumstances and should take place only after the candidate has had previous successful interviews. The candidate should be prepared for this type of interview, and there may need to be a moderator to manage the flow of conversation.

Tip: the keys to successful interviewing

- Prepare.
- Maintain rapport.
- Create a relaxed, friendly environment.
- Use relevant and effective questions tailored to the position.
- Use a consistent process and set of questions among all candidates.
- Listen 80 per cent of the time; talk only 20 per cent – the most common mistake of inexperienced interviewers is talking too much.
- Cover all the must-have aspects of the position.
- Explore the nice-to-have qualifications as well.
- Follow up on candidates' answers to learn more. Avoid drilling or interrogating them.
- Use open questions that require more than 'yes' or 'no' answers.
- Ask for examples of skills, experiences, and qualifications.
- Avoid leading, confusing, or long, involved questions.
- Do not assume anything – if information is unclear, or if answers are vague or inconsistent, ask more questions.
- Allow the candidate to ask questions – pay close attention to what he or she asks for indicators of concerns, challenges, or important areas of interest.
- Adhere to organizational policies, legal requirements, and custom.

When preparing for an interview:

- review the candidate's application file;
- develop questions to ask, both the consistent set of questions to cover with all candidates and possibly specific questions related to an individual candidate's résumé;
- confirm the time and date of the interview;
- set up a clean, quiet, and private area for the interview;
- bring paper and a pen for taking notes – notes are essential for later review and comparison.

A list of sample interview questions appears at the end of the section.

At the start of the interview:

- introduce yourself and anyone else in the area, whether they are involved in the interview or not;
- offer refreshments, if appropriate and customary;
- review the purpose and process of the interview, including the expected amount of time it will take;
- begin with relaxed topics of conversation, such as hobbies or recent work experiences. Avoid sensitive topics or tough questions at the outset.

And, when concluding the interview:

- keep to the scheduled time if possible – pay attention to whether your energy or the candidate's is declining, and come to a close if it is;
- make sure the candidate has no further questions for you;
- take the initiative to end the interview, since you are the host;
- review what will happen next;
- return to pleasant, informal topics as you assemble papers, find coats, or put away coffee cups, and see the candidate out to a public area of the building;
- avoid gossiping with co-workers about any topic, laughing about any joke, or discussing the interview while there is any possibility that the candidate will overhear you.

Using behaviour-based interviews

Behaviour-based interviewing asks candidates to talk about and reflect on specific, detailed accounts of their past experiences on the assumption that their past behaviour gives strong indicators of their future behaviour. It is an effective technique when used well, and some behaviour-related questions should be included in all interviews.

Typical behaviour-based interviews ask candidates to describe a circumstance that required a competency such as leadership, effective communication, problem solving, or innovation. Sample behavioural questions that can be included in interviews are given at the end of the section.

From the field: developing interview competencies

Prasthan, an MFI based in India, has two or three people responsible for interviewing new applicants, typically one HR professional, the direct manager of the position, and a technical staff member. To ensure that they conduct effective interviews, all interview panel members go through a two-day training session on how to define and focus on the applicants' competencies and rate them on an applicant scorecard.

Initially, interview skill training was offered only to regional and branch managers, because at first they were the individuals who conducted interviews. But as the institution grew and interviewing was carried out by a wider range of people, the training was also expanded. This has been the approach at Prasthan for four years.

Evaluating the candidate after the interview

In advance of the interviews, prepare copies of the major criteria for the position, and make notes on a copy as soon after each interview as possible. This is especially important if several candidates are being interviewed on the same day. Record observations and conclusions accurately and carefully.

Be sure to have a consistent list of criteria, to facilitate comparisons between candidates and help to document views about how well the candidates fit or do not fit the position requirements and the organization.

Each person involved in the same interview or in separate interviews should make notes on a separate criteria list, so that all points of view are captured.

A refinement of the candidate evaluation process is to prepare a post-interview candidate assessment form before interviewing begins, and have each interviewer complete one as soon as possible after the interview. A sample form appears at the end of the section. It should be customized to reflect the must-have and the nice-to-have requirements of the position and the key factors of the organizational culture.

Assessments

Assessing applicants through activities other than interviews can be helpful in determining actual skill levels. Candidates may exaggerate their experience and skill on a résumé, but it is harder to overstate them during a test.

Assessments may be pencil-and-paper or online tests of knowledge, and of the application of some mental skills such as maths, language, or accounting.

Larger, sophisticated organizations sometimes use experiential or activity-based assessments to test interpersonal skills, communication skills, and judgement. Occasionally the question arises about whether to use personality tests.

Testing and assessment are especially useful in a situation where none of the applicants possess the must-have skills, but some may have skills and knowledge that will allow them to learn what's needed more readily. Maths aptitude tests, reading comprehension tests, writing samples, and accounting exercises allow you to discover where along the continuum of skill level, from prerequisite to advanced, the applicants are situated.

The most effective assessments are the ones that can directly, clearly, and objectively show knowledge, skills, behaviour, or attitudes related to the job. Some standardized, off-the-shelf assessments are available and meet those criteria. The drawbacks associated with them can be their cost and the need to translate them into the local language. Some of them may also have cultural biases that distort the results.

The direct link between the content of the test and the content of the job is also important for legal reasons. If the link is not clear and a candidate is excluded because of his or her results, there may be a legal protest. For this reason, great caution is advised when using personality tests. If there is any question about using any assessment, consult an expert in assessment or obtain documentation that the test has been verified through research as valid and reliable.

Conducting an assessment. Conduct the assessment in the office to ensure that it is the candidate who gives the answers, even if the assessment is online. Observe the candidate during the testing process to learn about his or her confidence level, focus and concentration, work pace, ability to follow instructions, and willingness to ask for clarification.

Pre-employment training. In situations where the talent pool is very limited and applicants lack the required skills, consider screening for those who are capable of learning the job. One method of doing this is to implement a pre-employment training programme.

In this kind of programme, applicants spend an extended period, from a full day to a week or more, in an intensive training session during which they are observed for aptitudes and required attitudes and tested for the knowledge and application of basic-level skills.

Pre-employment training builds goodwill and publicity for the institution, since participants are likely to learn something of use whether they get the job or not. It may also supplement what is provided by local academic or training institutions.

Pre-employment training can also build a talent pool. Not all participants may be hired immediately, but they are identified and pre-screened for future recruitment.

Although it is an expense that may seem daunting to a new or small organization, it is an investment and a creative approach to a significant challenge. It is also likely to be less costly than hiring and relocating non-local or expatriate recruits, or than leaving positions unfilled and preventing or slowing the growth of the organization.

Tip: transitioning from pre-employment training or internships

Pre-employment training can be combined with an internship, to provide a more extended work experience. It is essential that expectations are set clearly about the implications of pre-employment training or internships.

If they are intended to be precursors to employment, ensure participants know the criteria and the process for moving from training or internship into employment.

If pre-employment training or internship is not intended to lead automatically to employment, that fact needs to be stated when people apply, when they start, and during their programme. They also need to be informed of the steps they can take to apply for employment.

Checking references

Checking references is the process of confirming that a candidate is and can do what he or she says. It is also a security measure.

One of the predictors of future behaviour is past behaviour, so talking to people who have known a job candidate gives you a view of the candidate's past behaviour. Talking to others can help confirm or change impressions from the interview and assessment process.

Evaluate reference comments carefully

When talking to character and experience referees, remember that they have their own relationships with and points of view about the candidate. Consider their motivations in praising or condemning the candidate.

Sometimes it is challenging to find people who can give a reference. Perhaps the candidate has little or no formal work experience; perhaps their former supervisor is unwilling to talk; or perhaps a colleague distorts the reference because he or she does not want to hurt the candidate's chances of getting the job.

It is usually easier to confirm the facts of schooling, professional certifications, and work experience. In regard to security measures, it may also be easier to check on factors such as licensing, police record, military service, and even government security clearances (if relevant to the position). All of these references or background checks are critical for employees who will handle money, who have information about customers' accounts and businesses, and who could be vulnerable to corruption or fraud.

Methods for conducting a reference check. There are three methods for conducting reference checks:

1. *By mail or email.* This is the slowest method. It does not allow for any rapport or give-and-take in conversation.
2. *By telephone.* This is sometimes the easiest and fastest. There is opportunity for follow-up questions, but, of course, not for reading body language.
3. *In person.* This is the most effective method but not always the easiest to arrange.

Tip: contacting referees

If possible, have job candidates ask their referees to call HR. At the very least, have them inform their referees that HR will be calling them.

Referees will be more willing to share information if they have been contacted by the candidate, and even more so if the contact initiates the call.

Questions for a reference check. As with the candidate interview, it is important to develop a set of questions so that the same questions are asked of all referees and about all candidates. The questions should be based on the must-haves and the nice-to-haves for the position. They should also allow you to verify information provided by the candidate.

Conducting the reference check conversation. Start with rapport building and questions that are easy to answer. Remember that the person giving the reference typically wants to help the candidate. Think of ways to allow the referee to mention weaknesses or gaps without seeming harsh. Listen for hesitations or for what is not said and follow up. Take notes during the conversation.

Sample reference check questions are included at the end of the section.

Whom to contact. The best source of references is the candidate. Inform him or her when you intend to talk to the referees provided. It is also possible to ask the candidate if you can contact people not on the list of references, such as a previous employer. If the candidate is unwilling, try to find out why. The reasons may be valid or concerning – poor relationships and poor performance are important to learn about, regardless of their implications for hiring.

Former supervisors, especially the most recent ones, are the best sources of information, since they have seen the candidate's performance on a daily basis. Other referees may be current or past co-workers or subordinates.

Personal referees are less valuable, since they are most likely to give positive feedback and are least likely to have observed the candidate in a work setting.

How many referees to contact. Generally, it is best to contact as many as possible: two is the minimum number. Do not necessarily disqualify a candidate on the basis of one weak reference. There may have been a personality conflict, or the referee may have been a poor manager. Multiple references allow you to check whether a poor report is unique or confirmed by others.

When to check references. The reference check must be conducted before an offer of employment is made. The usual process is to conduct reference checks after the first round of interviews, to confirm the desirability of the top candidates, and before the second round, so that it is possible to follow up any feedback from the referees in the later interviews.

If a candidate is working currently, if the employer is unaware that he or she is looking for another position, and if the candidate does not want the employer to be contacted, be sure to state clearly that a job offer may be contingent on a positive reference from the employer.

Template 3.9: Sample interview questions

Select **some** of these questions. Choose thoughtfully and focus on the must-have requirements for the position. Think about how the answer will help you assess the candidate.

General employment experience

1. Briefly tell me about your current job responsibilities.
2. What are the three most important duties of your current job?
3. What do you like most about your current job?
4. What have you learned from this job and others you have held?
5. What problems do you encounter in doing your job, and what do you do about them?
6. What do you dislike about your job?
7. Why do you want to leave your job?
8. Have you ever been fired?
9. Have you done the best work you are capable of doing?
10. What areas of your skills/professional development do you want to improve at this time?

Technical skills

1. What is your understanding of our business [be specific here]?
2. What experience do you have with [a businesses of our size/of our clients' size]?
3. What challenges do you think businesses our size face in this area?
4. What do you think makes a small business successful?
5. Tell me about your maths skills. Your analytical skills? [And other major skills required for the position.]
6. When you go shopping, can you easily add up your total purchases in your head, or do you rely on the vendor to tell you your total?
7. When making a major purchase, how do you make your decision? What factors do you consider? (For example, buying a TV, a car, a place to live.)

Personality, motivation or interpersonal skills

1. Tell me what your three major strengths related to work are and how they are expressed.
2. What have you done that shows initiative?
3. Do you prefer working with others or alone?
4. If I were to meet one of your friends on the street, what would that person say about you?
5. What personality characteristics are necessary for success in your field?
6. What kind of people do you like to work with?
7. What would motivate you to come into work at 6:00 am and not leave until 8:00 pm?
8. If you could change one thing about yourself, what would that be?
9. Describe your ideal boss to me.
10. What kind of people do you find it difficult to work with? How have you worked successfully with this type of person?

Specifically related to the organization

1. Why do you want to work here?
2. What interests you most about this job? About this organization?
3. What personality traits, skills, and experiences do you have that will make you successful with our organization?
4. What other jobs/organizations are you pursuing?
5. What would be the 'ideal' job for you?
6. What would be the most challenging aspect of this job for you?
7. What would you like to be doing five years from now?
8. Why should we hire you?

Template 3.10: Sample behavioural questions

[The following questions are the type that can be used for behavioural interviewing. The key to selecting appropriate, effective questions is to focus on behaviours that are essential for the job. Then ask questions that cause the candidate to talk about specific previous experiences.]

For initiative

1. Give an example of a situation in which you had to overcome major obstacles to reach a goal. What was the goal? What were the obstacles? Describe the steps you took to overcome the obstacles.
2. Describe a situation in which you were not as successful as you wished as you worked towards a goal. What obstacles did you encounter? How did you get around each of the obstacles? Why was the situation not as successful as you wished?

For influencing

1. Describe a situation when you had to 'sell' or convince others about an idea or a concept. Describe the process you used. What was the outcome?
2. Describe a situation when you persuaded someone to change his or her mind or to do things in a different manner. What did you do? How did you do it?

For innovation

1. Describe a time when you were able to find a new and better way of doing something. What was it? How did you discover the need for improvement? How did you come up with the new and better approach? How did you implement it? What was the outcome?
2. Think about your last three assignments or projects. On which one were you most able to be innovative? What encouraged you to be innovative? What did you do? What was the outcome?

For leadership

1. Describe a time when you had to take a leadership role, formal or informal. What was it? How would you assess your effectiveness as a leader in that situation? What did you do that was effective? What would you do differently next time, to be more effective?

For problem solving

1. Describe a time when you had to solve a specific problem or handle a crisis. What was the situation? What was your role? What approach did you take? What did you do that worked well? What would you do differently another time, and why? What was the outcome?
2. Describe a time when you had to do an analysis of important issues and information. What was the situation? What was your process of analysis? What led you to choose that approach? What was the outcome?

For teamwork

1. Give an example of a time when you were working with a group and succeeded in developing good rapport with most people. What did you do that was most effective? What would you do differently another time? Why?
2. Describe a situation when you were in conflict with a team member. How did you handle the conflict? What steps did you take? What was the outcome? What worked, and what would you do differently another time?

Template 3.11: Post-interview candidate assessment form

Candidate:__________________________________ Date:______________

Interviewer: ____

Understanding/ background in microfinance	Poor		Lacks experience but has potential to learn		Well demonstrated
	1	2	3	4	5
Interpersonal skills/manner	Weak, timid, rude, withdrawn, overbearing		On the whole, positive		Sensitive to others, pleasant, self-assured
	1	2	3	4	5
Motivation	Apathetic, just wants any job		Interested but lacking in fire		Highly motivated, long-term commitment to development
	1	2	3	4	5
Initiative/ problem solving	Tends to wait for direction		Shows potential, could learn		Results-oriented, shows leadership
	1	2	3	4	5
Maths skills	Weak		Some skills, could acquire more		Highly skilled, could do the job
	1	2	3	4	5
Philosophy/ values	In conflict with organization's		Under-developed, not discernible		Consistent with organization's
	1	2	3	4	5

General comments:

Template 3.12: Sample reference check questions

[Provide the person giving the reference with information about the position before your conversation with him or her.]

1. For how long did you work with the applicant? In what capacity? Were you co-workers, or did you supervise him or her? What was his or her job title when you were colleagues?
2. Given the description of the position (written or explained orally), in what ways was the applicant's position similar to this one? In what substantive ways was it different?
3. For these major responsibilities [describe them one at a time or refer to the written description], how would you rate the applicant's knowledge and skills?
4. Describe the applicant's style of interacting with other team members and with external stakeholders.
5. How would you assess the applicant's ability to comprehend directions or new situations, form a plan for handling the work, and then complete it thoroughly and on time?
6. How would you describe the applicant's ability to use job-related tools or resources? Give an example.
7. What would you give as the applicant's three most significant strengths? What three areas relating to this kind of work does he or she most need to improve or learn about?
8. If you had a position open in your business now, would you rehire the applicant? Why/why not?
9. Given what you have heard about the organization and the position, do you believe they are a good fit for the applicant, for his or her style, skills and knowledge, and interests?
10. Is there anything you would like to add?

Selection and job offers

The culmination of the process of putting the right person into the right job is selecting the person and making an offer. This section addresses the steps to take depending on whether a single final candidate has been identified, several final candidates, or no final candidates.

Process

If there is a single final candidate:

1. The search committee agrees that there is only one final candidate.
2. The hiring manager and the HR professional discuss the terms of the offer and the room for negotiation, if appropriate. They also decide who will make the offer and whether in person or in writing first.
3. The offer is made. Negotiations are conducted, if appropriate.
4. The agreement is confirmed in writing, and all follow-up steps related to payroll, benefits, start date, and on-boarding are set in motion.

5. The hiring manager, the HR professional, and others from the organization may have friendly, 'get acquainted' meetings or social contacts with the candidate before the start date, if appropriate or customary.

If there are several final candidates:

1. The search committee goes through a rating process – examples are given in the tip box that follows – and selects the candidate with the highest rating.
2. If this process is inconclusive, options include undertaking additional reference checks and conducting additional interviews. The process should not be rushed, and it may be helpful to bring in fresh perspectives.
3. Once the decision is made, the process goes through steps 2 to 5 above.

If there is no final candidate:

1. First review the must-have requirements to confirm that they cannot be adjusted. If not, it may be necessary to return to the recruiting process and look for additional sources of candidates, through advertising, contacts, or networking. If it is possible to adjust the must-haves, then review candidates who have already been interviewed and reference checked. If there are still no suitable candidates, then the search resumes.
2. If the only option is to work with a pool of partially qualified candidates, the challenge becomes determining which of them has the best potential for learning his or her way into the position, and how the organization can accommodate that approach. Focus on the candidates' ability to learn and their attitude towards work; this decision will be based more on character and potential.
3. Discuss the terms of the offer, including contingencies, such as a probation period and willingness to go through training. It may be necessary to adjust the salary offer to reflect the candidate's status.
4. Proceed with steps 3 to 5 above.

Table 3.12: Responsibilities for selection and job offer

Business manager	*HR professional*
Must • Take the lead in identifying the final candidate or brainstorming a solution when there are no final candidates • Participate fully in setting the terms of the offer and deciding whether there is scope for negotiation • Ideally extend the offer orally • Coordinate with the HR professional and others regarding aspects of the start date, such as work space, introductions, and on-boarding **May** • Prepare and send the offer letter • Be involved in negotiations, depending on the level of the job and the nature of the terms being negotiated • Have informal or social contact in advance of the start date	**Must** • Take an active role in identifying the final candidate or brainstorming alternative solutions • Coordinate the terms of the offer, including elements determined by policy, procedure, or usual practice • Clarify the options for negotiation and their scope • Prepare or review the offer letter and ensure it is sent • Ideally, negotiate with the candidate in most situations • Prepare all paperwork and arrangements for payroll, benefits, etc. • Participate in setting a start date • Take the lead in arrangements relating to the start date • Plan on-boarding • Encourage the new hire to visit or call with questions or needs **May** • Extend the offer orally • Participate in informal or social contacts in advance of the start date, if customary

The two-up rule

As an extra measure of perspective and security, it is valuable to consult the supervisor of the hiring manager, who must approve the final selection prior to making an offer.

In addition, the supervisor's supervisor is informed, although he or she is not required to contribute to the decision.

For example, if the position of credit officer is being filled, the branch manager, who is the hiring manager, participates and makes the final selection. The branch manager's boss, the operations manager, must approve the selection. The executive director, the boss of the operations manager, is informed about the decision.

Tip: methods for selecting among several candidates

Choose the candidate with the highest score, based on a rating scale or charting:

- *Rating scale.* Give numerical ratings from 1 to 10 to each candidate, based on the must-haves and the candidate profiles.
- *Charting.* List the must-have requirements and the nice-to-have features in order of importance. Include other factors, such as potential for promotion, long-term goals, or salary considerations. Give each candidate a rating on each factor, and add up the scores.

Stay committed to a sound choice

After all the tips and guidelines about making logically sound hiring choices, the other advice that all HR professionals would offer is to listen to your intuition! If there are nagging doubts or lingering concerns about a job candidate, think hard before committing to hiring him or her.

Avoid the temptation to 'just hire someone'

The temptation to 'just hire someone' – the best candidate currently on hand, regardless of fit or qualifications – can be strong when there is pressure from business growth, eager executives, or organizational change. One of the signs of HR leadership is being able to stand firm in the face of that pressure.

Seasoned HR professionals have found that, in a large percentage of situations when they had reservations, their hesitation was justified. Once they gave in to pressure, though, it was too late to make a change.

The desired outcome of recruitment is to put the right people in the right positions at the right time. Learn to trust your professional intuition and avoid rushing the process. Reflect, probe, research, and make sure the organization is making the right decision.

Making the offer

The hiring manager and the HR professional speak personally to the candidate and outline all the details of the offer. Issues such as salary, benefits, start date, work conditions, and work hours should have been discussed in the second interview, so the candidate could consider them while the organization was going through its decision-making process.

It is important to remember that candidates have the choice to accept the offer or not, and they need to do so on a fully informed basis. The hiring manager and the HR professional are responsible for providing as much information as possible about organizational culture, job details, training opportunities, working conditions, and performance expectations. They need to be prepared to revisit any of these topics during the offer and negotiation process.

After the offer has been made orally, it is wise to follow it up with a letter covering the main points.

Allow the candidate time to consider the offer, but give a date by which the offer will expire. The HR professional is the best contact for the candidate during this period if the candidate wants to challenge any policies or negotiate for different terms.

Negotiating terms

While this terminology sounds strong, often the negotiation is a simple matter of adjusting a start date or selecting one form of benefit over another, in instances where benefits are flexible.

In other cases, especially for specialist employees or senior-level managers, there may be more extensive conversations about salary, bonuses, office space, support staff, an early vacation, or perks. Whoever takes the lead in handling these negotiations should prepare carefully, and should have a clear understanding of his or her limits of authority to change the terms and a fall-back position if the negotiation becomes difficult.

Contract

A written employment contract is a 'must have' for all employees, no matter how new or advanced the financial institution. Each new employee signs an employment contract and a package of documents relating to benefits and perks. The HR office prepares, administers, and files these documents.

CHAPTER 4

Making a good start

A carefully designed on-boarding programme can help ensure that the well-matched new employee becomes a productive, loyal, and satisfied long-term staff member. Making a good start is key to how employees are positioned to perform well from the beginning.

The institution has spent considerable time and money to recruit, interview, and hire a new employee. Although everyone may feel confident that the new person is a perfect match for the job and the organization, if there is no proper introduction to the institution and the work expectations, the new hire may not perform well. All employees must be introduced to the organization's values and culture. They must be told and shown what behaviours are acceptable, and they need to learn how to survive and thrive.

An effective induction session provides answers to many of the questions a newly hired person has. More crucially, it sends a strong message to the new person about the importance of the human element in the organization and the employee's role in the business's success.

Several components need to work together to provide that good start. The on-boarding or orientation experience provided by the manager, the HR department, and others is important. Linking new hires to an employee-partner or a mentor helps them learn about the informal side of the work and the culture. All the initial interactions with the manager set expectations, work habits, tone, and relationships in the right direction. Formal and informal training activities are essential to initiating good performance.

A successful on-boarding experience comprises a series of phased activities that set the initial tone and provide valuable information. These include the following basics:

1. receiving an initial orientation manual written for new employees and a series of position-specific 'first 90 days' manuals;
2. going through a series of on-boarding activities;
3. meeting with the manager to learn what is expected, what the job consists of, what the initial goals are, and how to perform the tasks;
4. having one or more colleagues and/or mentors, on a formal or an informal basis, available to provide more casual, personal guidance;
5. participating in training and receiving coaching to acquire the knowledge and skills needed to perform the job.

http://dx.doi.org/10.3362/9781780447926.005

Table 4.1: Alignment of people management responsibilities

Business manager – typical contributions	*People management responsibilities*	*HR professional – typical contributions*
Structure and flow of tasks Job descriptions Quality, productivity, and timeliness expectations for the individual and team Documentation of procedures and rules Job manuals Information about employees' training needs Training content and delivery On-boarding On-the-job training, coaching, and guidance	Organizing the work Helping new employees make a good start	Templates, forms, support for job descriptions, and manuals Training and review of expectations Compilation of training needs On-boarding Training delivery

Connections to other components of the performance management system

Making sure newly hired employees get off to a good start puts the person in touch with several other components of the performance management system.

Setting expectations and performance goals is critical. New employees need to know immediately what their managers expect and what their performance goals are so they can begin to perform appropriately.

Training, coaching, and feedback are required to start the new hire off with the right skills and knowledge, and then to make sure he or she stays on the right track and makes progress as expected.

The new employee's success in his or her first *performance review* will be very much affected by the quality of the introduction to the work, the organization, and the culture.

High-potential new employees will be observed and directed into more rapid development towards leadership positions.

Development planning can influence the kind of formal and informal initial training a new employee receives, to reflect his or her future interests.

On-boarding

Definition

On-boarding is also known as orientation. It covers the set of activities and materials that helps a new hire learn about the organization, including its values, culture, and policies, and begin to settle into the job and the community of fellow employees.

It is important to remember that the recruiting, interviewing, and hiring processes have already communicated a lot about how the organization treats and values employees.

Orientation is an ongoing process that takes several sessions and may last several weeks; it is the start of the process of the new employee becoming acclimatized to the institution. Becoming fully proficient in a new position and completely familiar with a new organization takes much longer than the initial on-boarding period, and both managers and HR professionals need to pay attention to the subtler needs that come up after the programmes end and the first 90 days have gone by.

A checklist of activities for the first 90 days is included at the end of the section.

Table 4.2: Responsibilities for on-boarding

Business manager	*HR professional*
May announce the start date of the new employee Contributes to the process and content Knows all the content covered by others Introduces the new employee to the work space and fellow employees	May announce the start date of the new employee Develops and schedules the on-boarding activities Prepares on-boarding materials Conducts sessions relating to general policies, philosophy, structure, and history Acts as a guide Introduces the new employee to others involved in on-boarding, such as IT staff, trainers, and office manager

Involving the whole organization

Many parts of the organization are involved, formally and informally, in bringing on a new employee. His or her start date will be announced, and the business should encourage employees to introduce themselves to new people.

Some staff have formal roles, for example:

- IT provides training on the computer systems and services;
- accounting staff may train on financial procedures;
- an office manager will provide information on office systems;
- a colleague or manager may take the role of employee-partner or mentor.

Policies

It is appropriate to have a set of policies relating to on-boarding. The primary policy will be the requirement for the organization to provide an orientation. There may also be a policy about a mandatory set of topics to be covered, such as legal and ethical requirements relating to the industry and the position, safety, security, and confidentiality.

Criteria for effective on-boarding

1. *Create a sense of belonging.* New staff want to feel a sense of acceptance and belonging within the business. Orientation needs to create opportunities for them to interact with a range of other staff.
2. *Keep the induction programme lively and engaging.* A week of 'talking heads' quickly deflates a new person's sense of excitement on starting the job. A variety of activities, such as lunch meetings, field trips, individual conversations, reading, and online work, keeps the experience energized.
3. *Be thoughtful about introducing the organizational culture.* New hires want to understand the culture of the business so they can fit in with its values and norms. Explain policies, talk about the vision and mission, go over the organization's history, and share stories.
4. *Ensure clear understanding.* Explain the most important policies, norms, and practices fully and more than once. Give new employees several chances to ask questions. Consider using case stories or role play to make sure they have clearly understood the parameters that will point them in the right direction and help them avoid trouble right from the beginning.
5. *Be candid.* Everyone knows that no organization is perfect and every business has challenges. Be forthright about problem areas. Make sure the orientation is not a wishful picture or a sales pitch. If the situation seems too good to be true, new employees are likely to wonder what's really going on.
6. *Complete the paperwork* ... just not all at once! Spread the experience of form-filling over a series of short sessions.

Location of orientation

At the head office. Where possible, it is valuable for new employees to have some or all of their orientation at the head office. The headquarters location is likely to reinforce the history, philosophy, and values of the organization, and being there helps the new person feel like part of the larger group.

For on-boarding in a newer or smaller institution, being at the head office also means that the HR director or HR manager can make sure that a consistent message and complete and consistent information about the institution are delivered.

In the regions. In a larger institution with multiple locations, on-boarding may take place in stages. When a person has been hired to work in a branch, it is sensible and cost-effective for the first stage of on-boarding to take place there. The branch is where the manager and co-workers are; it is the space in which the employee will work; and its systems are the ones he or she needs to learn.

In larger institutions with regional as well as local branches, it may be worthwhile for the new employee to spend some time at the regional office, especially if he or she needs to interact with people, systems, and functions in that office to perform the job. Face-to-face meetings build collegial connections, which tend to facilitate good communication and work flow. The visit to the regional office can be treated as a special occasion in the orientation process.

It is also recommended that new employees in branches or regional offices have an opportunity to visit the head office sometime within the first six months on the job. This can be done as an annual or semi-annual event, and, in addition to the points previously mentioned, the opportunity to meet the CEO or president as well as see the building and facilities can be a memorable experience for a new person.

What to cover in the on-boarding process

The checklist below gives a number of activities and topics to be covered in the on-boarding process. The position manager and the HR professional will each have items from the list to cover. Topics such as expectations and work goals are discussed in detail in later sections of this chapter.

At the end of the section is a checklist for the contents of a new employee manual, some of which are described in detail below.

Schedule for the on-boarding process: include details for the first session and at least headline information about subsequent sessions, including any formal training. Talk the employee through the plan, explaining the activities, naming the people involved, and answering questions.

Maps and/or diagrams: the building where orientation is held, the building where the employee will work, and the locations of local and regional offices of the institution. Point out key locations relevant to the orientation – toilets, cafeteria, car park, offices to be visited that day and the next, sites of key functions such as payroll or office supplies – that the new person might need in the first week.

Organization chart and employee directory: explain the organization chart and orient the employee to his or her place in it, the manager, and the chain of management beyond his or her direct boss. Point out features of the employee directory, such as emergency numbers, security, special services, or services the employee may need in the near future. Provide the employee with his or her work address and phone number.

Work location, co-workers, equipment, and supplies: relatively early in the orientation, make sure the new person gets to the place where he or she will work and meets immediate co-workers. If appropriate, this is where the new employee could leave a coat. Depending on the physical set-up, make sure all typical work supplies are at the location, so that it is ready for the new person to begin work. If a name badge or sign, or a uniform or coverall is required for the job, have such items ready even if the new person is not required to use them the first day or so of on-boarding.

Tour: take the new employee on a tour of the building where orientation is happening, as well as of the building where he or she will work, if it is adjacent. Relate what he or she sees to the map or to aspects of the job. Be sure to point out even ordinary features of the building, such as elevators, corridors to the car park, and supply cupboards. Ensure there is a tour of the job location if it is distant from the orientation location.

It is a friendly gesture to point out to the new employee local transport, cafes, and restaurants, and any other services in or near the organization's location. Ensure that he or she knows where the canteen or cafeteria is, if there is one in the building.

Calendar of national and institutional events: let the new person know about holidays the organization observes, especially any upcoming ones, and any special days the business acknowledges, such as the anniversary of its founding.

Employee manuals: the material for an employee manual may be in one or more publications or binders. At a minimum, the contents need to include the following items:

- corporate statements of vision, mission, purpose, and values;
- company history and philosophy;
- general policy guide;
- general procedures – safety, security, sick leave, vacation time, and so forth;
- resource list.

It is a warm gesture to have a welcome letter from the CEO, with his or her picture, expressing hopes for the new person's success and reiterating some of the key points from the vision, values, or philosophy. Take the employee through the manual's contents, explaining items rather than reciting them. Cover the most important policies and procedures and the ones that are most likely to affect a new person. Try to allow time for the employee to read the rest on his or her own and to ask questions.

Systems training – equipment: computer, telephone, credit card or cash register equipment, copiers, and so forth. This is where specialists can be involved. However, do not assume that an IT person automatically knows what to cover or how to talk about it to a new employee. Have each specialist do a preparatory run-through before the first time he or she assists with the on-boarding process.

Systems training – procedures: signing up for payroll and benefits; filing for sick leave or vacation leave; receiving mail; sending faxes; and so forth. Have other specialists cover these topics, pointing out where the policies and procedures are addressed in the employee manual (or job manual, if the tasks are job-specific).

Systems training – resources: references, libraries, online materials, training, and so forth. Visit the physical locations, and some of the most useful online locations. Explain how training is provided, and point out any forms or typical announcements an employee might use to get information or register.

Job manual: a job manual describes the tasks of the job, general requirements, and expectations. It also gives a diagram or description to show how the job fits into the operations of the department or branch. It may also include inputs and outputs. It forms the basis of the tour, explanation, goal setting, and on-the-job training that the position manager provides.

Office or departmental manual: this manual lays out procedures and policies that apply specifically to a particular office, department, or other work group. The position manager will take the new person through this information as well, and the employee-partner or mentor may supplement the document with informal information.

Tip: successful on-boarding

The orientation needs to reflect the institutional culture. The priority given to on-boarding, the attention to detail, and the enthusiastic participation of others will be meaningful to the new employee.

- Imagine you are welcoming the friend of an old friend into your home, expecting the person to settle in and stay for a long time. Warmth, courtesy, and sensitivity to the new person's experience will make an indelible impression.
- Get ideas from new employees about what is most useful and important to cover in the on-boarding process.
- Prepare ahead of time and review what people other than the manager and the HR professional will be doing, to make sure it is accurate, complete, and easy to understand.
- Have others read through the documents to make sure they are accurate, free of typing or spelling mistakes, and easy to understand.
- Let other staff know that the person is coming, and encourage them to introduce themselves.
- Consider including co-workers at coffee or meal breaks.
- Meet the employee at the door on the first day.
- Prioritize the on-boarding schedule.
- Schedule all important activities, and allow enough time for each of them, remembering that the new person needs time to absorb all the new information.
- Pace the orientation gradually.
- Emphasize the human side of the organization by introducing people, by interspersing information or systems training sessions with visits or introductions, and possibly by including a small, informal social gathering at coffee break, lunch, or the end of the day.
- Provide smooth and complete handovers from one person to another, especially at the point when the HR professional steps back and the position manager moves into job-specific orientation and initial training, or when the new person moves into a classroom training session of one or more days' duration.
- Follow up after the official on-boarding is over – visit, call, or email to allow the employee to ask questions and to acknowledge that there is a lot to learn.

Success indicators for initial on-boarding days

- The employee asks enough questions, some of which show that he or she has been thinking about the job or the organization and its culture.
- The person is tired but has some energy left at the end of the first day and the first week.
- The co-workers of the new hire know his or her name and have learned something about him or her by the end of the first week.
- Everyone who helps with on-boarding has generally positive things to say.
- The new person seems comfortable to ask a 'silly' question or express mild confusion or concern with all there is to learn.

From the field: orientation to build institutional culture

Indian microfinance institution BWDA conducts an intensive three-day introductory programme. It covers BWDA's vision, mission, and core values, what the new hires can expect from the job, and what BWDA expects of them. The operations manual and the HR manual are reviewed, to make sure that employees are introduced to all the institution's policies and procedures. Both new hires and experienced employees of BWDA cite this intensive orientation as a central element in building the internal culture of cohesion, clarity, and focus, especially when they are caught up in everyday tasks.

Table 4.3: Concerns during the first on-boarding days

Concern	*What to do*
The new person is passive, makes few comments, or asks few questions	• Ask questions and wait for the answers • Offer a quiet moment, with a refreshment or a chance to read • Point out the lack of response and ask if there is a problem or something that you can do to help
He or she seems aggressive, defensive, or arrogant, or talks and acts in ways that are likely to create a poor first impression with the manager and co-workers – notably different from behaviour shown in the hiring process and references' comments	• Guide the person to a private area and use neutral language to point out what you see • Ask if there is something you can do to help with the on-boarding • Express your concern, if necessary
The process is disorganized, too rushed, or too slow	• Pause to organize • Prioritize and postpone some activities, if it's too rushed • Include reading time, or, if the process is too slow, contact others about moving activities forward in order to speed up • Ask the new employee what he or she needs
The manager seems unprepared	• Avoid this with advance planning and communication
Other presenters in the on-boarding process seem unprepared	• Avoid with advance planning and communication • Reschedule if a problem has come up

Template 4.1: New employee package – content checklist

- Name, position and job title, office address, work location, phone number, email address, and fax number
- Welcome letter
- On-boarding schedule – time, activity, location, and person/people involved
- Routine work hours
- Maps
- Organization chart
- Employee directory
- Corporate vision, mission, philosophy, and values
- Company history
- Brochures explaining the organization, products and services for customers, and services for employees
- Key points of business strategy
- Calendar of holidays observed and important institutional events
- Telephone and computer 'quick reference' guides
- Important procedures and policies for the first 90 days
- Employee manual and job manual

The first 90 days – checklist

First week
- All on-boarding activities, including all paperwork
- Name badge, nameplate, and uniform (if applicable)
- All manuals – new employee, general employee, job manual, and any others
- Introduction to mentor/employee-partner (if applicable)
- Introductions to or meetings with appropriate senior-level managers/executives
- Initial conversation with manager about goals and expectations
- End-of-week check-in with HR professional

First month
- At a minimum, weekly interaction with mentor/employee-partner
- At least one check-in conversation with HR professional
- Possible visit to another office – head office, regional, or branch
- Ongoing on-the-job training and coaching

First three months
- Possible tapering off of interactions with mentor/employee-partner, depending on need and inclination
- At least one additional check-in conversation with HR professional
- Communication between HR professional and manager to touch base about new employee's settling into work, group, and environment
- One or more visits to other locations, as appropriate to the position and institution
- First classroom training has occurred or is scheduled
- First interim review, with an update/upgrade of initial goals
- Probationary period ends, or a discussion of conditions for the remainder of the probationary period
- If possible, participation in at least one formal or informal work-group social activity
- At least one explicit professional development conversation – may be related to classroom training

Mentors and employee-partners

Definition

A mentor is usually a slightly more senior person who takes a more junior person – in this case, the new employee – under his or her wing, to help the junior learn his or her way around, to give advice, and to make introductions.

An employee-partner is more often a peer – a co-worker doing the same job and of the same age – who also helps the new employee learn his or her way around and gives informal advice.

Either of these relationships can develop on their own, but making sure that a new employee has a mentor or an employee-partner as an explicit part of the on-boarding process – for the first few weeks, at least – is another effective tool in helping new people make a good start.

Table 4.4: Responsibilities for the mentor/employee-partner system

Business manager	*HR professional*
Must • Agree and contribute to setting up the mentor and employee-partner system • Participate in selecting mentors or employee-partners **May** • Brief the mentor or employee-partner • Introduce the new employee to the mentor or employee-partner	**Must** • Determine whether a mentor/employee-partner system would be useful • Propose and/or contribute to setting up the system • Participate in selecting mentors or employee-partners • Follow up with the mentor/employee-partner to make sure the process is working **May** • Brief the mentor or employee-partner • Introduce the new employee to the mentor or employee-partner

Role of the mentor or employee-partner

The mentor or employee-partner makes a point of keeping in touch with the new employee, providing information about both the formal and informal processes and procedures, and answering questions. They are the ideal individuals for a new hire to talk to about matters that he or she might feel are too trivial or not sufficiently work-related to bring up with his or her manager or with HR.

Sometimes the employee-partner or the mentor has some assigned tasks, such as accompanying the new employee to a company meeting or departmental social event. The contact between the new hire and the employee-partner or mentor should be planned to continue for four to six months.

Formal mentoring. Some organizations have a formal mentoring programme for their high-potential employees. This is a different kind of programme, with a more explicitly developmental purpose. However, if a new employee is identified during the hiring process as having high potential, he or she might move directly into the formal mentoring programme upon starting with the organization.

Other involvement. Other employees may informally become 'buddies' or mentors for a new hire because they were at the same university, worked in another business together, live in the same neighbourhood, or play on a sports team together. If the manager or the HR professional is aware of any of these points of contact, he or she can encourage the experienced employee to become acquainted with the new hire.

Choosing a mentor or employee-partner

As with other orientation activities, interactions with a mentor or an employee-partner can strongly shape the new person's view of the organization. For that reason, it is wise to select the mentor or employee-partner carefully. Consider the following criteria:

- good worker;
- good representative of the organization's culture and values;
- knowledgeable about all the policies and procedures the newcomer is likely to have questions about;
- positive attitude towards the job and the organization;
- reasonable match of temperament with the new hire;
- outgoing enough to take the initiative in the acquaintance;
- sensible enough to judge when the new person might need help and when he or she is moving towards making other friends.

Guidelines for having a mentor or employee-partner system

- Select such people wisely; allow them to decline to participate.
- Brief them on their role.
- Make sure they have all the information on basic policies and procedures.
- Check in with them to make sure the process is working successfully.
- Allow them to withdraw from the role if necessary.
- To support the new hire's trust in the organization, do not ask for or listen to 'reports' about him or her from the mentor or employee-partner unless there is a serious problem – some kind of danger or risk to him or herself, to another person, to the work, or to the organization.

Setting expectations and initial goals

Although every aspect of the on-boarding and start-up processes contributes to setting the expectations of the new employee, it is the role of the manager to talk about his or her specific expectations as they relate to the job. Managers need to talk about their general expectations of someone in the new employee's position, and they need to talk about their initial expectations as the new person learns the job. To make their expectations explicit and concrete, managers need to set goals for the initial period of the new hire's employment.

Definition

Expectations can relate to job performance, participation in the team, appearance, interaction with customers, and administrative procedures. They can be general, such as 'active participation in meetings', or specific, such as 'returning customer phone calls within an hour'. Expectations express how the job should be done and what the work environment should be like.

Goals are targets that the employee is expected to meet, and they can typically be expressed in numerical terms. For example, a teller may be expected to complete a particular transaction within a certain amount of time, and a credit officer will be expected to manage a given number of loans.

Initial expectations and goals

Managers usually have some expectation of how their employees will behave in regard to certain matters from the first day, as well as other expectations that vary depending on the qualifications, experience level, and job level of each employee. For example, a manager might expect all employees to arrive by the designated start time and stay until the designated end time, from the first day of work. On the other hand, the manager might expect an experienced staff member to volunteer to lead a committee and expect a newer employee to join a committee, only once he or she is confident in the basics of the job.

Similarly, performance goals for a new employee will start off at a percentage of the target performance for someone who knows the job and has done it for a substantial period of time.

Probationary employment

Some organizations require that some or all new employees start on probation. Probationary periods may be one, three, or six months. Policies for probationary employees are different, as are salaries and benefits.

This practice may make sense in business environments where statutory benefit requirements are onerous, where termination of regular employees is limited or impossible by law or custom, or where the candidate pool consists of only under-qualified individuals or people without work experience.

There are drawbacks to probationary employment. New employees may feel less than welcome, they may not develop loyalty, and they may feel short-changed and poorly rewarded. Other employees may look down on them and treat them poorly.

For under-qualified new hires, the probationary period should include a sufficiently intensive level of education and training that will be valuable to them regardless of whether they remain with the organization.

The terms and conditions of probationary employment need to be spelled out fully and clearly when screening applicants and in interviews. There needs to be a clear probation contract that defines the time period, any gradations, and the requirements for moving from probationary to regular status.

Managers and HR professionals need to comply diligently with the terms and conditions, ensure that probationary staff are treated well, and keep one another accountable.

Table 4.5: Responsibilities for setting expectations and initial goals

Business manager	*HR professional*
Must • Identify and document expectations – prioritize for communication to new employees • Outline performance goals for new staff, staff after three months, and proficient staff – and document them • Communicate expectations and goals to new employees • Describe support and follow-up activities • Describe the first interim review of goals	**Must** • Provide training and/or coaching to managers **May** • Provide a template for identifying expectations and goals • Provide advice and counsel

How to set expectations and initial goals

When preparing to discuss expectations, the manager:

- needs to think through what his or her expectations are – what is important for success on the job, with the team, and in the work environment;
- then needs to prioritize these expectations, identifying the ones that are most critical for a new person to know immediately and the rules that it would be very serious for even a newcomer to break – for example, timeliness, security, and accuracy in cash handling might be the 'make-or-break' expectations;
- finally decides how many expectations to talk about in the first conversation – enough to be helpful but not so many as to confuse or

overwhelm the new person. The expectations should be documented in the job manual or the branch or departmental manual.

Reminder: Managers' expectations must be in line with company policies and expectations as well as with legal and regulatory requirements.

A work sheet to help with reviewing and documenting expectations is included at the end of the section.

Preparing initial goals. When preparing initial goals, the manager needs to review the tasks cited in the job manual or the job description – the main tasks, the most important results, and the success measures. The manager then needs to think about the goals for experienced employees and the stages of performance they went through. If it took six months for most of them to become fully proficient performers, what was their level of performance at three months? At six weeks?

On the other hand, the manager may be under pressure to set aggressive performance goals for new employees. Perhaps overall results are down, and the business needs to recover; perhaps competition in a new market is intense. In such circumstances, the manager still needs to set initial and interim goals for new hires, but he or she needs to think creatively about how to help the new people become proficient rapidly.

Whichever the case, the manager finishes his or her preparations by planning how to discuss performance goals – all at once or in stages. Outlining goals all at once gives the new person a complete picture of what he or she will have to accomplish. It is wise to put goals in writing and to talk about them more than once, to make sure that nothing is overlooked. Covering goals in stages helps the new staff member focus on certain areas of performance initially that may be more appropriate for the position. For example, establishing a goal relating to accuracy and speed of transaction might be at stage one for a teller; adding a goal relating to looking at the customer or using the customer's name may come at stage two.

There is a work sheet to help with documenting performance goals at the end of the section.

Talking about expectations and goals. The most important thing for the manager to remember is that talking about goals and expectations is an ongoing process, not a single conversation. This is especially true for new employees in the first week or so, while they are taking in a vast amount of new information.

It is reasonable to tell a new employee about expectations and performance goals for experienced staff and then goals and expectations for the new hire. This approach provides an immediate goal and an idea of what is to come in the future.

Tip: discussing goals and expectations

- Combine talking about goals and expectations with explaining tasks, demonstrating them, and providing instructions or a manual. Give the employee the 'what' of the job along with the 'how well' aspect.
- Let the employee know how on-the-job training will proceed so that he or she realizes that there will be ongoing support to help reach the first stage of goals.
- Be sure the employee knows how and when the first evaluation of performance will occur. This is particularly important if the institution starts employees on a probationary basis.
- Make it clear that questions and requests for help are acceptable and even encouraged until it is time to establish an expectation that the employee will handle some or all of the tasks of the job independently.

One manager's guide for setting expectations

Mr Singh, a senior manager at BWDA, builds his expectation-setting conversations with staff around three elements:

1. explaining the organizational structure and growth strategy – where we are, where we're going;
2. describing the experiences of staff who have reached higher levels in the institution – how people achieve success here;
3. emphasizing the pillars of the institution's culture: discipline, faithfulness, client focus, community development – what guides all of us in our work.

In Bala Singh's experience, employees need to be motivated by the institution's values. What BWDA finds is that its employees are motivated both by success in their positions and salaries and by satisfaction with the institution's social mission and approach to working with clients.

Think carefully! How often should you set goals?

Staff at Sampoorna had initially been asked to set goals every 30 days, and then, as they gained experience, every 90 days. They received feedback and guidance for improvement at the end of every 30- or 90-day period. Staff gave mixed reports about this approach. Some found it supportive and helpful to have feedback, know how they were doing, and be coached for improvement. Others found the frequency of making plans and being appraised nerve-wracking and anxiety-provoking. They felt as if they spent all their time planning and worrying about feedback rather than doing the work.

Expert commentary: We might recommend to Sampoorna managers that they adapt their process. They could adopt shorter cycles of goal setting and feedback for employees who need that level of monitoring and those who flourish with the attention, while for employees who seem to prefer more autonomy and are performing reasonably well, the longer cycle would be appropriate.

On-the-job training, coaching, and the probationary period

An Indian MFI brings new hires in for a six-month probationary period. The first month is spent in on-the-job training. The typical entry-level position is 'cluster coordinator', responsible for forming and maintaining joint liability groups. For example, a new cluster coordinator spends a week working closely with the assistant internal auditor, learning accounting and audit procedures. For the next three weeks, the new coordinator works alongside a senior cluster coordinator to learn the intricacies of group management and loan processing. During the same period, the cluster coordinator learns about administrative skills from a branch manager.

In the second month, the probationary employee gradually begins functioning independently, building confidence in his or her skills and performance. The branch manager gives regular feedback. This is a good example of how new employees may be given more independence as they grow more proficient and familiar with their responsibilities.

Following up. Give encouragement, help, and feedback regularly as you assess the new person's capacity to learn and feel comfortable in the job. Making every effort to ensure that a new employee is able to meet initial goals and live up to initial expectations makes sense in light of the investment made in recruiting, hiring, and on-boarding him or her.

A checklist for setting expectations and initial goals appears at the end of the section.

Characteristics of effective goals

Effective goals are those the employee can understand and act on with some reasonable expectation of success. When talking about and documenting goals, be sure the goal statements have the following characteristics:

- *Specific.* What needs to be done and the expected level of performance. An example of a goal for a staff member in administrative services would be: document in writing what each department needs to do to evacuate its area of the building when the fire alarm sounds, with a description and a map of the exit routes and assembly areas. To be completed by the end of the week.
- *Measurable (or observable).* It is possible, in an objective, concrete way, to determine whether the goal has been achieved. (See Template 4.4 at the end of the section.) An example goal would be: have the evacuation plan reviewed by the office manager for accuracy and completeness.
- *Actionable.* It is clear what needs doing; something that can be performed. A bad example would be: figure out why we're losing money. A good example goal for an employee in the accounting group would be: analyse all the small business loan accounts and tally up the delinquencies, the length of delinquencies, the number of defaults, and the amount of money not repaid. Prepare a written analysis for review with the branch manager by the 20th of the month and every month for the next quarter.

- *Realistic*. Something that can be achieved. A bad example would be: be more of a people person. A good example for an employee with a customer service role would be: look customers in the eye, smile, and use their names. Speak confidently and courteously.
- *Time-bound*. How much time to spend on the task or the deadline for its accomplishment. The examples given for 'Specific' and 'Actionable' would also work here.

To keep these five characteristics in mind, just remember the first letter of each – SMART.

Table 4.6: Problems in setting expectations and initial goals

Problem	*Consequences*
There is a failure to discuss expectations and goals at all	The new employee has to figure out what to do, how to do it, how to behave in the workplace, how to get along with others, and what quality level is expected on his or her own or by observing and asking co-workers. His or her performance will most likely be unsatisfactory to everyone, including him or herself, and relationships will be damaged Subsequent performance reviews will have limited or no validity
Discussion of expectations and/or goals is incomplete, vague, or too general – important points are missing, are not discussed, or are not specific enough to be actionable	As in the first point, the new employee will be at a loss, but the manager may have more difficulty understanding why, since he or she may believe that everything was spelled out
There is no support and no follow-up to make sure that the new hire can achieve the set goals	The new hire may know what is expected, but is unable to perform because of a lack of skills or knowledge. In some cases, the manager may be unaware of the level of support a new employee needs, but at other times the organization may have a tacit belief in 'sink or swim: that's how I learned'. In either case, there will be frustration on all sides

Success indicators

Success in communicating expectations and goals will be clear when the following circumstances apply:

1. The new employee can do the job well within a reasonable time.
2. The new person seems comfortable and fits in.
3. His or her comments about enjoying the job sound genuine.
4. Co-workers are comfortable with the person and make positive comments about him or her.

Template 4.2: Checklist – setting expectations and initial goals

If no manuals for the department, branch, or position are available

Preparing to discuss expectations:

- List expectations – get input from others
- Prioritize the expectations to be covered initially and later on, depending on the position and the new employee's experience level

Holding the conversation about expectations:

- Explain expectations, discuss them, and answer questions
- Review expectations

Preparing to discuss performance goals:

- Document performance targets for the department, branch, or work group
- Document performance targets for the position
- Distinguish and document appropriate performance goals for three levels: the proficient, skilled, experienced employee in the position; the employee who is gaining skills, experience and proficiency; and the new employee who has been on the job for six to eight weeks.

Determine and document the timeline for reaching each level – the number of days, weeks, or months.

Plan follow-up: for example, daily on-the-job coaching, daily/weekly observe-and-do, and periodic feedback and coaching.

Holding the conversation about performance goals:

- Outline performance goals to the new employee
- Explain support mechanisms – on-the-job training, employee-partner, observe-and-do, classroom training, feedback and coaching, manuals and reference materials
- Set a date for the first informal performance review
- Link initial expectations and goals to conditions of probation and related procedures
- Provide support and follow-up

If manuals are available

Preparation

- Review expectations and prioritize what to cover initially and what later, depending on the position and the new employee's experience level
- If the three levels of performance goals have already been documented, review them and prepare to explain them to the new employee

Proceed with conversations and follow-up, as indicated above.

Template 4.3: Work sheet – setting expectations and initial goals

Getting ideas together

Remember the basics that the business expects – safety, security, legal and regulatory requirements, ethics, and other policies.

With regard to working with you at the specific position and with the current team, ask yourself what it takes to be successful. Here are examples:

- Doing the job at the most competent level.
- Demonstrating to you, the manager, the expected level of commitment and competence.
- Getting along well with customers.
- Getting along well with co-workers.
- Thriving in the culture and the work environment.

Ask managers who report to you and/or your most successful employees for their input on these points.

Use the categories in the table below to stimulate your thinking and to record notes.
My expectations of employees on:

Safety – equipment, fire, falls – review safety manual	
Security – cash, personal ID, credit card and account numbers, client files, company files, etc.	
Security – before/after hours, intruders, other	
Legal/regulatory requirements – review manual(s)	
Ethics – security issues (see above), fraud, corruption	
Company policies relating to the inappropriate use of authority, harassment, threats, workplace violence, intimidation, discrimination – review codes, manuals	
Timeliness	
Appearance – guidelines, dress code, uniform	
Work space neatness, personal items	
Amount of personal conversation with co-workers	
Volume of conversation, noise level	
Use of headphones, listening to personal music selections	
Personal telephone calls, visits from family, friends, outside colleagues	
Drinks in the work space	
Food in the work space	
Attendance at meetings	
Participation in meetings, on committees	
Participation in work-related sports, social events	

Template 4.4: Work sheet – setting initial performance goals

The typical measures of performance are in terms of:

- *Productivity.* Amount of service provided, tasks, or transactions completed per unit of time
- *Volume.* Total level or amount of service, product, tasks, or transactions
- *Quality A.* Completeness, accuracy, freedom from of errors
- *Quality B.* Effectiveness, success, production of promised results
- *Time.* By deadline, within allocated time
- *Cost-effectiveness.* Within budget, lowest-price option, at or below expense target
- *Speed A.* At the required or requested rate, at a faster rate than competitors
- *Speed B.* At a rate that prevents a problem or resolves a crisis

Performance on a task is typically measured in some form of three parameters:

- how good;
- how much;
- on time or how fast.

Identify the most important tasks of the position – the work that requires at least 80 per cent of the employee's time, contributes to at least 80 per cent of the position's responsibilities, and is responsible for at least 80 per cent of the employee's success.

	Proficient, experienced employee	Employee gaining skills and proficiency	New, inexperienced employee
Key task: *Productivity*			
Volume			
Quality			
Time			
Cost-effectiveness			
Speed			
	Proficient, experienced employee	Employee gaining skills and proficiency	New, inexperienced employee
Key task: *Productivity*			
Volume			
Quality			
Time			
Cost-effectiveness			
Speed			
	Proficient, experienced employee	Employee gaining skills and proficiency	New, inexperienced employee
Key task: *Productivity*			
Volume			
Quality			
Time			
Cost-effectiveness			
Speed			

	Proficient, experienced employee	Employee gaining skills and proficiency	New, inexperienced employee
Key task: *Productivity*			
Volume			
Quality			
Time			
Cost-effectiveness			
Speed			
	Proficient, experienced employee	Employee gaining skills and proficiency	New, inexperienced employee
Key task: *Productivity*			
Volume			
Quality			
Time			
Cost-effectiveness			
Speed			
	Proficient, experienced employee	Employee gaining skills and proficiency	New, inexperienced employee
Key task: *Productivity*			
Volume			
Quality			
Time			
Cost-effectiveness			
Speed			
	Proficient, experienced employee	Employee gaining skills and proficiency	New, inexperienced employee
Key task: *Productivity*			
Volume			
Quality			
Time			
Cost-effectiveness			
Speed			

On-the-job training and coaching

Definition

On-the-job training and coaching are closely linked. The main difference is likely to be in duration and purpose, but there is no value in making fine distinctions for everyday operating purposes.

On-the-job training occurs when a manager or a co-worker teaches an employee how to do something related to his or her current position in the workplace and at the workstation. There should be some thought given to what to teach and how to teach it, and the session should be scheduled, but it may last only 20 to 30 minutes and may be presented informally.

Coaching happens when one person helps another person do the job or do the job better, whether by providing information, helping to solve a problem, answering a question, troubleshooting, or showing the person how to do something. It is likely to be spontaneous, in the moment when the two people are talking about the work; such a coaching conversation might last 5 to 10 minutes and is likely to be very informal.

Table 4.7: Responsibilities for on-the-job training and coaching

Business manager	*HR professional*
Must • Identify all the procedures, processes, tasks, skills, and knowledge a new employee needs to learn • Develop the sequence of learning • Decide when, how, and who will facilitate training • Train, observe, and coach the new person **May** • Ask a co-worker to train or coach the new person	**Must** • Provide training for managers on how to train and coach **May** • Provide a template for identifying training needs, and for outlining training content and steps • Consult with and advise managers • Confirm that on-the-job training is occurring

Checklist for on-the-job training

- Use the task outline developed for goal setting (see the previous section).
- For each task, document what procedures, processes, skills, and knowledge the employee needs to master.
- Plan how to teach the employee each component – using a manual or online source, explaining it, demonstrating it, talking the employee through doing it independently, or having him or her watch someone else.
- Plan how to make sure the employee understands each component and can perform it – talk it through, ask him or her to demonstrate it to you or perform while you observe, or videotape the employee.
- Determine how much time it will take to teach and 'test' each component.
- Plan a sequence of training sessions.

- Prioritize teaching tasks by urgency, importance, ease of learning, or how one task builds on another.
- Finalize the training programme by clustering task training based on priorities and on the amount of time needed to do the training.
- Provide the training, or have one or more co-workers do it.

There is an on-the-job training preparation work sheet at the end of the section.

Tip: successful on-the-job training

1. Prepare. Do not do training on the job or ask another employee to do it with no advance thought about what to do, how to do it, and when. Assemble all the materials you will need before you start a training session, and write a job manual if one does not already exist.
2. Get input on what it takes to do a task by observing employees performing and/or by asking them to describe what's involved. Even if you have had that job, do not assume that you remember accurately everything that a new person needs to know.
3. Make sure that either you or the employee who will provide on-the-job training has some basic training skills such as: the ability to break a complex task into simple parts; the ability to explain a procedure or process clearly and in more than one way; sufficient knowledge to answer questions; knowledge of different ways of teaching something; and knowledge of the different ways in which people learn. (See Chapter 5.)
4. Plan when to do the on-the-job training to ensure you don't let other responsibilities take over.
5. Start on-the-job training as soon as possible during the on-boarding, at least by the second day.
6. Provide training in increments to give the new person time to absorb and possibly to practise. However, give him or her enough information to start performing the job as promptly as possible.
7. Provide a coach or observer if the new person is working with customers or on sensitive tasks at an early stage in his or her learning.
8. Pay attention to how the person learns, and adapt to that style. Let experimenters try doing things themselves. Let readers go through the manual. Let observers watch you or someone else.
9. Combine learning methods – explain, demonstrate, observe.
10. Check back, observe, coach, and add more information.
11. Encourage and praise.
12. Be patient and stay positive.

How to give coaching 'in the moment'

Coaching can happen as a spontaneous, informal, short conversation about a specific question, problem, or need to know, or it can be a longer, planned, more formal conversation in a meeting-style setting.

Most managers know how to give coaching 'in the moment' and do it without any training. What they do is:

- notice their employees, observe them working, and talk to them while they work and on breaks;
- pay attention to the possibility that an employee is having difficulty with an aspect of the job, wants to learn more, or has lots of questions;

- ask their staff what they're doing and how it's going;
- offer help as soon as they see a problem, and intervene more definitively if the problem is serious;
- ask questions that allow them to hear their employees describe how they're doing their work and offer information or advice if it's needed;
- step back when the employee is back on track;
- give their employees opportunities to learn and work independently without micromanaging or over-coaching.

Table 4.8: Pitfalls of on-the-job training and coaching

Pitfall	*Consequence*
Not doing enough; stopping too soon; or not reinforcing what was trained	The new employee struggles to perform, gets discouraged, and feels frustrated with the manager or co-workers
Starting training without preparation or planning	The new employee is confused or acquires bad habits and fills in knowledge gaps by making things up or by gleaning from co-workers. Performance is uneven, and the employee is frustrated
Over-training or over-coaching – continuing to teach the same points and continuing to stop by to observe and give suggestions after the point when the new employee can demonstrate his or her ability to do the tasks properly and on his or her own	The new employee may get bored and may wonder whether the manager or co-worker distrusts him or her or has concluded that he or she is not intelligent or is unmotivated. This is frustrating and demotivating as well as wasteful of the manager's time

Indicators of success

One or more of these criteria would indicate that the on-the-job training and coaching are having the desired results:

- The new employee makes reasonable or rapid progress learning the tasks of the job and performs the job as expected for his or her level.
- The new employee asks questions that suggest that he or she is interested in performing well or that help deepen knowledge.
- The new employee seems confident and comfortable with the work, with co-workers, and in the workplace.

From the field: more is better!

A field study of the effectiveness of on-boarding and training included three MFIs. One of them, MicroInd, provides two weeks of training at head office and then sends its new credit officers out into the field, with performance targets. The result has been that the credit officers do not properly learn how to form and manage their joint liability groups, and their performance is poor.

On the other hand, Andra Loan and JLG Services provide continuing on-the-job training to new staff for three months before those staff are expected to perform independently and meet targets. The work is up to standard much more often, and the lending groups perform substantially better.

Template 4.5: Work sheet – preparing for on-the-job training

Task. Duties or components of a job. Examples include completing a loan application form, interviewing the loan applicant, and finalizing the granting of the loan.

Procedure or process. Specific activities or steps to follow to perform a task. An example is: obtaining loan form XXX for an agricultural applicant and form XXY for an equipment dealer applicant; entering information in all the spaces on the form, then signing and dating it; and having the credit manager review the form.

Knowledge. Information, data, and facts. This can include the steps of a process.

Skill. A set of actions or behaviours that are required to do a process or a task. Examples are reading, writing, and mathematical calculations.

Part 1: Requirements for learning how to perform a task

Task	
Procedures or processes required to perform the task	
What does the employee need to know or be able to do to perform the procedures and processes of the task?	
Knowledge	Source for learning – manual, online, teaching
Skills	Observe, demonstrate

Task

Procedures or processes required to perform the task

What does the employee need to know or be able to do to perform the procedures and processes of the task?

Knowledge	Source for learning – manual, online, teaching
Skills	Observe, demonstrate

Task

Procedures or processes required to perform the task

What does the employee need to know or be able to do to perform the procedures and processes of the task?

Knowledge	Source for learning – manual, online, teaching
Skills	Observe, demonstrate

Task	
Procedures or processes required to perform the task	
What does the employee need to know or be able to do to perform the procedures and processes of the task?	
Knowledge	Source for learning – manual, online, teaching
Skills	Observe, demonstrate

Part 2: Planning how to provide on-the-job training and check progress

What to be trained and how	When	Follow up and check progress

CHAPTER 5

Sustaining performance

Once the right people have been found and have got off to a good start, the ongoing work of managing them and sustaining their good performance moves ahead. During this process, it can be easy to focus on tasks, results, production, quality, crises, and changes – what is referred to as 'the work'. That approach falls short.

In fact, sustaining performance by managing people is the foundation for completing tasks, hitting results targets, producing services, delivering competitive levels of quality work, minimizing crises, and handling change with aplomb. The primary and most important responsibility of managers, therefore, is managing the people who do the work.

Aspects of people management were introduced in the chapters on getting the right people and making a good start. This chapter will give more depth and additional tools appropriate to the ongoing responsibilities of managing people and their performance.

Managing people consists of several regularly repeated activities:

- giving feedback regularly, in informal and formal conversations;
- coaching employees to fix performance problems, develop additional skills, and prepare for future responsibilities;
- motivating people to persist in spite of difficulties and to raise their level of performance;
- giving incentives for important areas of performance and rewarding success;
- developing the right training experiences, getting the right people into them at the best time, and evaluating their success in learning.

http://dx.doi.org/10.3362/9781780447926.006

Table 5.1: Alignment of people management responsibilities

Business manager – typical contributions	*People management responsibilities*	*HR professional – typical contributions*
Stating training needs and training content Delivering training sessions Maintaining performance expectations, standards, and goals Monitoring performance and enforcing standards Giving feedback Motivating people Coaching and mentoring Designing incentive schemes and performance review processes Implementing performance review processes and incentive plans Maintaining performance records	Make sure employees learn to do the work Make sure they perform Make sure people get better at doing the work	Conducting training needs reviews Organizing, documenting, or creating training content Arranging delivery of training sessions Training managers – expectations, standards, goal setting, feedback, coaching, and motivation Producing forms and templates Advising and counselling Designing incentive schemes and performance review processes Developing policies and manuals as support Establishing a calendar Tracking the use of incentives and performance review Monitoring completion Serving as appeals forum Maintaining data

Connections to other components of the performance management system

Sustaining high levels of performance starts when the tasks and responsibilities are organized, defined, and documented. Other links include those listed below.

Thorough and comprehensive recruiting, interviewing, and selection enable new employees to arrive with an idea of what is expected of them and the capabilities needed to perform the role.

On-boarding sets the new employee on the right track to perform at expected levels.

Setting expectations and performance goals from the beginning helps employees focus on the right activities and learn the right habits.

In addition to coaching, feedback, motivating, and training, *holding performance reviews* is essential to sustaining strong performance. They are covered in Chapter 6.

Certain aspects of the people management system motivate employees to improve performance – *development planning, career development, high-potential programmes, stretch assignments, and opportunities for advancement and promotion.* They are discussed in Chapters 7 and 8.

Giving feedback and coaching

Definition

Ongoing feedback and coaching are typically combined. Giving feedback means letting an employee know how he or she is performing – what's going well and what needs improvement. Coaching is a personal, one-to-one, on-the-job interaction that helps an employee do the job and do it well by giving information and guidance, answering questions and showing how something is done, helping to solve problems, and explaining the reasons to do or not do something.

It is important to give both positive and negative feedback. Positive feedback tells employees what they are doing well and motivates them to continue or perform even better. Negative, corrective, or 'constructive' feedback lets employees know when their performance isn't on the right track. Positive and corrective feedback can often be combined, but it is important to give them separately when only one or the other is what is needed.

For feedback to be effective, it usually has to be combined with coaching so that people know how they're doing and what to do to perform correctly or more effectively. Coaching often includes both positive and corrective feedback.

Formal and informal feedback and coaching

Managers and their direct reports often mistakenly associate feedback only with annual performance reviews. While it is the case that the performance review is a formal, extended opportunity to give feedback, there is a range of occasions for giving feedback. Employees need to know on a regular basis how they are doing and what their manager thinks of their performance, so quarterly scheduled feedback meetings should be set up. In addition to the structured occasions, there are many quick, informal opportunities to let employees know when they've done a good job and what exactly they're doing well, and there are many opportunities to point out how performance could be improved.

Similarly, there are various opportunities to coach employees that emerge during normal daily activities. For example, when a manager delegates a new task to an employee, there is a suitable opportunity to coach the employee on the new skills needed for the task.

Coaching can happen in a more structured way, in connection with a performance review discussion or as part of on-the-job training. It can occur at the beginning of a new project or a new assignment, or as an employee takes the next step in a new process. Managers also need to take advantage of many informal, brief conversation moments to give information, explain the reasons for a particular method of handling a task, or give encouragement.

Coaching will be effective when the manager understands that his or her role is to help employees perform well, teach new competencies, and keep employees motivated to both learn and perform.

Table 5.2: Responsibilities for giving feedback and coaching

Business manager	*HR professional*
Gives direct reports and feedback in formal review conversations and on an ongoing basis as employees do their work Coaches employees as part of formal discussions of performance, development, promotion, or career options Coaches employees on an ongoing basis as they perform their jobs	Trains managers in giving feedback and coaching Gives managers feedback and coaches them on providing feedback and coaching to their direct reports Trains staff on how to ask for and make use of feedback and coaching

The role and responsibility of direct reports

Giving feedback and coaching is a primary responsibility of the manager, but direct reports are also responsible for requesting feedback and seeking out coaching. They need to be encouraged and expected to ask how they are doing and how they could improve. The culture needs to support staff in asking questions, asking for help and guidance, and speaking up when they want to learn more or enhance their performance.

Involving the whole organization

At first glance, it would seem that giving feedback and coaching involves just managers and their direct reports. However, the organizations that receive the most consistently high employee satisfaction ratings and that have the highest rates of retention are typically organizations that constantly emphasize the expectations for feedback and coaching.

In that sense, feedback and coaching need to be part of the organization's culture, and everyone needs to see himself or herself as giving and receiving feedback and coaching. It also needs to be part of the culture that people ask for feedback and let it be known that they want coaching.

Policies

The primary area of policy relating to feedback and coaching is the institution's requirement for regular performance reviews, which will be discussed in Chapter 6.

Reason for giving feedback

Feedback is used both to encourage an employee to continue productive activities and to help him or her to improve or alter actions that are counterproductive.

When to give feedback

Feedback is effective only if the employee can act on it, i.e. if he or she is **capable** of continuing productive performance or changing poor performance and is **willing** to do so.

Initial feedback and coaching sessions may provide the opportunity for the manager to determine whether an employee is capable of and willing to make use of the input. Before investing extensive efforts in feedback and coaching, the manager needs to discern whether the direct report has the prerequisite skills, experience, or resources to make the necessary changes. Otherwise, both the manager and the employee may be frustrated, and the feedback will be unproductive until the gaps are filled.

Several occasions lend themselves to feedback:

- *Performance reviews.* The regular performance review meeting is often the most extended feedback discussion a manager and an employee have.
- *Interim reviews.* Depending on the position, the employee, and his or her performance history, managers should plan to give feedback on overall performance at least quarterly, perhaps even monthly or weekly.
- *Transition points.* Any time when a significant change is under way – when employees take on new or increased responsibilities, when their jobs are restructured, or when their group is reorganized – is a good time to review good performance, areas needing improvement or continuing attention, and the relevance of past performance to the new situation.
- *At the end of a task, project, or assignment.* When a responsibility is concluded, especially if it is the employee's first experience with the task, project, or type of assignment, feedback about what went well and what could be improved is meaningful and helpful.
- *At the earliest indications of poor performance or misalignment.* When performance does not meet expectations and standards, it is imperative that the manager gives prompt, complete feedback, to prevent the performance from getting worse and to assist the employee in improving. Similarly, when employees conduct themselves in ways that are out of line with the culture, policies, or expectations, they need immediate feedback to avoid repeating or worsening unacceptable behaviour.
- *At many of the moments when employees perform well and achieve goals or make a mistake and are struggling.* These are the informal feedback opportunities that should be seized as often as possible. Given how busy most managers are, they do not need to worry about giving too much feedback!

How to give feedback

For feedback to be effective, it needs to be prompt and specific. The following framework is useful for structuring a short feedback statement or a more extensive conversation. It works for both positive and corrective feedback.

1. *Situation.* What is the context or situation being referred to? Provide enough information for the employee to recall what was happening, but avoid overloading the story.
2. *Behaviour.* What was the employee doing/not doing or saying/not saying? Give as many relevant and specific details as possible. Be complete enough to reconstruct the successful or problematic aspect of the behaviour and focus on what was either highly effective or ineffective.
3. *Impact.* What was the effect of the employee's behaviour on the manager or on others? Be specific and explain sufficiently for the employee to grasp why the impact was positive or a problem.
4. *Request.* What should the employee do? In positive feedback, the request may point out other situations in which to use the same approach. In corrective feedback, there may be multiple requests: a request to apologize or make immediate amends in some form, and a request to change behaviour in a specific way. The request may lead directly into setting a goal for improved performance along with coaching about how to make that happen.
5. *Check for understanding.* Use open-ended questions to ensure the employee's full understanding of all parts of the feedback statement.

Examples of how to give feedback:

- 'This morning when we found out that the credit officer was sick, you stepped in to substitute without anyone asking. That helped out several of us. I appreciate it, and I hope you'll continue to show that kind of initiative.'
- 'Last night, when we had to work late to reconcile the gaps in the accounts, I overheard you complaining frequently, and when I came to ask you questions, you were never at your desk. It began to look as if you were there but not helping much to get the situation taken care of. I was frustrated, and I think the rest of the staff were too. I do want to know what you were doing, and I also want you to recognize that we need everyone to help out when we have these kinds of problems.'
- 'Congratulations on doing well in your first six weeks in the branch. You have clearly learned to handle all the transactions at the teller desk. Your speed has picked up, and there have been no errors at all in the last two weeks. That's a great start.'
- 'When you started, I said I wanted you to focus on learning the transactions, doing them quickly, and doing them accurately. I have noticed that you don't say much to the customers at your desk, and I want you to start doing more to relate to them. Let's go over some specifics, and maybe you can watch Arvid and Rana to see how they do it.'

Preparing for a feedback meeting

For more formal feedback meetings, it is a good idea to prepare.

- Review goals from previous conversations.
- Refer to notes about the employee's performance, and recall all positive and negative aspects of his or her performance since the last meeting.
- Consult with others who might have more direct knowledge of the employee's performance.
- Make a list of points to be covered in the conversation, including accomplishments, areas for further growth, and problems to be taken care of.

The keys to effective feedback

- *Promptness.* Give feedback promptly, while the situation and the behaviour are still clear in everyone's minds and before the employee can become embarrassed or upset others by continuing poor performance or ineffective behaviour. Research finds that feedback should be given within 48 hours to be fully effective.
- *Self-evaluation.* Provide the employee with an opportunity to give a self-evaluation first. Often, employees are more critical of themselves than the manager would be. Likewise, if the employee is focused on the wrong things, the manager is alerted to the difference in perspectives that needs to be addressed.
- *Objectivity.* Be as objective, factual, and neutral as possible. If personal offence is involved, take time to regain composure and emotional control before giving the feedback. It is appropriate to talk about emotions, but it needs to be done without being overly emotional. If you or the employee are in a highly emotional state or use emotive language in the conversation, the feedback is likely to be ineffective, and the conversation is at risk of becoming unprofessional.
- *Respect.* Be respectful. Sarcasm, insults, or disrespectful language will not lead to improved performance.
- *Behaviour.* Focus on the behaviour and not the person; on what he or she did, not who he or she is. Base the feedback on actual results or observed behaviour, backed up with evidence or specifics.
- *Constructive.* Be constructive. Include the request for the kind of performance that is expected.
- *Listening.* Listen to the employee's perspective on situations, both out of respect and as a way of understanding how the person got into difficulty or how the person plans to get out of it.
- *Actionable.* Make sure the request for change is actionable, something the employee can actually do. Asking employees to do what they have never been asked or trained to do is unreasonable, and asking them to change some aspect of their nature or basic appearance is unlikely to be successful.

- *Fairness.* Be fair and take responsibility if you or the organization contributed in some way to the problematic situation.
- *Ownership.* Use the first-person pronoun 'I' when stating opinions and talking about the impact of the employee's actions on yourself. Avoid using the pronoun 'you' in a harsh, accusatory way, although it is appropriate to use it to make neutral, factual statements about what the employee did or is expected to do. Be thoughtful about assigning responsibility for negative impacts or outcomes without discussing the situation fully with the employee.
- *Simplicity and directness.* When the employee has done something well and you want to give positive feedback, give it simply and directly. Do not feel that you must combine it with negative or corrective feedback to somehow be balanced or keep the employee from becoming overly proud. By the same token, when an employee does something problematic, simply and directly give him or her the corrective feedback. Some people think it is better to include a 'dose' of positive feedback to help smooth over the negative feedback. In fact, this approach sends a mixed message, confuses the employee, devalues the positive feedback, and leaves the employee suspicious when positive feedback is offered at other times.

What is coaching?

Coaching is any interaction that helps someone do the job, do the job better, and meet his or her goals. It can be as simple as the following actions:

- Answering a question.
- Explaining a task.
- Showing how to do something, whether simple or complex.
- Giving information.
- Giving background details.
- Explaining the reason for a decision or a procedure.

Coaching can also be a more complicated or extended conversation to address a specific need:

- Introduce a new job.
- Explain a new assignment and how to do it.
- Solve a complex problem.
- Establish goals and how to accomplish them.
- Review a development plan and how to put it into action.
- Improve performance.
- Correct a mistake.

In some cases, coaching consists of a series of interactions and conversations. This would be the case if the manager were coaching the employee through on-the-job training, on a complex or demanding special assignment, to solve a particularly challenging problem, or to correct a complicated performance problem.

These conversations might take place when the manager and employee are meeting to start the project, when consulting at checkpoints, when jointly solving problems, and so forth.

Types of coaching

Managers coach employees for several reasons. Performance and developmental coaching need to be done in all institutions; career coaching may not be offered until an institution has matured.

Performance coaching is done when the employee is performing poorly or has made a mistake. It includes feedback, and the goal is to correct the performance or avoid future mistakes.

Developmental coaching occurs when the manager is helping the employee learn the job at the beginning (as described in Chapter 4), learn a new aspect of the job as he or she is ready for increased responsibility or the position changes, or prepare for a more advanced level of the position.

Developmental coaching may also be offered in conjunction with working out the employee's development plan or to support the employee during developmental experiences such as training or special assignments.

Career coaching is sometimes called 'career counselling' and happens when managers talk with their employees about career interests, career paths, and requirements for lateral movement and advancement. This type of coaching will be covered in Chapter 7.

Benefits of feedback and coaching

There are a number of benefits to the individual manager and for the organization when managers consistently give feedback and coaching to employees.

- *Improved quality.* The work is done to a consistent and often higher standard, with fewer errors and greater improvements.
- *Improved customer satisfaction.* External and internal customers receive the services and products they want more consistently and more promptly.
- *Improved productivity.* More work gets done in the allocated time, tasks are finished more quickly, and there is less rework or fixing of errors
- *Improved retention.* Because they are learning, being guided and supported, and being given care and attention, staff stay longer in their jobs, there are fewer expenses for recruitment and hiring, and profit margins go up.
- *Improved loyalty.* Employees feel that their managers care about their success, so they want to work for them and are willing to do more.
- *Enhanced reputation.* The institution becomes known as a place that takes care of its people, gives good service, and operates efficiently; the

individual manager becomes known as someone whose group does good work, whose people are loyal, and who develops future leaders.

- *Greater attractiveness to job applicants.* The good reputation attracts job applicants for all levels.
- *Greater leverage for managers.* With better-developed staff, the manager can give them more work and is able to do other, more strategic, leadership activities.
- *Greater satisfaction for managers.* The more the manager can delegate, the more he or she can work on tasks that interest him or her or develop new competencies.

Giving coaching every day

Here are some of the opportunities for managers to coach staff while they are working.

Before the person starts a task or assignment, the manager can coach him or her when giving instructions, setting expectations, and explaining the task or process. This coaching helps the employee know what to do, how to do it, why it is important, what has worked in the past, and what has not worked in the past.

While the employee performs the task or assignment, the manager can coach him or her when giving more information, solving a problem, finding resources, answering questions, and giving feedback. Coaching during performance helps the employee know what to do, how to do it, what is working now, what is not working now, and what to do about problem areas.

After a person finishes a task or assignment, the manager can coach him or her when giving feedback, debriefing after a meeting, and evaluating results. This input makes sure that the person knows what worked well and why, what did not work as expected and why, what might have been done differently, or what to do better next time.

The following list illustrates some of the situations in which managers can coach their direct reports:

- preparing a presentation or report together;
- planning an assignment or an event together;
- checking on the progress of a large assignment;
- attending a meeting or a conference together;
- giving the person part of a task the manager normally does;
- asking the employee to explain how he or she did a task;
- asking the employee for his or her opinion;
- asking the employee what he or she would do in a given situation;
- having the employee conduct some or all of a meeting or give some or all of a presentation;
- showing the person how the manager approaches a managerial task.

The six-step coaching model

Regardless of the type of coaching or the occasion when it takes place, there are six steps to follow. Sometimes the steps run together and are done very quickly; sometimes they are distinct and time is taken with each one; sometimes the middle steps are repeated several times as the conversation touches on two or three different issues.

1. Opening
2. **G**oal
3. **R**eality
4. **O**ptions
5. **W**hat, where, when, how
6. Follow-up

The well-respected British business coach Sir John Whitmore gave the four middle steps the acronym GROW, which helps managers who are coaching to remember both what to do and why they are doing it.

Step 1: Opening. Make sure it is a suitable moment for coaching (if it's a spontaneous opportunity), and make sure the employee wants coaching rather than merely someone to listen or a briefly stated piece of information. *Examples:*

A. Manager: 'It sounds as if there's a problem with this loan analysis. May I suggest something?'
B. Manager: 'Sure, come in, sit down. How can I help? What do you need me to do?'

Step 2: Goal. What the employee needs to accomplish.
Examples:

A. Manager: 'What's the question?'
   Employee: 'I need to fill in the new expense report form.'
B. Manager: 'The plan is to have the market analysis for the new credit product completed by the end of the week.'

Step 3: Reality. Current status – what's going on and what the employee knows or is capable of doing right now.
Examples:

A. Employee: 'I read the instructions, and I think my expenses don't fit the categories. Suri is out today, or I would ask her.'
B. Employee: 'I helped with the analysis for the special savings account publicity campaign, but I wasn't in charge. This is different. I have to figure out the whole process – I'm leading this one. I need to think through the right way to organize things.'

Step 4: Options. What the employee could do. In some cases, there is only one option, and this step is simple. It requires only being clear and complete about what the option is. In these situations, it may be the manager who explains the option.

In other cases, especially in developmental coaching, the employee can think of several ways to address the problem or work on the task. In those cases, the manager needs to allow for some discussion and evaluation of the best choices. The more involvement the employee has in generating and evaluating the options, the better the learning and the stronger the commitment to following through.

Examples:

A. Manager: 'The simplest thing is for you to tell me which items you don't know how to enter on the report, and I'll tell you what to do.'
B. Manager: 'What can you do to figure out how to organize this campaign as the team leader?'
Employee: 'I could ask Solongo, who worked on the last campaign. I could talk to Director Mehdi – he's had a lot of experience with them. Do we have any files from the last couple of product launches? I could look at them. I guess there's something in the business library or on the internet that I could look at, too. What would be the best options?

Step 5: What, where, when, how. For coaching to produce results, each conversation needs to end with commitment to an action plan. Depending on the complexity of the situation, that may be a simple sentence that summarizes what the employee will do next, or it may involve a written plan.

For the more complex situations, this step needs to cover all four elements:

- *What*, specifically, the employee will do, in a single action or a series of steps.
- *Where* the employee will do it, if locations other than the usual workplace are involved.
- *When* the employee will take the action – starting time, length of time, and, most importantly, completion time (the 'due date' for the action or each step).
- *How* the employee will do it, including the tools, resources, equipment, budget, and other people he or she might need. It may also include how the manager will help; for example, sending out an announcement or finding a temporary support person. If the action will take place over more than a couple of weeks, the 'how' component will include an agreement for a progress update and a check-in conversation.

In thinking through the 'how' component, the manager should help the employee anticipate problems, barriers, and any pressures to go back to old ways of doing things. It may also be necessary to consider contingencies – fall-back plans – if something goes wrong and adjustments to the action plan need to be made. Then the manager and the employee should discuss how to address those concerns.

The manager needs to establish the expectation that the employee will let him or her know promptly if the employee is having difficulties or is at risk of not completing the action plan. Being accountable overall includes being accountable for speaking up when help is needed or when there are questions.

Step 6: Follow-up. The manager provides any support that has been agreed. The manager also monitors performance and morale, offering more coaching if there appear to be significant difficulties. He or she keeps an eye open for problems and contingencies. Finally, the manager helps to hold the employee accountable for completing what was agreed to by the time it was agreed.

Tip: effective coaching

- *Relationship and environment.* First and foremost, effective coaching takes place in the context of a respectful, professional relationship between the manager and the employee. It also takes place within a work environment that supports the growth of all employees and recognizes that people must ask questions and may make a few mistakes on the road to high-quality performance.
- *Learning orientation.* Equally important is that coaching is intended to help employees learn, grow, and become increasingly independent and autonomous. It is *not* the same as managing or giving direction; it is not an excuse for micromanaging.
- *Timing.* Pay careful attention to when it is appropriate to step in to help and when it is better for the employee's learning to allow him or her to struggle and then come for help.
- *Self-directed learning.* Pay careful attention to when it is appropriate to tell the employee what to do or provide information, as opposed to when he or she will learn more by figuring out the answer or finding the information independently.
- *Questions.* Use lots of questions to draw out useful information and encourage the employee to figure things out on his or her own or with light guidance from the manager.
- *Listening.* Listen to the employee's questions and ideas, especially if they are different from what is usually done.
- *Easy access.* Be accessible for informal coaching conversations. Make coaching opportunities a regular part of management interactions.

Documenting feedback and coaching

Feedback and coaching will be documented in the annual or semi-annual performance review process, using the appropriate forms.

It is also helpful to make notes about interim reviews and other, more informal conversations, especially if expectations and goals with specific results and deadlines are involved. These notes help busy managers remember what they requested and allow them to hold staff accountable. The notes also provide the key points to cover in formal review meetings and allow both the manager and the employee to follow progress throughout the quarter or the year.

As mentioned earlier, sometimes managers give feedback and coaching because of employees' poor performance or unacceptable behaviour. In these cases, it is critical to document the situation and the key points of the feedback and coaching.

Documented records are helpful for several purposes:

- They are necessary to track improvement and progress.
- Memory tends to be selective and can be affected by frustration, disappointment, hope, personal likes and dislikes, and the elapse of time (see also Chapter 6).
- It is usually required by policy, regulation, and employment law that there be a record of poor performance, attempts to change it, and persistently poor results to justify terminating employment.
- They help the manager and the employee stay accountable for what needs to be done and by when.

The documentation relating to poor performance needs to cover the following components:

- specific data relating to the performance problem or unacceptable behaviour, including the performance goal and standards or the statement of policy or expectations, as well as the report of what actually happened;
- what was said and done in response to the problem – reprimands, penalties, feedback, on-the-job training, coaching, etc.;
- details of what the employee was asked to do to improve results or stop the unacceptable behaviour – what, where, when, and how;
- specific data about performance or behaviour following the request for change or improvement;
- tracking of the ongoing process of feedback, coaching, and requests for improved performance;
- criteria for deciding whether the change is satisfactory, whether penalties should be applied, or whether employment needs to be terminated.

More details relating to termination will be covered in Chapter 9.

A sample form for documenting performance problems appears at the end of the section.

Problems with giving feedback and coaching

The worst problem with feedback and coaching is when there is none. Managers who fail to give their employees the most basic information required to perform their jobs are defeating all the efforts of the organization to produce high-quality, profitable performance through its people.

Other problems include the following:

- giving feedback in harsh, demeaning, or disrespectful terms that destroy the professional relationship and interfere significantly with employees' learning;
- giving vague, indefinite feedback that prevents employees from recognizing what was ineffective about their behaviour;

- telling an employee that there have been complaints about him or her, but the problematic situation cannot be identified because the manager believes that the privacy of others needs to be protected;
- delaying the feedback until it is no longer useful or the employee is embarrassed to realize how long he or she has continued to make a mistake or upset co-workers;
- coaching as a form of micromanaging, by frequently intervening to tell employees how to do their work;
- overdoing feedback to the point where the employee cannot discern the priorities or take in the information;
- giving feedback about areas the employee cannot change or does not control;
- taking control of a problematic situation for an employee when the person could be coached to handle it independently, unless the situation is an emergency or there would be a serious negative effect on the business;
- failing to hold the employee accountable for not following through, or for not asking for help if he or she is unable to follow through.

Troubleshooting

The best means of troubleshooting managers' difficulties with giving feedback and coaching is to make employee performance a topic of discussion in several kinds of meetings:

- *Executive committee meetings.* Review general performance and employee progress, looking for trends that suggest that training, advice, or other support is needed in a department or branch, or at manager level.
- *Management committee meetings.* Confirm that formal and informal performance reviews are taking place, and be alerted to specific, important performance problems so that the committee can monitor progress.
- *HR advisory groups* or other committees and councils in which business managers and HR professionals meet regularly. Discuss successes and difficulties as well as how to help specific groups of managers, and sometimes individuals.
- *HR professionals' conversations with first-level managers.* Provide opportunities to touch on the challenges of management and the techniques that managers use to ensure that their employees perform successfully.
- *HR professionals' conversations with middle managers.* Identify areas where first-level managers need coaching from their managers, advice from HR, and training related to coaching and feedback.
- *HR professionals' visits to departments and branches.* Give employees opportunities to talk about their managers and any difficulties they may have with feedback and coaching.
- *Assessments and satisfaction surveys.* Provide an alternative way for employees to indicate whether their managers give feedback and coaching at all, and whether they do it well.

Template 5.1: Form for performance problem feedback, coaching, and goals

Employee: **Manager:** **Date:**

Expected performance Performance goal/standard Policy or departmental/ branch expectation	
Performance Performance/behaviour problem – what was said/not said or done/not done	
Initial response Conversation, reprimand, penalty – as required by policy and regulation	
Manager's feedback and request for change or improvement *[Give specific, detailed points]*	

Other support Coaching, on-the-job training, classroom training	
Monitoring How the manager will track change and improvement	
Criteria for success Indicators that the employee has improved or changed	
Criteria for continued monitoring Indicators that the employee has not made sufficient improvement	
Criteria for termination Indicators that the employee's performance is not improving or is getting worse	

Motivation, rewards, and incentives

Definitions

Motivation is the enthusiasm, commitment, and sense of purpose that keeps employees coming to work and performing well. An important factor in managing people and their performance is maintaining their motivation at a high level, using both monetary and non-monetary means.

Rewards and incentives usually refer to money or other tangible awards given for performance that is above the satisfactory level. They are given in addition to contractual salary and benefits, which employees receive regardless of performance.

Effective reward and incentive systems are clearly linked to performance and achieving business targets.

Table 5.3: Responsibilities for motivation, rewards, and incentives

Business manager	*HR professional*
Identifies and uses varied methods for motivating direct reports	Provides training, coaching and advice for managers on motivation methods
Contributes to the design of reward and incentive policies and systems	Tracks motivation levels in conjunction with performance results
Contributes to deciding or designates who will receive rewards and incentives	Contributes to the design of reward and incentive policies and systems
Gives rewards and incentives	May coordinate the process for designating who receives rewards and incentives
	May coordinate the process for giving rewards and incentives
	Documents recipients of rewards and incentives

Involving the employee

Typically, reward and incentive systems are designed jointly by managers and HR professionals, and employees may not have significant input. However, in challenging environments or difficult economic circumstances, it can be more effective to involve employees to ensure that rewards and incentives meet their needs and to allow them to understand the constraints on the system.

Motivating employees is a less formal activity, primarily under the control of individual managers. Since different employees are motivated by different means, to be most effective, the manager needs to use the methods that best motivate each individual. For example, some employees enjoy group attention when they have achieved an important goal or made a special contribution. Others would find that form of recognition painful and embarrassing. They might prefer a personal thank-you note from their boss's boss.

One way to tailor the use of motivation is to observe and ask questions to find out what is meaningful to each direct report. This can be done in a poll, in a staff meeting, or in individual conversations.

A sample motivation survey is included at the end of the section.

Involving the whole organization

The design of reward and incentive systems should involve the whole organization and must be in alignment with the organization's culture. A cross-functional committee of managers representing branches and the head office, along with HR professionals, can propose the system, design it, or approve a draft design.

The reward and incentive system will need approval from the executive or senior management level, and if it includes investment options or other rewards for executives, it will involve the board of directors.

The awarding of some rewards may involve the whole organization as well. Announcing recipients of top rewards, posting names or photographs in a public place, designating a special parking place, and holding an awards luncheon are all ways that the whole organization honours top achievers. These activities communicate the culture, values, and goals of the organization to all employees, and the opportunity to participate can be motivating.

Policies

Since budgeting and spending are involved, and since rewards and incentives involve issues of equity, there must be clearly and completely documented policies that are distributed and explained to all managers.

There may also need to be policies in place relating to spending for motivational activities by managers; for example, what can be spent for a departmental social outing or sports activity and how managers get clearance for those activities. Policies may also need to spell out criteria for acceptable motivators and what is off limits. For example, a policy may state that gifts need to be professional or work-related and of modest cost, and personal gifts or outings to nightclubs are unacceptable.

What motivates employees

Employees are motivated by a variety of factors. Managers tend to think that money is the primary motivator, but studies show that, as long as employees make a fair salary, other factors are the strongest motivators. Once employees are receiving salaries that meet their living needs, they put more emphasis on other, non-monetary rewards. For example:

- an inspiring institutional mission and the opportunity to contribute to the community, the country, or society in general;
- interesting work that is challenging, presenting new problems to solve;
- a compatible, friendly group of co-workers;
- a fair boss who has a positive relationship with each employee;
- the opportunity to contribute ideas on how the work is done or how the team is managed;
- a feeling of doing something that matters and that makes a difference;
- being part of an exciting, important, or well-regarded organization;
- opportunities for professional learning and growth;
- career opportunities.

Other motivators to consider include:

- perks or special benefits, such as parking, transportation, or meal vouchers;
- appreciation – spoken and written thank-you cards, letters, or certificates;
- recognition announcements or events, including with the team, or with more senior managers;
- conferences and conventions;
- a friendly atmosphere and compatible culture;

- social events;
- special assignments;
- trust from teammates;
- independent work and autonomy;
- regular increases in responsibility and opportunities for leadership.

It is important to recognize that motivators vary by culture as well. For example, in some places, canteen vouchers or a company-subsidized cell phone would be considered basic requirements of the job or standard benefits. In other places, special meal vouchers or an upgraded cell phone would be seen as a motivating reward.

From the field

Different motivators for different positions

A well-established Asian micro- and small business financial institution has found two high-impact rewards. Employees with direct sales responsibilities in particular respond to large financial rewards for achieving aggressive targets. Managers (who do not have sales or business development goals) respond better to being in high-potential development programmes, which enhance their status in the institution and through which they are given value-added tasks, roles, and visibility.

Motivation and retention – a long-term view

An African microfinance institution (MFI) uses a long-service incentive scheme to promote retention and conducts annual surveys to identify other important factors that employees find motivating.

Being creative with non-financial motivators

A south Asian institution uses recognition from the chairman of the board as a tool in its selection of rewards and incentives.

The human touch

Everyone at BWDA (India) knows that the founder and managing director learns and remembers the names of every employee at every level. This accomplishment has inspired his managers. As one of them said: 'If Mr Thambi can know my staff people's names, then I should know their families.' With this personal touch, based on having relationships with employees, many of BWDA's staff have remained with the institution since its founding in 1998.

Supporting your people beyond the workplace

An Indian MFI uses a variety of incentives that provide care for its people and contribute to high retention numbers:

- Employees can receive education support. Those who complete their education in their own time are rewarded with salary increases.
- There are welfare schemes, housing loans, general loans, and social functions.
- Family issues are given consideration; for example, staff may be reassigned to another work location so as to remain close to the home they share with their family.

This is an interesting example, but each institution needs to find its own mix of incentives that work within its financial constraints and cultural requirements.

Designing the rewards and incentive systems

Setting up systems to provide rewards and incentives is a strategic decision, since they will represent the organization's values and drive employees' behaviour. These systems also need to be thought through carefully to ensure fairness and to prevent opportunities for 'playing' the system – getting around it or taking advantage of it.

When designing these systems, you should consider the answers to key questions such as the following:

- What employee behaviours are essential for the institution to meet its goals?
- What are the organization's targets in these areas? Are there rates of change or incremental steps that are worth recognizing, in addition to the final targets?
- What kinds of rewards and incentives are meaningful in the national culture and current economy and are in line with the company's values and culture?
- What can the business afford? How can the business be creative about designing rewards that fit within its budget?
- Would the institution be able to make the awards if everyone achieved the targets?
- Is there a risk that the goals are unattainable or the incentives are not sufficient?
- How would the monitoring and decision-making happen? How do the managers avoid favouritism, keep the system fair and open to all, and make sure it cannot be taken advantage of?
- What are the time periods involved?
- How will we evaluate the success of the system – ease of use, effectiveness, perceived fairness, and so on?
- How long should we try the system? (Recommendation: minimum of 12 months unless dramatic unexpected effects are observed.)

Pitfalls of reward and incentive systems

For the system to be effective, employees must be able to see the clear and direct link between the rewards and incentives and their own performance. The most significant problem in any reward and incentive system is a failure to make that connection obvious and consistent. Several other kinds of problems can also occur in reward and incentive systems:

- *Favouritism.* Employees come to believe that rewards and incentives go only to certain individuals or groups based on status or relationships.
- *Arbitrary or random implementation.* Employees do not know the criteria for receiving the awards, believe the criteria are not followed, or observe

that the criteria are followed or ignored at the whim of the executive or manager.

- *Inadequacy.* Rewards are not seen as substantial enough.
- *Secrecy.* Overdone attempts to provide total confidentiality around pay and benefits can eliminate the clear connection between incentives and performance necessary for them to be motivating and rewarding.
- *Punishment.* Rewards are withdrawn for unclear reasons, but in circumstances that appear punitive.
- *Threat.* Managers try to motivate employees by threatening them with not receiving a reward.
- *Unmotivating.* Employees are not interested in the reward, or they consider it a contractual benefit they are entitled to receive.
- *Too easy.* Anyone can earn the reward simply by coming to work and doing the basics of the job.
- *Too hard.* Employees have no control over the circumstances that would allow them to earn the reward.

These pitfalls can be addressed through policies, careful design, piloting, documentation, training, and information systems. The success of the initiative partly depends on a strong code of ethics in the organization. It is also important that the reward and incentive systems be monitored by a credible cross-functional group of managers and HR professionals.

Caution! An example of what can go wrong when rewards are not carefully thought through

Sanskar Finance was expanding, opening new branches every month. To open a new region, the company hired a regional manager with banking experience but no background in microfinance, and his salary was double that of his peers. Sad to say, this action was only the first in a series, as new middle and senior managers were brought in at pay rates substantially above the 'old' ones. Resentment exploded, and performance deteriorated.

Template 5.2: Sample motivation survey

This survey is intended to help your manager understand what factors motivate you – help you do your best work and stay with the task or project even when it becomes frustrating or difficult.

Select the five to seven most important factors that motivate you.

1.	Working in an innovative, exciting business.
2.	Working with interesting people.
3.	Work that is interesting and challenging, with new problems to solve.
4.	Friendly atmosphere where people know and like me, and I fit in.
5.	A boss who listens to my ideas, and who uses my suggestions to do the work and run the team.
6.	Attending a conference or a class to learn for the job.
7.	Seeing possibilities for a good career here.
8.	Getting a personal thank you from the boss when I do something well or finish something especially difficult.
9.	Having fun and socializing with my co-workers.
10.	My boss tells my co-workers when I do an excellent job.
11.	My boss tells people higher up in the organization, maybe even the CEO, when I do excellent work or complete an especially difficult assignment.
12.	Being assigned to a special project that senior managers consider important.
13.	Being able to travel within the country or outside for special, important assignments for the institution.
14.	Feeling that my co-workers count on me to do an excellent job.
15.	My boss is interested in my success, speaks up for me, guides and protects me.
16.	My boss provides opportunities for me to grow professionally, and to improve my skills.
17.	My boss trusts me and lets me work independently.
18.	My boss supports me when others question my work or decisions.
19.	My boss makes sure I have everything I need for my work, and clears away barriers to the work.
20.	A good salary compared with people in other businesses.
21.	Good benefits, such as sports club memberships and access to education.
22.	Regular increases in responsibility and promotions to higher positions.
23.	Other:

Training and education

Definitions

Training refers to activities intended to help employees acquire the knowledge and skills related to their work. It can be formal, such as classroom sessions, or informal, such as on-the-job training provided by the manager or lunch talks.

Training may be delivered by various people:

- specialist trainers brought in from outside the business;
- experts within the organization;
- the institution's own trainers;
- managers.

Employees also attend training programmes conducted by external training groups and held outside the organization.

Education sometimes means the same as training, and sometimes it refers to learning that is not exclusively related to the job. For example, learning a language that is not required for work but could become useful later in the employee's career might be called education.

The Handbook focuses on training, which is a complex topic; achieving sufficient expertise to design, develop, and deliver training internally is a substantial task. The Handbook gives an overview of this process and is more specific about the aspects that managers and HR professionals can readily do to plan for, select, prepare for, support, and follow up on training activities.

Involving the whole organization

One way the whole organization is involved in training is through policies that promote training for all employees and a culture that encourages learning on the job.

In addition, executives and senior managers need to review and approve the training curriculum, and both branch managers and functional managers should be fully involved in defining training needs and the parameters of specific training courses.

Table 5.4: Responsibilities for training

Business managers	*HR professionals*
Must • Identify training needs • Collaborate with HR to develop competency profiles • Provide on-the-job training • Prepare employees for training • Support employees during training sessions • Debrief and help employees apply learning to the job • Give HR feedback about the effectiveness of training **May** • Collaborate in developing training policies • Collaborate with HR to select appropriate training programmes	**Must** • Deliver classroom training sessions • Collaborate in developing training policies • Conduct job analyses and training needs analyses • Draft the training curriculum and review it with managers • Identify sources for training – both internal and external • Propose external training sources, and review these with managers • Finalize training arrangements – both internal and external • Distribute training information • Administer a system to track and approve employees' training selections • Conduct training registration • Monitor training in progress • Make sure pre-work and other materials are distributed • Conduct training evaluations • Follow up with managers about the on-the-job application and effectiveness of training **May** • Initiate drafts of competency profiles • Design and develop internal training • Work with internal experts to develop internal training

HR involvement in training

As the organization grows, a designated person, and eventually a department, will take responsibility for training. In some businesses, training is included in the HR department; in others, it is a separate department.

The level of involvement of internal HR or training staff in training will be different for each institution.

On-boarding, orientation, and on-the-job training are usually provided in-house, as a collaborative effort of HR and the business managers.

Even if the organization is not ready to provide training using internal resources, the HR professional has two important responsibilities:

1. Find out what the external resources are and build a curriculum of those offerings.
2. Assemble a library of self-study materials. These may include books and manuals as well as online learning programmes. The HR professional vets the materials for suitability and then creates a catalogue of resources accessible to everyone in the organization.

Managers' involvement in training

Approximately 70 per cent of employees' learning happens on the job, through experience, feedback, coaching, and relationships with managers and co-workers. External training can be helpful, but its value should not be overestimated. The greatest learning impact comes from managers managing their employees, giving feedback, and finding new and challenging tasks for them.

Using external resources to provide training

The company should take advantage of external training resources under the following circumstances:

- HR and/or the rest of the organization does not have the expertise to provide the required training.
- External training is more cost-effective.
- The training is offered by a credible institution on a regular basis.
- The training is specific to only a few staff; for example, accounting certification.
- The organization will benefit from having its employees interact with others in the industry.
- HR does not have the capacity to organize and administer an in-house training programme.
- An outside expert or institution can provide the necessary level of credibility or reputation.

From the field: integrating external resources with internal needs

A number of Indian MFIs have set up relationships with Adyayan in Delhi, an institute that prepares people to be field officers and branch managers. Through the relationship with this organization, an MFI can reduce the time required to recruit and screen job candidates as well as the time for initial training.

Types of training

Technical training covers the technical knowledge, skills, and processes required for each position, such as handling cash, underwriting, or managing a loan portfolio. This is the training necessary for the organization to perform its work, and proficiency in technical areas is the organization's initial definition of success.

Some areas of technical training may be mandated by regulation, and ongoing professional education in technical subjects may be required for some specialized qualifications such as accounting or law.

Customer service training may be included with technical training. It covers the skills and behaviours needed to interact effectively with the institution's customers of all kinds.

Business management training covers topics such as budgeting, using information systems, analysing capacity, results analysis, and reporting – the competencies needed by all managers to run their areas of the business.

Specialized training refers to the competencies needed by the specialist functions of the organization, such as finance, IT, marketing, or law.

Project management training focuses on the planning, budgeting, resourcing, tracking, and implementation competencies required for individual projects. It is sometimes provided for individuals with responsibility for setting up large-scale new operations, and components of this training can be useful for any manager.

Communication and organizational skills training covers competencies such as written communication, giving presentations, and time management.

People management training covers all aspects of managing employees (as distinct from managing their work), such as motivating, giving feedback, conducting performance appraisals, building teams, and giving direction and setting priorities.

Leadership training addresses the competencies needed by senior managers, such as leadership communication, sustaining the vision, leading change and innovation, working with the board, defining strategy, and interacting with external constituents. Leadership training can also be valuable for more junior managers, individual professionals, and staff in promoting initiative, strategic thinking, and an entrepreneurial mindset.

Evolution of the training curriculum

A curriculum is a series of courses that prepare trainees for a designated specialty, such as accounting or underwriting, or for a level or type of position, such as loan officer or branch manager. A curriculum may include both internal and external courses. There is no single fixed or standard business curriculum, but there are trends in how a curriculum evolves that parallel the evolution of the business.

An *initial curriculum* is created in the earlier stages of a business's development, with formal and informal courses. It will include technical training and customer service training. It is unlikely to include business management, specialties, project management, communication and organizational skills, people management, or leadership.

The start-up organization usually hires people who are already trained or gets by with what its people can pick up in self-study.

The second stage curriculum comes together as the business grows and becomes more established. This is likely to include technical training, customer service training, business management, and communication and organizational skills. It is unlikely to include specialties, project management, people management, or leadership.

The third-stage curriculum is likely to include technical training, customer service training, business management, communication and organizational skills, and people management. It is unlikely to include specialties, project management, or leadership.

People management skills training tends to come in later. Some organizations are able to include it along with business management, but technically oriented managers and leaders do not always see the need for these competencies until the organization is larger or there are problems with retention or performance.

The fourth stage curriculum is the most advanced. It is likely to include technical training, customer service training, business management, communication and organization skills, people management, project management, and leadership. It is unlikely to include specialties.

Typically, the last component that institutions attend to is formal training in leadership. The need arises as the founder considers retirement or the first leadership team experiences turnover. It also becomes important when the organization grows to 1,000 or more employees with a large number of branches in many different regions, a more complex structure, and a more challenging or competitive environment.

Specialty training is rarely conducted internally, even by very large organizations, because of the small numbers of possible trainees and the availability of education through universities and academies.

Getting ahead in the evolution of the training curriculum can be a competitive advantage for an organization.

Notes on the curriculum of an established MFI

An established institution offers a curriculum that includes a variety of training, with different offerings suitable for different levels and functions. The courses are sponsored by government, academic, and development institutions as well as by the MFI itself. The courses include:

- individual lending;
- livelihood promotion;
- cluster development;
- business planning;
- financial modelling;
- housing microfinance;
- capacity building;
- management skills;
- train-the-trainer skills.

Caution! A challenge in providing advanced training to more senior managers

One of the challenges that MFIs can encounter as they provide advanced training to their senior managers is the loss of the training investment. In other words, once trained, the senior manager leaves the MFI to work elsewhere – where he or she is desirable because he or she arrives well prepared.

From the field

Training policy

An African bank has developed the following policy to avoid losing its training investment in senior managers. Before final approval is given for a senior manager to attend a longer, advanced training programme at a degree- or certificate-giving or foreign institution, the manager must do the following:

- sign an agreement to continue working at the bank for one to five more years, depending on the length and cost of the training;
- identify a valid guarantor who will repay the entire cost of the training if the manager leaves before completing the agreed time commitment;
- in the absence of a guarantor, demonstrate his or her ability to repay (in some cases, collateral provides the guarantee).
- This kind of policy can tend to favour the institution over the individual, and it must be communicated and deployed with care. It must also be used in the context of other developmental activities for senior managers so that advancement is not limited only to those who can potentially pay for the preparation.

Mandatory training

A leading Indian bank mandates that all employees must attend as a minimum one 10-day training session each year. This event is based on recommendations from supervisors and managers about what employees need to maintain and enhance performance. It combines refreshing and advancing technical and managerial skills. The institution's evaluation is that mandatory training has contributed to a steady improvement in performance.

Keeping training relevant

Both Grameen Koota and BWDA keep their training curriculum current and relevant by linking needs assessments to performance appraisals. At the end of each appraisal cycle, the training manager finds out from each department head the competencies on which he or she believes the staff need refreshing or enhancement. The training manager prepares a list of courses, both internal and external, and resources required to develop or access them. This list forms the basis for the training budget, to be approved by the managing director. The information is then posted as the year's training calendar.

Designing, developing and delivering training

The HR department needs to be able to perform some basic training design, development, and delivery tasks even if all its training is provided by external sources. Here are the musts:

- Conduct a job analysis, based on job descriptions prepared by managers – what are the tasks and activities required to perform the job, and what skills, knowledge, and ways of thinking are needed to do it properly and effectively?
- Provide all information required for on-boarding.
- Present all the technical knowledge and skills, based on the expertise of the organization's management and available consulting resources.
- Make a curriculum outline of training provided internally or by external sources that is relevant to and used by employees or managers currently at the institution.

- Conduct a training needs assessment based on the skills and knowledge required to perform each job at a satisfactory (or better) level to determine which training needs are currently being met and which are not.
- Review training offered by external resources, whether in classrooms or online, against the needs assessment and the job descriptions to determine its suitability.
- Research additional training resources to fill gaps or improve training quality.

As the HR department develops and includes one or more dedicated training professionals, it will bring in more of the competencies needed to design, develop, and deliver high-quality training. At that point, its activities may include the following:

- predictive training needs analyses for positions that are planned but do not yet exist;
- basic course design specifications that cover the characteristics of the people needing the course, the desired learning objectives or outcomes, the content (facts, concepts, tools, skills, and mindsets), and the learning methods;
- use of generic competency models to structure training course curricula.

A large and well-established organization may develop a training department or learning centre, with one or more individuals with specialized training expertise in designing, developing, and delivering training. In those circumstances, the institution may implement the most advanced training activities. For example:

- arranging train-the-trainer courses to equip non-trainers to prepare and present technical material in the most effective ways;
- conducting competency modelling, a performance-based process that analyses what the highest-performing individuals in a designated position do that distinguishes them from average performers;
- producing complex design specifications, including more involved and experiential learning methods, and covering other aspects of the context and environment for the training course;
- conducting management and leadership training with internal resources;
- developing and administering training evaluations internally.

Why needs analysis and training design matter

At a certain time, Manyata decided to require all managers to attend a course on calculating ratios for financial statements, income statements, and balance sheets. Managers who had already been through the basic accounting course learned much more about controlling costs, using financial projections, and running their branches more effectively. However, managers who did not have the prerequisite training were confused and frustrated, unable to benefit from the course. For them and the institution, the training was a waste of time and money.

Training design. The keys to good training design are that the programme does the following:

- prepares people to perform on the job;
- uses a variety of learning methods to accommodate different learning styles;
- keeps learners interested and engaged;
- moves at a pace that is appropriate to the learners and the organizational culture.

Job analysis or needs analysis. HR professionals can conduct their own job analysis or needs analysis by working with the job analysis form in Chapter 3 (Template 3.1). The quickest approach is to talk to one or more managers of the position. In that case, select managers whose staff consistently produce the best results.

A more reliable approach is to talk to managers and high-performing staff, asking them to identify the factors required for high performance. Staff can be interviewed individually or in small focus groups.

Basic competency outlines. A basic competency outline can be built in a similar fashion, by holding behavioural event interviews with top performers and average performers and then analysing the results for the important differentiators. It is preferable to have this work done by an outside expert who has experience in behavioural event interviewing and has no assumptions about the distinguishing characteristics of different levels of performance.

In order to produce an effective training design, some specialized training and experience are required. A well-prepared HR professional can perform a thorough and thoughtful review of a training design created by an expert trainer or by a training or educational institution.

A sound training design will cover all relevant factors:

- The essential characteristics of the people the training is intended for: prior experience needed, appropriate job level, education level needed, specific skills required, such as maths; any prerequisites, such as certification or advanced reading; and other considerations to ensure a good match between the training design and the people from the institution needing this training.
- What people who take the training will be prepared to do when they finish: observable or measurable results; realistic goals given the nature of the trainees and the amount of time allotted for the training; recognition of limitations on performance, such as needing to use a manual or be coached by a manager; and other considerations to ensure a good match for the work the trainees are in now or are preparing to start.
- What content the course will include: skills, knowledge, processes, and mindsets or attitudes; other considerations to ensure a good match for the results of the needs analysis.

- What methods the course will use to conduct the training: appropriateness for the trainee group and the culture; varied and interesting enough to keep most people's attention; and reasonable for the content and the performance objectives.

> **Tip: reviewing training designs**
>
> Involve managers in reviewing designs. It is much easier to reject a content expert or revise an internal plan at the design stage rather than later in the process.

Training materials development. Development usually refers to the process of preparing or acquiring the materials, equipment, and space needed for the training session.

Materials include books, articles, videos, case studies, games, and PowerPoint slides. They usually need to be reviewed and critiqued by internal managers or experts to ensure that they present the content in ways that are consistent with the business's practices, whether they come from an outside source or have been created internally.

Equipment ranges from tables and chairs, through flip charts and markers, to electronic equipment and slides or videos.

Internally developed materials are materials that are prepared in-house. They do not have to be fancy, but they do need to be well formatted, use graphical elements for interest and business identity, and be free of spelling and typographical mistakes.

They need to support the learning process by leaving room for notes as well as space to do written exercises – but they should not have the 'answers' to discussion questions. They also need to serve as reference materials that the trainees can turn to later, on the job. Tables of contents and labels on pages help with this requirement.

Purchased or externally acquired materials need to meet the same criteria, but the expectations for graphical design may be higher. Review purchased materials for completeness and ease of use in the classroom as well as their value and accessibility as workplace references.

> **Tip: reviewing training materials**
>
> Involve others in reviewing materials as a way to ensure that the materials are relevant and useful and as a way to build interest in the training.

Delivery. Delivery is the presentation of the training itself, whether it occurs at the organization's premises or off-site, perhaps at another institution. The quality of the delivery can make or break the experience, no matter how sound the design or the materials.

If a programme has been developed internally and is intended for a large audience or has high visibility with senior managers, consider holding a pilot session. A pilot session takes place with a small audience and includes opportunities to stop and evaluate how the programme is going. Everyone knows it is not the finished version, so mistakes are accepted, and revisions can be made before the major roll-out happens.

Tip: training delivery

For internally developed training, bear the following in mind:

- Before the delivery, have internal experts and trainers give a 'dress rehearsal' to make sure they are prepared, the timing is right, and the activities work as designed.
- Try out any unusual activities, such as games and adventurous exercises, to make sure they work as stated without unintended problems; for example, will they work for someone with limited vision or short legs?
- Internal people who are designated to lead training sessions should have training in presentation skills. If possible, they should practise and be coached.

If you are using externally developed training, the following is a useful suggestion:

- Ask the outside source to give a demonstration to get a sense of pace, style, voice, and other factors that can affect success.

Evaluation of training

There are two kinds of evaluation relating to training. One type is for determining whether the investment in the training was worthwhile, and the other is to find out whether each individual trainee learned what was expected.

Pre-tests are given to find out what level of knowledge or skill the trainees have before the training starts.

- Useful: They are worth doing if the training is intended to upgrade or enhance existing skills and knowledge or allow trainees to expand what they do in their current job.
- No use: But they are pointless for new hires or anyone else with no knowledge of the job.

End-of-course learning evaluations are like tests in school, intended to find out what trainees know at the end of the training.

- Value: These can be beneficial if the work requires employees to have knowledge of facts, policies, or procedures.
- Limitations: But they are less valuable if the primary job requirement is for skills. (However, some end-of-course evaluations do include application activities in which trainees use new skills.)

End-of-course training evaluations ask trainees to give feedback on their subjective experience of the training.

- Value: They are beneficial for assessing the impact of the trainer, the materials, the environment, and the learning methods. They allow for feedback on trainees' perceptions of how relevant the content is to their jobs.

- Limitations: But treat the findings with caution, since a trainer who gave tough but relevant feedback or put trainees through a challenging exercise can receive unwarranted criticism, and a course full of fun activities can be highly rated even though it taught relatively little.

On-the-job evaluations ask managers and trainees to report on what skills and knowledge they are using on the job, how well they are performing, and what difference the training has made to quality, productivity, confidence, or other important measures.

- High value: This is a very useful evaluation method for determining whether the training was effective and whether individual employees learned what was expected.
- Limitations: These evaluations require expert development, as well as a time commitment to conduct and analyse the feedback.

Impact on business results

- Highest value: This is considered by some to be the ultimate measure of the effectiveness of a training programme.
- Limitations: Given the large number of factors that affect business results, it can be hard to determine the contribution of the training to the whole picture.

Preparation for training

Information and registration. The first step in preparing for training is getting the information out to managers and staff and asking people to sign up. In some cases, everyone in a group, in a specific position, or at a given level is expected to attend, and signing up consists mainly of selecting which dates to attend, if various options exist.

In other cases, trainees have to be nominated, and the process is more complex. The people who nominate need to be identified and briefed about the criteria for selection. Their candidates may need to go through an application process or be reviewed by HR professionals or by more senior managers.

These processes are usually administered by HR or training department professionals.

Trainee preparation and pre-work. If a training session is standard and straightforward, there may be no need for preparation other than a confirmation of registration and the date, time, and place for the first day of training.

If the training is a special opportunity or a high-visibility experience, then trainees may need to receive an explanatory letter. Sometimes a letter from the CEO or other senior manager goes out to impress trainees with the importance of their training and to motivate them to perform well.

Some training courses depend upon the trainee doing work in advance – reading something, assembling sample documents, collecting data, or interviewing people. Trainees need to receive clear instructions far enough in advance to be able to complete the pre-course work along with their regular work.

Manager preparation. In the end, managers benefit from the training their employees receive. Managers should be provided with details of the training and suggestions for how to prepare their direct reports, support them, and follow up with them.

In some cases, managers complete an assessment for or provide data to the employees to use in the course, and they need adequate time to do their part.

Support during training

Part of preparing managers for their employees' training is to request, or require, that the managers do not distract the trainees or pull them out of the training with work demands. In this case, being 'supportive' means not interfering.

It can fall to the HR professional to have to intervene with managers who persist in interrupting their employees' training experience.

Follow-up after training

Both managers and HR professionals can provide follow-up.

Managers can:

- talk to employees individually about their training experience – find out what they learned;
- ask an employee who attended training to share something from the experience with co-workers;
- designate the trained employee as the 'expert resource' for the group;
- follow up during a feedback or performance review, to reflect on how the training affected the employee's performance.

HR professionals can follow up training by:

- administering an impact evaluation, four to six months after the training;
- circulating additional articles or podcasts relating to the training;
- holding informal lunchtime discussions of topics related to the training, to keep it fresh in everyone's minds and to provide a forum for bringing up questions and difficulties.

CHAPTER 6

Evaluating performance

Evaluating performance is where the responsibility for managing people and the responsibility for producing results come together. On a regular basis, all employees and all managers need to consider whether their performance is producing the desired business results and what kind of development steps should be taken to either remedy performance problems or enhance or broaden strong performance.

> **From the field**
>
> The chief operating officer of an east African MFI spoke at length about the critical need for developing a performance culture – a mindset throughout the institution that cares about excellent performance, coaches and trains for it, evaluates it frequently, and rewards it. In her experience, a performance culture and the accompanying consistently high performance cannot be achieved through a half-hearted, inconsistent, vague annual performance review. To have a performance culture, the organization must require and enforce frequent formal and informal performance reviews.

Evaluating performance and planning development are also the points at which concern for the organization and concern for the individual need to be balanced. The organization's vision, mission, and values will help set that balance; the HR philosophy and strategy also give it definition.

Organizations must achieve results to survive and thrive, and employees must meet goals and expectations to produce results, follow policies, and support the organization's culture. Organizations need to review and evaluate performance to be sure that they are on track with their strategic goals.

At the same time, employees need to know how they are doing, whether their performance is meeting expectations, and how they are contributing to the organization's success. At the individual level, they need to know that they are on track.

Organizations must also develop the people who work for them so that all employees can achieve the required results and behave in alignment with policies and culture. Beyond results and alignment, providing development is one of the ways in which organizations recognize, motivate, and reward employees. It is in the organization's interest to plan and provide development.

Likewise, it is in the employees' interest to plan and participate in development. It is their path to success, improvement, and advancement. It is also one of the ways in which they know they are recognized and valued by the organization.

http://dx.doi.org/10.3362/9781780447926.007

Each conversation about performance and development tests the manager's alignment with the organization's culture and values and also highlights the manager's individual values.

Performance evaluation and development planning are addressed together because the two activities need to take place in closely linked conversations. It is logical for an employee and a manager to review existing expectations and goals, evaluate the employee's performance against those goals, and then plan the next steps.

- If the employee achieved the existing goals, the next steps address future goals and any development needed to achieve them.
- If the employee exceeded the goals, the next steps could be expanded responsibilities, a promotion, or other career moves, supported by the appropriate development activities.
- If the employee's performance fell short of the goals, the next steps are to examine the reasons, the changes needed so he or she can meet those goals, and the development required to support the changes.

Table 6.1: Alignment of people management responsibilities

Business manager – typical contributions	*People management responsibilities*	*HR professional – typical contributions*
Reviewing performance and documenting results, goals, and next steps Rewarding strong performance and good results Planning development for increased responsibilities and promotion Remedying weak performance Applying consequences or penalties for failure to meet standards Documenting measures taken with regard to addressing performance problems Identifying indicators of potential termination, documenting behaviour and steps taken to address problems Recommending putting an employee on a short-term improvement plan	Measure people's results Maintain performance standards Reward people for good work	Collaborating on designing the performance review process Maintaining the performance review calendar Providing training, coaching, and counselling for performance reviews Monitoring compliance with performance review meetings and documentation Collaborating in defining policies and procedures for giving rewards, consequences, and penalties Monitoring the use and impact of rewards and penalties Advising on and monitoring performance problems, remedy measures, and supporting documentation Advising on and monitoring potential termination situations, and ensuring documentation of behaviour and remedy steps Advising on and monitoring decisions about and use of improvement plans

Connections to other components of the performance management system

Evaluation and development are introduced on an employee's first day with the business.

On-boarding is an employee's first development experience, during which he or she learns a great deal about the organization and the job, including culture, policies, and behaviour expectations with which he or she must be aligned (see Chapter 4).

Setting expectations and performance goals from the beginning lets the new employee know what performance he or she will need to produce and what will be measured and evaluated in reviews (see Chapter 4).

Feedback and coaching on a day-to-day basis require the manager to pay attention to the employee's performance and address questions, mistakes, or concerns before they become problems, or to reinforce correct or exceptional performance promptly (see Chapter 5).

Training, whether formal or informal, on the job, through self-study, or in the classroom, is a major component of individual development plans and can contribute significantly to employees' ability to perform successfully (see Chapter 5).

Career development and advancement build on insights gained from evaluating performance (see Chapter 7).

High-potential programmes and succession planning also depend on the information that is consolidated and documented in performance reviews and the growth that results from development planning (see Chapter 7).

Compensation may be directly linked to performance and therefore requires careful evaluation and documentation (see Chapter 5).

Performance reviews

Definition

Performance reviews typically refer to the formal conversations between a manager and an employee about how well the employee has performed during the preceding quarter, half-year, or year (the review period). Giving performance reviews is a planned process that requires measurement, feedback, positive reinforcement, dialogue, and agreement. Another way to think about a performance review is that it is an extended, formal, comprehensive feedback session.

Along with reviewing past performance, managers and employees typically discuss future goals and the support and development needed to make it possible to meet those goals.

As long as the manager has clearly communicated performance expectations, regularly monitored performance throughout the review period, and given open, honest, and consistent feedback and coaching, the formal review meeting should be a straightforward wrap-up within an ongoing process.

Importance

The importance of performance reviews cannot be overemphasized. They are the points in the business cycle when both the manager and the employee summarize what has been accomplished, whether work performance is on track against goals, and whether behaviour is aligned with expectations and organizational culture.

Performance reviews are the foundation stones of organizational success. Individual performance goals are supposed to be structured to enable the business unit to achieve its goals. The business unit's goals contribute to the success of the organization's strategic goals.

Performance reviews are also critical for the success of the individual employee. Goals direct the employee's efforts; feedback keeps those efforts on track. The performance review conversation provides recognition of and reward for strong performance, reassurance that efforts are on target and paying off, and redirection if needed.

The performance review conversation is also a very significant opportunity for the manager and the employee to maintain and strengthen their working relationship.

Ongoing loyalty and commitment to staying in the job with the organization – in a word, retention – can be heavily influenced by a programme of regular, timely, and successful performance review conversations.

Risks

Without regular performance reviews, each business unit and the organization as a whole will not have a clear view of the internal factors that are promoting or interfering with the achievement of strategic goals.

Without regular performance reviews, the individual employee has only a subjective and vague idea of whether he or she is doing the job properly, achieving the required results, satisfying the boss's expectations, and working well with the team.

Without regular performance reviews, the individual employee is likely to feel neglected and undervalued.

Table 6.2: Responsibilities for performance reviews

Business manager	*HR professional*
Must • Schedule and hold performance review conversations at designated intervals, documenting achievements and poor performance • Set goals with each direct report for the future period, and document these • Discuss, document, and follow up on rewards, consequences, or penalties, depending on results • Identify and prepare to build a case if termination is a possibility or if the employee qualifies for promotion **May** • Collaborate with HR professionals to design the performance review process, calendar, and forms	**Must** • Collaborate with business managers to design the performance review process, calendar, and forms • Maintain the appraisal calendar and issue reminders • Train, coach, and advise managers on holding performance reviews • Monitor and collect documentation, as needed, for other performance management processes (high-potential identification, succession planning, etc.) • Collaborate with managers on the administration of rewards, consequences, and penalties • Collaborate closely on identifying and building termination and promotion cases

The role and responsibility of direct reports

In most organizations, employees contribute equally to the performance review conversation, and their input matters. They are expected to document achievements; describe results achieved; recommend a rating, according to the organization's system; and propose goals and performance standards for future periods.

The full engagement of employees in the performance review process is critical, since their efforts determine the results, and their perspective is essential to understanding how the results were or were not achieved. The manager can determine the employee's engagement through several measures:

- the level of preparation and documentation that is shown;
- the extent of participation in the performance review conversation;
- his or her readiness to propose ideas and take the initiative on evaluation and development planning;
- the promptness and completeness of follow-up actions.

The extent to which employees participate equally and are given consideration in the conversation mirrors the extent to which they follow through on development, fix performance problems, and remain loyal to the unit and the organization.

Involving the whole organization

In preparing for the review meeting, the manager and/or the employee may ask others with appropriate connections to the employee's work to contribute their assessments of the employee's performance. This additional input can be critical in situations where the employee works in a different location from the manager or has worked on assignments with other managers. It is valuable in all cases for the more fully rounded perspective it can provide.

In some organizations, the manager may preview his or her appraisal of the employee with his or her direct manager. In challenging situations or with challenging employees, the manager's manager can provide the manager with objectivity, strategies for conducting the review, and clarity on authority or limits relating to rewards or negative consequences. This review step can also reassure to employees that their manager's assessment has received a potentially objective appraisal.

In other institutions, there may be a review of the results of the manager–employee conversations by senior managers. The second review step gives senior managers an overview of employee performance. It also allows them to administer ratings, rankings (if done), salary increases, promotions, performance problem plans, and potential termination cases from a less personal perspective and with the overall organizational needs in mind.

Other than reviews with the senior manager or with an HR professional, the content of performance review conversations is kept confidential, since sensitive topics may be discussed. It is important that the whole organization respects the confidentiality of sensitive aspects of performance reviews.

Input from clients

A northern Indian MFI collects feedback about its field staff from clients. This input gives the managers and the field staff direct data on performance and has the added benefit of serving as a fraud prevention mechanism.

Policies

The organization needs to have policies on all relevant aspects of the performance review:

- how often performance reviews are held – quarterly or semi-annually is recommended;
- how the manager and the employee prepare, including the documentation to be assembled;
- what the conversation needs to address;
- the documentation of performance against goals, ratings, reasons for ratings and poor performance, rewards, consequences or penalties, performance plans or remediation, and future goals;
- who needs to be involved in providing input and in addressing problems;
- which situations require the involvement of the manager's manager or an HR professional;
- what matters will be kept confidential;
- documentation to be provided to the HR department;

- the consequences for managers who fail to conduct performance reviews according to the organization's review calendar.

When to hold performance reviews

Formal review conversations should be held at least twice a year, at six-month intervals. One of these reviews should coincide with the business's fiscal year-end. Interim quarterly reviews are recommended, especially if there is rapid intake of new employees because of rapid growth, or if there is volatility in the structure or direction of the organization. The reviews held every other quarter are more informal.

Rating systems

Most performance management systems have a rating scale of some kind. A rating summarizes the level of quality of performance. The simplest rating systems summarize the outcome of the review by using one of three categories to describe the employee's performance: exceeded expectations; met expectations; and fell below expectations.

Number of rating levels. Rating scales may have between three and six levels.

Three-level scales are built on one of the following models:

- overall achievement: exceptional/acceptable/not fully acceptable;
- achievement of objectives: exceeds/meets/fails to meet.

Employee competencies may also be rated on three-level scales; for example:

- competence level: highly capable/fully capable/less than fully capable;
- relative ability: above average/average/below average.

Four-level scales use only positive definitions to give positive reinforcement of achievements regardless of level. This approach reflects a culture of positive thinking and continuous improvement, and is not suitable in all environments:

- individual performance: very effective/effective/developing/basic.

Organizations with large numbers of employees or complex levels of compensation or responsibility may use a *five-level rating system*, reserving the highest rating to flag high-potential employees and the lowest rating to flag employees at risk of being terminated for poor performance:

- 5 = consistently exceeds standards;
- 4 = good performance, meets standards, often exceeds standards;
- 3 = satisfactory performance, consistently meets standards;
- 2 = weak performance, sometimes doesn't meet standards, needs improvement;
- 1 = unacceptable performance, consistently doesn't meet standards.

Five-level scales are the most commonly used scales in performance management systems. They provide for two levels of strong performance, and the nuance of two levels of below-average or less-than-acceptable performance.

Six-level scales eliminate the tendency in five-level scales to focus mainly on the central rating or to drift upward. A six-level scale may use terms such as the following:

- individual performance: exceptional/excellent/well balanced/reasonable/ barely effective/unacceptable.

The *behaviourally anchored rating scale* (BARS) is an entirely different way of rating performance, since it is not reduced to numbers or single words. Instead, it contains the key behaviours that constitute successful performance and gives specific measures or descriptors for satisfactory performance. The BARS approach requires separate rating sheets for each type of position. Those rating sheets can be closely linked to performance standards and key performance indicators.

For example, the rating scale for a receptionist might include the following comments:

- answers incoming calls within four rings;
- gives every customer a greeting and a smile;
- logs visitor names and communicates them accurately to their hosts.

Communication. Whatever the rating system is, it needs to be clearly explained to everyone in the organization and consistently and fairly administered.

Making judgement calls about which rating to give

The more concrete the goals and performance standards, the easier it is to decide whether performance meets, exceeds, or falls below expectations. However, there are some common dilemmas that arise when rating performance.

Deciding whether the performance fell below expectations to a mild or serious degree – choosing between the lower two points on a five- or six-point scale. Sometimes performance falls below expectations, but as a result of understandable circumstances or not to a serious degree. In these cases, the rating may be given for the sake of fairness and for the effect of stimulating the employee to make improvements, but it should be annotated to reflect the less serious nature of the shortfall.

Situations of this nature include the following examples:

- Inconsistent performance: the employee has shown the ability to meet the standard, but not consistently enough to warrant 'meets expectations' and not so inconsistently to cause more serious concern.

- Goals or standards were unclear initially or changed during the quarter or half-year, and so the inability to meet expectations has been to some extent outside the employee's control, and the manager is confident that the employee could meet the clarified or revised goal.

Sometimes performance falls below expectations to a serious extent, without extenuating circumstances, and the manager is not confident that the employee could improve performance. In these cases, the rating needs to be given as a clear signal to the employee and to the rest of the organization of a problematic situation, a potential case for termination.

Situations like this include the following examples:

- Consistently poor performance: the employee has regularly failed to perform as expected, in spite of feedback, coaching, training, and warnings.
- Negative impact on co-workers or the unit: the employee's periodic or regular below-standard performance has prevented others from completing their work or performing up to standard and has affected the overall results of the business unit.

Deciding whether the rating merits a 'meets expectations' or an 'exceeds expectations' on a three-level scale. Goals and performance standards need to be written in such a way that meeting them would result in a rating of 'meets expectations'. This rating acknowledges solid, good work with which the manager and the employee can be satisfied. Deciding whether to give an employee an 'exceeds expectations' rating is determined by the extent to which the employee demonstrated exceptional initiative, dedication, and commitment, unusual creativity, leadership, steadiness in a crisis, or exceptional good judgement in a challenging situation. Here are the key questions the manager can consider in making the distinction:

- Did the employee exceed expectations more often than not? Or only occasionally?
- Did the employee's exceptional performance result in improved operations for co-workers or higher-than-expected results for the business unit?

Regardless of the manager's decision, instances of exceptional performance should be noted in the employee's permanent record, specifying what behaviours and impacts were above expectations.

What does and does not get rated

Performance review conversations need to cover the full range of relevant performance relating to goals, expectations for behaviour in a business unit, and company policies and culture. The ways in which an employee meets goals and is aligned with the policies and culture should definitely be discussed in formal and informal feedback and review conversations.

Performance ratings need to be based on goals and expectations that have been documented and discussed fully with the employee over the period before the performance review.

What this means is that exceptional performance or performance problems relating to areas not covered in documented goals and expectations cannot be rated unless the issue is clearly integrated with a documented goal. For example, a worker's poor personal hygiene cannot be rated 'below expectations' unless hygiene standards, grooming, or appearance had been included in goals and expectations (perhaps because the position requires constant interaction with customers or team members).

However, limiting performance ratings to documented goals and expectations does not prevent the manager from discussing the problem with the employee. And, of course, the additional goals or expectations should be documented for the next review period.

The following items typically fall outside the rating system:

- use of vacation or medical leave – how much time was used (within the policy limits) or how it was used;
- appearance, grooming, and hygiene, unless covered in expectations;
- personality and 'style' (although behaviours may be set out in goals and expectations);
- self-expression and social behaviour that is not covered by policies and does not impact on the ability of co-workers to perform at their best.

Cumulative ratings

In some organizations, a separate rating is given for each major performance goal, and then the individual ratings are added up for a single, final rating.

In these cases, it is important that the manager and employee establish at the beginning of the review period the weighting of each goal, to clarify priorities and avoid later disappointment.

The process

The usual performance review process follows these steps:

1. Manager schedules the review meeting, with a reminder of what data or documents are needed as well as what the components of the conversation are.
2. Employee and manager collect data, prepare assessments, gather documents, and ask for input from appropriate others.
3. Employee and manager prepare by looking over goals, results, and feedback and noting points to be covered and questions to be raised. They write their review points (achievements, gaps) and assign ratings.

4. Employee and manager meet, covering all components of the conversation, documenting designated points, and agreeing on next steps or follow-up.
5. Employee and manager retain their documentation of the review process and submit copies to the HR department.
6. Employee and manager follow up with next steps.

Every review conversation (Step 4), whether formal or informal, needs to cover the full range of components:

- goals and expectations set in the previous meeting; the job description may also be reviewed;
- where performance met, exceeded, or fell short of goals and expectations, in objective, concrete terms, with examples and results data;
- factors that contributed to performance, both strong and poor;
- development activities undertaken during the time period to support or improve performance, and their impact;
- feedback from others;
- the rating;
- what will be done in response to performance – remedy performance gaps, expand goals and responsibilities, move towards promotion, etc.;
- the next steps or follow-up to the meeting – documentation, further reviews, development activities, performance plans, redeployment, termination, or promotion.

Preparation for the meeting – the manager

One view is that managers should be preparing for performance review conversations throughout the review period (the quarter or half-year) by communicating and updating goals and expectations, giving feedback and coaching, saving emails and notes to track performance, and providing developmental opportunities (see the section on 'Development planning' below).

If the manager keeps up with these responsibilities, there should be no major surprises for either the manager or the employee during the performance review meeting.

Specific preparation activities by the manager include the following:

- Schedule sufficient time (at least one hour) during the business day, and reserve a private meeting location.
- Give the employee advance notification and a reminder to bring the appropriate materials.
- Ask the employee to complete a self-evaluation form and bring notes on his or her achievements, concerns, and questions (see the performance appraisal template at the end of the section).
- Request input from others, as appropriate.

- Help the employee arrange work coverage for the meeting time.
- Review the job description, documented expectations, and goals.
- Read the employee's self-evaluation form.
- Review any documentation collected during the period and input provided by others, making a note of examples and statements that substantiate the employee's self-rating.
- Make notes of questions, concerns, and other points to raise in the meeting.
- Identify the best examples to use in positive and negative feedback, reviewing context, behaviour, and impact.
- Make notes of requests for improvement or change, and prepare to state them clearly and specifically.
- Have a copy of the performance appraisal form (see the template at the end of the section).

Preparation for the meeting – the employee

- Confirm the meeting and clarify any uncertainties about time or materials needed for the meeting.
- Complete a self-evaluation form and forward it to the manager.
- Request input from others, if appropriate.
- Confirm any arrangements for work coverage.
- Review the job description, expectations, and goals from the previous period.
- Make notes of achievements, questions, concerns, and other points to bring up in the meeting.
- Be prepared to talk about performance, achievements, areas for improvement, and development needs.

Tips for review meetings

- Make the review meeting a priority that is scheduled and planned.
- Do **not** permit interruptions.
- Set a tone of collaboration – encourage the employee to participate and keep up a free-flowing, two-way dialogue.
- Be 100 per cent clear about key details: the purpose of the meeting; points to be discussed; goals and performance standards – both general and specific to the employee; specific examples of the employee's below-standard performance; next steps and follow-up actions.
- Understand clearly the employee's perspective, questions and concerns – confirm your understanding, asking questions if necessary before moving ahead.
- Discuss **performance** and **behaviour**, not personality.
- Listen for explicit and implicit questions, and answer them, checking that the answers meet the employee's need.
- Keep asking the employee for his or her assessment and suggestions for what to do to build capability.

Covering positive and negative points

- Keep positive and negative feedback in proportion to actual performance and its impact.
- Outline a positive/negative balance in the introduction: 'There are a number of strong aspects of your performance to discuss, and two or three results that were not up to expectations. I plan to review the strongest points first and then, with them in mind, look at the weaker areas.'
- Avoid overplaying the positive to make the employee feel good.
- Do not focus only on the negative in the belief that it is only worth talking about what needs improvement.
- If there is a good balance of positive and negative feedback: give the positive first, and make sure the employee knows there is plenty of both.
- If there is primarily good feedback, point that out and then get to areas of improvement.
- If there is bad news or an uncomfortable message, get to the point and talk about the problem. Managers may have been told to talk about something good, then give the bad news, and finally end with something good again. That approach just puts a pretty cover over a tough topic. Employees usually sense that there is bad news. Include positive comments only if they are appropriate to the context.

Content of the review meeting

Opening. As appropriate to national and organizational culture, open with general conversation to build rapport. The manager usually takes the lead. Be sensitive to the employee's possible anxiety about the substance of the conversation and avoid prolonging (or allowing the employee to prolong) the opening. The manager usually initiates the transition into the review discussion.

The manager also has primary responsibility for keeping track of the agenda.

In a non-controversial review meeting with a moderately confident employee, the manager should ask the employee to talk first about his or her performance. This approach allows the manager to hear what the employee thinks about his or her performance, determine whether there is a gap between their perspectives, and, in most cases, communicate validation and agreement on both positive and negative assessments. As a result, the employee feels empowered and supported by the manager, and may find it easier to address shortfalls and problems.

However, in a review meeting with a challenging employee or a difficult message, it may be more effective for the manager to maintain control of the conversation to ensure that it conveys the critical messages. This includes starting the review, bringing up all key points, and either pausing or moving the discussion along.

During the opening, review the agenda and remind the employee about the overall process: input from others, pre-meeting reviews, documentation, and next steps such as committee reviews or compensation reviews.

The review. The key points to be covered in the performance review are recapped here:

- all important goals previously set and performance against those goals, supported by data and concrete observations;
- feedback or input from others;
- reasons for performance or non-performance;
- rating;
- rewards or negative consequences (penalty, performance improvement plan, warning, etc.);
- strengths to be maintained, reinforced, or expanded, and how that might be done;
- remediation or improvement needed – who is responsible, how it can be done, time frames for observable improvement, etc.;
- future goals;
- development needs and interests relating to goals and beyond, and how they can be addressed.

As the conversation proceeds, keep track of needs, interests, decisions, and commitments to future action. Make sure that commitments to future action specify who, what, when, and how.

Closing. Review next steps, such as follow-up memos or committee meetings, and summarize decisions and action plans.

If appropriate, the conversation may end on a more general or social note, including appreciation and thanks.

Key skills for effective review meetings

A skilfully managed performance review can be an inspiring and energizing experience for both the employee and the manager. A poorly conducted review can lead a good employee to leave the business unit or the institution.

Below is a list of skills that make a difference. These are skills that managers need to develop and refine throughout their careers, no matter how simple or basic they seem:

- listening with patience, interest, and respect;
- allowing the employee to give his or her views, assessment, and ideas for improvement or next steps;
- asking useful, thoughtful questions;
- giving specific, concrete examples of both effective and ineffective behaviour;
- making clear, unambiguous, concrete requests for improvement or change;
- staying constructive, especially in relation to weak performance;
- setting concrete, actionable, measurable goals, whether for the next period or for improving performance;
- checking that the employee understands what has been said;
- checking that you understand what has been said.

Following up

After the performance review meeting, the manager should:

- supply answers, information, or resources agreed to in the meeting;
- complete documentation and submit it to HR;
- get signatures, if needed;
- take next steps, as agreed – further meetings with the employee, contacts with training or a mentor, etc.;
- work with the direct manager or HR professional to address performance problems or difficulties that occurred in the review meeting.

The employee needs to:

- supply answers or information agreed to in the meeting;
- complete documentation, if necessary;
- provide signatures, if needed;
- take next steps, as agreed;
- use the appeals process to address concerns or difficulties relating to the review or the meeting.

The HR professional must:

- supply any information requested;
- obtain documents, and check for signatures, if needed;
- confirm his or her role in any next steps – for example, a performance improvement plan, high-potential programme, or compensation review;
- counsel the manager and/or the employee if there are problems;
- survey managers and employees about all aspects of the process for future improvement and troubleshooting;
- work with senior management to ensure full compliance with the performance review process.

Feedback in a formal review

There are four main components of a feedback message, as cited in Chapter 5:

- situation – the context;
- behaviour – what the employee said, did, did not say, did not do;
- impact – on individuals, a group, the organization, the results;
- request – what the employee could or must do differently.

These same components should be present in the cumulative feedback given in a performance review. Whether the feedback is positive or negative, describing several instances of the context, the behaviour, and the impact relating to a key behaviour can be helpful. However, while two or three examples build the picture, be careful not to pile on an overwhelming number of examples.

In giving positive feedback, include a request to take specific actions:

- continue using the effective behaviour;
- do it in other situations;
- show someone else how to do it;
- combine it with other behaviours in relation to a new responsibility.

In giving negative feedback, ask the employee to provide his or her perspective of the situations, behaviours, and impacts. Be prepared to adjust your thinking if warranted.

For each behaviour that needs to change or be improved, be sure the employee understands what is expected. Discuss what can be done, and take the employee's suggestions into account.

In cases where the manager's feedback differs substantially from the employee's self-evaluation, it is essential that both views be documented.

Setting goals in a formal review

Once the employee and the manager have discussed performance against previous goals, they need to set goals for the next period or periods. There may be short-term (e.g. monthly or quarterly) goals as well as longer-term ones (12 months or longer).

The manager first needs to discuss the overall objectives of the business unit and the organization, including results and performance standards or quality levels, such as the size of a loan portfolio and level of on-time repayment. The individual employee's goal setting is a dialogue that includes how the employee and the manager see the employee helping the business unit meet its targets.

A structure for this part of the conversation can take the following form:

- current and future business unit goals, in the context of organizational strategy;
- previous goals;
- changes, if any, to previous goals to meet future targets;
- plans for achieving those goals – what, when, and how.

Confirm that the employee's goals are:

- written down;
- spelled out specifically and concretely, so there is no mistake about what is expected;
- stated in measurable terms, to allow for objective determination that they have or have not been achieved;
- achievable, given the individual, the resources, and the environment;
- relevant to the employee's job description, understanding of what is expected of him or her, and career interests (as much as possible);

- time-bound, so there is no uncertainty about when the goals are to be achieved.

Goals need to be documented. The performance review forms should include a section for future goals. Both the manager and the employee need to have copies of the goals.

Pitfalls to avoid in evaluating performance

There are a number of common errors that managers can make in evaluating employees' performance:

- *Unstated or undocumented goals or standards.* Failing to document some or all goals and standards, or having some aspect of the goals or standards implicit, with the assumption that 'everyone knows how to do this'.
- *Vague, ambiguous goals and standards.* Having written goals or standards in overly general terms or that can be interpreted in more than one way.
- *Halo effect.* Giving positive ratings to all aspects of performance based on impressive performance in just one or two areas.
- *Horns error.* The opposite of the halo effect, i.e. downgrading ratings across all dimensions of performance because of poor performance in one or two areas.
- *Relying on intuition and feelings.* Lacking facts and specific examples to support the appraisal and the rating.
- *First impression syndrome.* Developing a positive or negative opinion of an employee early in the review period and allowing that opinion to affect all subsequent perceptions of performance.
- *Recency error.* The opposite of the first impression syndrome, i.e. being heavily influenced by good or bad performance at the end of the review.
- *Leniency tendency.* For cultural or personality reasons, consistently rating performance higher than is deserved.
- *Severity tendency.* The opposite of the leniency tendency, i.e. for cultural or personality reasons, consistently rating employees lower than is deserved.
- *Central tendency.* Avoiding giving ratings at the highest and lowest ends of the rating scale or describing performance in superlative terms.
- *Clone syndrome.* Giving better ratings to employees who are similar to the manager in style, behaviour, or personality.
- *Spill-over error.* Continuing to give higher or lower ratings to a highly or poorly rated employee because of ratings in a previous review period.
- *Employee misunderstanding.* Possibly resulting from a lack of discussion when goals and standards were established.
- *Inconsistency.* Lack of agreement among ratings given by different managers, which usually occurs when goals have not been outlined

clearly, when there are no job descriptions, and when there is ambiguity about the employee's role.

There are three common pitfalls that occur during the performance review meeting itself:

- *Insufficient time.* There is not enough time for a full discussion, the employee does not understand everything, and the process itself may be incomplete.
- *The manager dominates.* The manager does all the talking, turning the experience into a one-way communication. The manager learns little about the employee's perspective, and the employee feels disengaged or overpowered.
- *Lack of documentation or follow-up.* New goals are discussed and development needs are identified, but there is no follow-up plan, with the result that later evaluation and accountability are impossible.

Avoiding pitfalls

- Keep documentation – notes, emails, memos – throughout each performance review period, on both positive and negative performance.
- Ask employees to keep documentation as well.
- Take time before the review meeting to reflect on the employee's behaviour over the last period and to review the documentation.
- Make sure the employee completes a self-evaluation form, and review it before finalizing ideas about ratings.
- Depending on organizational practice, get input from others on the employee's achievements and shortfalls.
- Allocate plenty of time, or break the meeting into two parts.
- Make sure the employee talks at least 50 per cent of the time.
- Plan the next steps for working on goals and doing development activities.

Preparing managers to conduct appraisals

At Reach Foundation, when individuals are promoted to manager, they attend a compulsory management training course that recognizes a significant shift in their responsibilities, from being 'doers' to being managers of others' work and performance. An important topic of the course is managing employee performance and holding performance appraisals.

Template 6.1: Performance appraisal form

Employee name:	Meeting date:
Manager name:	For review period:

Section 1: Review of performance objectives

Objectives agreed to in the last meeting and modified during the review period, as needed.

Sample rating scale
5 = Exceptional performance, consistently exceeds standards
4 = Good performance, often exceeds standards
3 = Satisfactory performance, meets standards
2 = Weak performance, improvement needed, sometimes/often does not meet standards
1 = Unacceptable performance, consistently does not meet standards

Performance objectives (goals for job tasks and standards)	Results and comments	Rating (1 to 5)
1.		
2.		
3.		
4.		
5.		
6.		
7.		
8.		

Section 2: General expectations

[The items below should be adapted to the organization.]

2.1. Values

- Attuned to organizational values

2.2. Interpersonal skills and communications

- Interacts effectively with all levels of staff
- Deals openly and straightforwardly with others
- Demonstrates a positive attitude, a team player

2.3. Initiative and problem-solving ability

- Assumes responsibility without being asked, resourceful
- Identifies ways to constructively deal with problems, creative

2.4. Professionalism

- Makes the extra effort to complete a project or task to a high level of quality
- Confidential, discreet, professional representative of the organization

Section 3: Updated, new or additional goals for the upcoming period

Performance objectives (goals for job tasks and standards)	Preparation and development needs
1.	
2.	
3.	
4.	

Development planning

Definitions

The last section of the performance appraisal template (6.1) relates to development planning. Development is a broad term that refers to all activities that help people do their jobs, improve in their jobs, and advance in their careers. Planning for development is a three-step process:

- identifying development needs in terms of performance goals and the skills, knowledge, and mindsets required to meet the goals;
- selecting activities that will build what is needed;
- making a plan to conduct the activities and review their impact.

Importance and value

As stated in the introduction to this chapter, development planning is important for the organization and the individual. The organization needs to give thought to the capabilities required to meet its strategic goals and how managers and staff will acquire those capabilities. It needs to make sure that each person is equipped to do their job and that performance shortfalls are addressed as promptly and effectively as possible.

The individual needs to know what it takes to perform the job to the required standards, both present and future standards, and he or she needs to know how to acquire those capabilities. No matter how informal the development process may be, having a development plan helps the individual focus on what needs to be learned or improved. Having a way to learn new skills and knowledge is both reassuring and rewarding.

Link to succession planning

One component of succession planning is the development of individuals identified as future successors to senior leadership or management positions. For those individuals, development planning is particularly critical, to enable them to be ready and to ensure that the organization will have continuity of leadership.

The development planning process associated with succession planning is the same. However, the plans may be more extensive and more detailed. A wider range of people may be listed to implement different aspects of the development. Implementation of successors' development plans is under the direct scrutiny of the organization's executive team.

Table 6.3: Responsibilities for development planning

Business manager	*HR professional*
Must • Work with employees to identify development needs linked to past performance, changes in goals and expectations, and career interests • Document development plans and send copies to HR • Link development needs with development activities, e.g. coaching, on-the-job learning, classroom training, and self-study • Implement development plans • Evaluate the impact of development activities **May** • Collaborate on the design of processes for planning and providing development	**Must** • Collaborate on design of processes for planning and providing development • Provide career development information to employees and managers (see Chapter 7 for more information) • Distribute development planning forms • Train managers on planning and providing development • Coach, advise, and counsel managers on development needs, development options, and development plans • Remind managers of the development planning calendar • Obtain copies of employees' development plans • Analyse development plans to coordinate training, succession planning, high-potential identification, and other development activities • Follow up with managers on the implementation of employees' development activities and success

Responsibilities

There are different schools of thought on who has the primary responsibility for planning and providing development for employees:

- Some believe the employee has the responsibility, since development is in his or her interest.
- Some say the HR or training and development department has the responsibility, since the formal aspect of development is managed in that department.
- Others believe the manager has the primary responsibility, because he or she knows what the work demands and capability needs of the business unit are.

All three schools are right:

- The employee definitely has a duty to pay attention to his or her own development needs, look for ways to meet them, and speak up to the manager, HR, and the training department.
- The HR and training and development departments have responsibilities for providing some development activities and for ensuring that all employees have a development plan and participate in some kind of development. They are responsible for following up if any employee

does not have a development plan or if an employee's plan is not implemented. They also have the broad, strategic view of the organization's capability needs and plans to develop people accordingly.

- Managers are responsible for thinking about individual employees' development from two points of view – the needs and interests of the individual and the demands of the business unit and the organization. They are also responsible for ensuring that development planning is appropriately linked to performance, future operational goals, and employees' career goals.

Involving the employee

Both the planning and the implementation of development require the full involvement or initiative of the employee for their success. The greater the extent to which the employee participates or takes the lead, the greater the engagement and commitment to the process and the outcomes. To that end, employees need to be involved in the following actions:

- assessing performance shortfalls and deciding what knowledge or skills need to be acquired or what mindsets need to be changed;
- discussing the demands of expanded responsibilities, higher performance standards, or preparation for advancement and the knowledge, skills, and mindsets needed for future success;
- brainstorming or selecting development activities;
- describing the ways in which the learning will be applied to and demonstrated on the job;
- establishing a timetable for the development experiences and for evaluating their impact;
- participating in the development activities;
- assessing their performance during and after the activities.

Involving the whole organization

The process of identifying development needs and planning ways to meet them is typically confined to the manager and the employee. However, the whole organization can provide resources and opportunities for the development activities (see 'Development activities' later in this section). On-the-job learning, self-study, shadowing assignments, special assignments, 'stretch' experiences, mentoring, and coaching all draw upon the expertise and experience of a wide range of people in the organization.

The whole organization is also involved at a strategic level. Development is not provided just to make employees happy or just to ensure that each manager has people fully qualified for the work of the business unit. Development must be planned and carried out in light of the organization's goals and future direction, and with a view to growth, transitions, and leadership succession.

To maintain this strategic perspective on development planning and provision, the executives or senior leaders need to make sure that everyone in the organization sees development as a critical, strategic activity that must be an ongoing part of their daily work.

An alternate approach to development planning

In Ascent, a separate team is entrusted with integrating the results of assessments with development plans and the training curriculum. The individual managers and employees remain responsible for specific development activities, and the development group takes responsibility for making sure that development programmes and resources are available for them.

This approach ensures that the very important tasks of development planning and integration take place while avoiding an undue burden on managers in the field.

Using a 360-degree approach and linking appraisal to learning

Innovators Inc. uses a 360-degree assessment approach for staff at all levels, a programme they call 'professional learning and review'. Each employee receives an appraisal from at least one peer, one junior, and one senior. Scores and comments are consolidated by HR and discussed with the person being appraised in a one-to-one meeting. Using these assessments of performance and skills, employees set targets for building their competencies and plan their development.

Policies

The basic policies relating to development planning cover the requirements that planning should take place at least once a year and that every person in the organization should be involved in some form of development.

Other policies may specify further conditions. For example:

- requirements that licensed personnel (underwriters, accountants, lawyers) keep their professional credentials current through designated professional education;
- minimum or maximum amounts of time or funding to be spent per person in formal, off-the-job development;
- consequences for managers who fail to undertake development planning or fail to make development plans available for other performance management processes such as training needs assessments.

Types of development

As has been previously indicated, development planning is done for several reasons:

- to remedy deficits in knowledge, skill, or mindset that have resulted in performance rated below expectations;

- to prepare or support employees for whom higher performance standards have been set – they are no longer 'beginners' and need to perform at the 'fully competent' level;
- to prepare or support employees whose responsibilities have been expanded within their existing jobs;
- to prepare or support employees who are on track for or have just received a promotion or a transition to a different position;
- to prepare employees for future career steps, such as moving into management, taking an assignment in another country, or working directly with board members.

Planning process

The process of planning employees' development involves five principal steps:

1. Identify the reason or reasons for development – see the list above.
2. Clarify the knowledge, skills, and attitudes needed to move to the new level of performance.
3. Come up with ways to develop the knowledge, skills, and attitudes, through formal or informal means.
4. Select specific activities and make a plan for doing them. The plan can include: what each activity is (see 'Development activities' later in this section); who is involved; when the activity starts, how long it lasts, when it will be evaluated, and when it might end; where it happens, if off-site or in a special location; what resources may be needed – funding, equipment, contacts, etc.; what support may be needed – work coverage, preparation, debriefing, etc.; what obstacles might come up and how to handle them; and what progress reporting, evaluation, feedback, or other reporting may be needed.
5. Attach the development plan to the performance review, as described in the section on 'Performance reviews' at the beginning of this chapter.

Employees and managers prepare for development planning at the same time they prepare for the performance review. They reflect, make notes, or complete a form in advance, depending on the organization's procedure. The following factors should be considered in preparation:

- what is needed to improve or advance performance;
- what kinds of experiences might provide the learning needed;
- how the employee learns best – by learning concepts first, by observing others, by getting involved alongside an experienced person, or by doing an activity on his or her own and then debriefing;
- development experiences – either past experiences or the experiences of others – that seemed particularly effective and ones that have been notably ineffective (what to try again and what to avoid).

To give an example, a teller has enough experience and sufficiently strong performance to qualify her for promotion to head teller. As she and her manager think about the development required to prepare her for and support her in that new position, two main topics come to mind: supervisory skills and communication skills. A person can learn supervisory skills by reading, taking classes, taking on assignments, or shadowing a supervisor. The teller seems to learn best from direct experience and does not find books to be helpful. Previous head tellers have had great success in preparing for their positions by attending two classes, debriefing extensively with an experienced head teller, and shadowing several different head tellers to learn the nuances of the job.

The work sheets provided at the end of the section may be helpful to managers and employees in preparing for the meeting or keeping track of ideas during the quarter or half-year.

Another component in preparing for a development planning conversation is career development information. In younger, smaller organizations, ideas about career options and career development may emerge informally, from the experiences of managers at all levels and from HR and training professionals. As the organization structures career-related information and activities, the manager and the employee can take advantage of those resources as they prepare to talk about development for growth, advancement, or lateral movement.

Development activities

Formal development activities are usually scheduled, require registration, and have an associated cost. For example:

- internal classroom training;
- speakers who come to the business;
- external classroom training, academic classes, or degree programmes;
- conferences and conventions;
- meetings of professional organizations or business groups;
- online courses or conferences;
- participating in an exchange programme with another institution or with another office or branch.

They are valuable because the content and focus can usually be anticipated and will be more or less targeted to a content area and a particular audience. Also, the formality may motivate a sceptical employee to take the experience seriously.

Informal development activities can be more open-ended, as well as more specific to the organization, and many have little or no direct cost. For example:

- frequent feedback from the manager or designated coach or mentor;
- regular performance reviews or interim reviews;

- thorough discussion of goals and performance standards;
- talking with experts or experienced people;
- reading articles or books by experts;
- studying and discussing business articles or case studies;
- doing online research;
- observing an expert or experienced person performing the task;
- shadowing an experienced colleague for a short period, with debriefing to understand how and why activities are performed;
- being consulted for advice or an opinion on a new problem;
- taking on a representative task relating to a responsibility to be learned and either experimenting outside the stream of accountability, or being supervised in performing it by an experienced person;
- sitting in on meetings and then debriefing afterwards with the boss, the person running the meeting, or another experienced person;
- going on a field visit to regional offices, with advance preparation and follow-up debriefing;
- helping to prepare an article or a presentation;
- giving a presentation;
- working with a coach or a mentor.

The range of informal development activities is limited only by the imagination and initiative of the manager and the employee. There is no valid excuse for not providing development, especially since many of the informal activities can be carried out in little time and can be combined with routine job activities.

Documenting the development plan

It is important to document development plans, for several reasons:

- The manager and the employee can keep track of what they planned.
- They can assess progress against the plan.
- The plan can be forwarded to HR or training managers to help them support and coordinate other aspects of development.
- The individuals and the organization are accountable for fulfilling their responsibilities for development. This is especially important where there is a risk of termination for poor performance or where development is a required element of a certification process or a professional licensing programme.

A template for a development plan appears at the end of this chapter (Template 6.4), as the final component of the performance appraisal form.

Following up

The employee, the manager, and the HR professional all need to follow up on development planning. They need to make sure that the plans are documented and distributed as required, and to do their part in setting up the activities.

Furthermore, development experiences do not automatically turn into learning and effective changes on the job. Discussion, experiments, demonstrations, and new assignments are all means of helping the employee integrate new learning, discover how it applies to the job, and prove that it is positively affecting his or her performance. Managers, coaches, mentors, trainers, and HR professionals can all play a part in following up.

Template 6.2: Development needs analysis – manager's work sheet

Use the work sheet to help think about and keep notes on the development needs of the business unit overall and of individual employees.

Goals for the business unit	Major work activities of the unit	Capabilities required: knowledge, skills, mindsets	Methods for building capabilities

Goals and major work activities of the individual employee	Capabilities required: knowledge, skills, mindsets	Methods for building capabilities
Refer to existing documentation. Add notes here only as needed to reflect new insights or changes.	*Refer to existing documentation if available. Add notes here only as needed because of new insights or changes.*	*Formal and informal. Refer to 'Development activities' in Chapter 6.*

Template 6.3: Development needs analysis – employee's work sheet

Use the work sheet to help think about and keep notes on your development needs as they relate to overcoming performance problems, increasing competence in the job, taking on new responsibilities, or preparing to make a lateral move or to take a promotion.

Work responsibilities and performance goals	Capabilities required: knowledge, skills, mindsets	Methods for building capabilities
How you want to perform better and what new goals you want to meet	*What you need to know or do and how you need to think to do the work successfully and meet the goals*	*What activities you might do to gain the knowledge, skills, and mindsets (consult your manager or HR professional for ideas if needed)*

Template 6.4: Development plan

A. Development activities to bring performance up to expected levels

Skill, knowledge or mindset to be developed or improved	Activity and success measures	Plan: what, when, how

B. Development activities for job growth/increased responsibility/advancement

Skill, knowledge, or mindset needed for new goals or responsibilities	Activity and success measures	Plan: what, when, how

____

Employee's signature **Date**

____

Manager's signature **Date**

CHAPTER 7
Building on performance

In addition to making sure employees perform well, the organization needs to offer them a future – a career. A career means different things to different people. It may be an interesting variety of assignments and responsibilities, it may be steady increases in responsibility and salary, or it may be a fast track to the top. All of these possibilities exist within a single organization, and all of these aspirations exist within different employees. The primary effort required is matching possibilities to aspirations.

From the organization's point of view, there is a need to ensure that the ranks of managers and executives are filled with the most talented, focused, experienced, and energetic employees. There is also a need to retain the best talent rather than allowing it to slip away to other organizations or, worse, be snapped up by the competition.

From all perspectives, defining career paths, offering career planning and development, identifying high-potential employees, planning succession, and grooming successors form an important and meaningful set of performance management activities. See Table 7.1 for the alignment of people management responsibilities between the business manager and HR professional.

Connections to other components of the performance management system

Building on performance with opportunities for a career and advancement is linked to several other components of the performance management system.

High-potential individuals are sometimes identified *during the recruiting and hiring processes*; when that occurs, the individuals need to be encouraged, coached, and developed for their future career opportunities (see Chapter 3).

Setting expectations and performance goals provides direction for success, whether that means exceeding standard expectations or succeeding with 'stretch' goals (see Chapter 4).

All employees need *coaching, feedback, training, and development* to succeed and advance; high-potential individuals and identified successors for senior positions need even more intensive attention (see Chapter 5).

The same is true for *performance reviews* – all employees need them, and high-potential individuals and executive successors need them to be thorough and rigorous (see Chapter 6).

Career planning should be a routine part of *development planning*, and career development activities are no different from other *development activities* (see Chapter 6).

http://dx.doi.org/10.3362/9781780447926.008

Identifying high-potential individuals, instigating career development, and planning for succession are inevitably linked to *opportunities for advancement and promotion* (see Chapter 8).

Table 7.1: Alignment of people management responsibilities

Business manager – typical contributions	*People management responsibilities*	*HR professional – typical contributions*
Proposing and implementing ways to redesign, enrich, and enlarge jobs	Find ways for people to do more work	Proposing and supporting the redesign, enrichment, and enlargement of jobs
Participating in mapping career paths Conducting career planning with employees	Find ways for people to do different types of work and take more responsibility	Taking the lead in mapping and documenting career paths Proposing and coordinating individual career planning conversations
Participating in career development activities Proposing development opportunities – plans, implements, monitors, and coaches Proposing and implementing 'stretch' assignments Contributing to the design of the system to identify high-potential employees Participating in identifying high-potential employees Contributing to the development of the leadership curriculum Providing training in the leadership programme Contributing to the design of the succession planning process Participating in general succession planning and in succession planning for his or her own position Identifying successor(s); Communicating with high-potential employees and potential successors	Prepare people for leadership	Proposing and coordinating career development Proposing and following up on development opportunities Proposing and implementing the development planning process and forms Tracking development needs and development activities Proposing the design of the high-potential identification system Coordinating the high-potential identification process and programmes, and maintaining documentation Developing the leadership training curriculum and other development activities Coordinating and providing delivery of leadership training – schedule and register Proposing, scheduling, and coordinating the succession planning process Developing succession planning tools Maintaining succession documentation

Career paths

Definition

Career paths are the typical routes that people in the organization follow to different ends. For some, a career path consists of promotions and advancement. For others, a career path is a series of assignments that provides variety, breadth, and stimulation as much as advancement. And for yet others, a career is an option for stable employment, perhaps with modest responsibilities that accommodate family care, and provide a sense of belonging and contributing.

In every industry, there are typical paths to advancement and typical 'broadening' assignments. In most businesses old enough to have had some turnover among the senior leaders, there are likely to be patterns in the kind of background, job assignments, and developmental experiences among successors that can be instructive for more junior managers and staff on the routes to the top. For example, the chief executive officer may typically have a background in the finance industry, while the chief operating officer might always have come from the ranks of branch and regional managers.

In newer, younger organizations, there may not be enough history to review for career path mapping. In those cases, defining responsibilities, expectations, and competencies for positions at all levels makes it possible to describe to more junior staff what they will need to experience and learn if they want to move to more senior levels.

Importance and value

As organizations look beyond salary and benefits as means to motivate and retain employees, they realize how important career opportunities are to many younger staff. Although it is not possible to promise advancement and a prize position to every younger person, transparency about how others have moved up and what is expected for someone else to follow in their footsteps is considered fair and reasonable. To that end, the organization needs to analyse and communicate that information as part of development planning.

Similarly, being able to discuss realistic career opportunities – stability, variety, or advancement – can give an organization an 'edge' in recruiting and retaining talent.

Table 7.2: Responsibilities for mapping career paths

Business manager	*HR professional*
Must • Describe career paths – his or her own, other managers', and senior leaders' – to employees, or articulate potential career paths (for younger organizations) • Contribute to career path descriptions and career development, including preparation and developmental experiences outside the organization	**Must** • Analyse career paths • Build 'maps' or responsibility and competency profiles of typical or potential career paths • Provide information to managers • Remind managers to discuss career paths with employees • Conduct formal or informal career forums

The role and responsibility of direct reports

As is the case with development in general, employees need to be encouraged to take full responsibility for learning about career options in the organization and evaluating which ones match their needs and aspirations.

Involving the whole organization

It needs to be part of the organizational culture that anyone in the organization is free to talk with anyone else about what his or her career path has been to date, what it took to be successful and to make lateral or upward moves, and how the person decided on the direction he or she took.

Policies

The policy requirement is that there be documentation and discussion of career paths, once the institution is mature enough for the directions and patterns to be discernible.

The process for mapping career paths

There is a template for mapping career paths at the end of the section. As shown in option 1 ('top-down') of Template 7.1, the process for mapping career paths involves reviewing the types of positions and responsibilities held by senior leaders throughout their careers and identifying both the common and the unique characteristics. Are there some leadership positions whose holders have always come from the ranks of accountants? Is the chief information officer an executive with a specialist background?

It is also useful to find out from the senior leaders how they assess the contribution of past positions to their current ones, to determine how critical it may be to ensure that future candidates for their jobs have the same or very similar experiences.

Option 2 of the template sets up a 'bottom-up' career mapping process. That process can be based on actual experiences of individuals in the organization, or on asking 'what if'?

To map from the 'bottom up', start with an entry-level position. List one or more alternatives for a next step from that position. For each of the possible next steps, list additional future options. The outcome is a branching structure that helps HR consider how to help employees prepare for the various options, and gives junior employees options to think about.

Table 7.3: Alternative steps in a bottom-up career map

Entry-level	*Next steps*	*Future steps*
Teller	Head teller	Agency manager Branch manager
	Customer service associate	Operations officer
	Operations associate	Product developer

The process for profiling positions

In addition to or instead of mapping career paths, it is possible to profile positions in terms of responsibilities and competencies. The responsibilities are drawn from the job descriptions.

One way to identify competencies is to interview people in the jobs and the people around them and come up with the five to seven most important competencies required for success in the position. Each competency may also be broken down into levels – first-level manager, middle manager, group or regional manager, senior manager, or executive. For example, effective communication may be an important competency for managers in the organization:

- First-level managers may be expected to communicate information, responsibilities, and feedback to individual staff and the team as a whole.
- The middle-manager level might, in addition, be expected to prepare clear, concise, and complete written reports for use by senior executives in monitoring progress and making decisions.
- The group or regional manager level might include written and oral communication with customers, board members, and professional groups.
- The senior manager level might add the requirement to communicate with senior government officials, investors, and international stakeholders.

Another way to identify competencies is to start with a reputable list of general competencies for managers or for technical areas (such as marketing or IT) and ask people in those groups to rank the generic competencies in terms of their importance to success in their groups within the institution. The HR professional can make a first draft of the profiles, including the competency levels appropriate to different job levels, and ask for colleagues to respond.

However it is done, the important result is having information for employees about what is required in other positions so that they can think about and plan how to prepare for the jobs that interest them. This kind of information also gives them perspective on what future positions might suit them best, as well as how long it might take them to be ready for their next career step.

Alternative career paths

Careers are often thought of as advancement, of moving up in rank, status, pay, and authority. However, for some individuals, a career path may mean lateral moves through varied responsibilities, or it may mean stability within a function or at a given level.

The 'variety' career path may be geographic or functional. Geographic variety means the individual is stimulated by working in different locations – different branches within the city, or different cities or regions. Functional variety means the person has a broad range of interests and talents, and may be stimulated by and contribute to positions in different areas – for example, product development, marketing, administrative services, and human resources. This career path can be offered to the extent that the institution can provide variety and the individual can perform and flourish in varied locations or functions.

The 'stability' career path can be seen in specialists and middle managers. With specialists, the career may consist of increasing specialized complexity, breadth, or responsibility, with management responsibilities limited to management of the specialized function. This can be the case with IT specialists, lawyers, and marketers, for example. This path succeeds as long as the position can be enriched in parallel with the specialist's needs and aspirations.

The other stability career path appears in middle managers, especially branch managers. Their competencies grow to suit branch management; their aspirations do not extend to riskier, more pressured senior management positions; and sometimes their family commitments tie them to a regional assignment rather than a head office one. The typical multi-branch, flat, moderate-sized organization needs to have a number of middle managers who are content to remain at that level, because it needs competent, experienced people in the mid-level positions, and it will never be able to offer all of them promotion to the very top positions.

Communicating career paths

Once the various career possibilities have been reviewed and laid out, the next step is to communicate the information.

- Communicating career path information to managers needs to include reminders that they should discuss career interests with their employees, preferably as part of development planning.
- Communicating the information to employees can occur in connection with quarterly organizational meetings, smaller staff meetings, relevant training sessions, or informal 'lunch and learn' sessions.

Career path information needs to be given to everyone who recruits and interviews for the organization. Job candidates are often interested in what their future options might be.

Guidelines

Although career path information is discussed separately here, it can be included as part of a more general review of development – what it is, how it is done, and what employees' interests are. Make conversations about careers a safe and normal activity. Use informal mentors to discuss careers and provide career path information in situations where the formal boss is unavailable or less focused on that activity.

From the field

In one organization, three distinct career paths emerged:

1. Start as a teller or customer service officer, hold two or three other positions of increasing responsibility within the branch, become a branch manager, and then become a regional manager. (This path worked well as a result of continuing expansion of branches and employees' willingness to move from one city to another.)
2. Start in an entry-level position in a branch, move to a non-managerial position in the head office, and advance in the head office.
3. Start in a junior or entry-level position in the head office, advance to a more senior position within the function, and then move into a more general management and leadership position.

Template 7.1: Mapping career paths

Option 1: Top-down

The 'top-down' approach involves looking at the preparation and progression of people currently within your organization to use as models for how others might advance towards their positions. There are two types of position to use for this approach: senior managers, such as the chief operating officer, the chief financial officer, or the head of banking services; and department or function heads, such as director of IT or internal audit, to provide a direction for people in head office groups.

Career paths do not have to follow a direct, single track – for example, from teller to loan officer, to credit underwriter, to director of the credit department. For career paths leading to senior management positions, it is usually valuable to have had at least one position in another area of the business, to develop broader, cross-business, general management skills and insights.

Position (senior leader or function head)	
Typical education and training experiences essential for being effective in the position (degree, licence, technical knowledge)	
Typical progression of jobs and work experiences contributing to readiness for the position (management, cross-functional, technical)	

Option 2: Bottom-up

The 'bottom-up' approach starts with entry-level or more junior positions and lays out possible directions a person might take from those starting points. As with the 'top-down' approach, it can be valuable or even mandatory for a career path to include work experience in other areas of the business.

Supplement the career path information with ideas about what people would have to do to advance from a given starting position to at least the next step, and, even better, through one or more typical sequences.

For example: How would a teller need to develop to become a managing teller versus becoming a customer service associate? And how would a managing teller need to develop to reach the next level of middle management?

Starting position *(junior level: teller/cashier, customer service associate, or loan officer)*			
Possible next step *(e.g. teller, managing teller, customer service associate)*			
For each possible next step above, possible sequences of future steps *(e.g. managing teller, agency manager, branch manager, senior operations officer)*			

Individual career planning

Definitions

Career planning is a component of development planning. As has been discussed, development planning involves thinking about next steps, identifying the competencies needed to take those steps and the ways to develop those competencies, and then planning how to implement the development. The scope of development planning can be relatively modest, such as preparing to take on an additional responsibility or being ready for an upcoming special project. It can also be broader and longer term, involving promotions or lateral job moves and three- or five-year career goals. The latter would also be considered career planning.

Individual career planning is the process of identifying a series of two or more job moves or an ultimate career level to which an employee aspires. For example, a loan officer might aspire to become a credit manager in the head office. The career planning involves not only discussing competency requirements and associated development needs, but also evaluating the implications for the person's life (longer hours or a move to another town) and the organizational navigation required (meeting people in the head office, or getting on relevant committees or projects).

Career planning requires readiness in the organization and in the individual to think longer term, and willingness to commit to longer-range goals.

Table 7.4: Responsibilities for career planning

Business manager	*HR professional*
Must • Advocate for employees in management discussions of careers and promotions **May** • Include explicit discussion of career interests and possibilities in development planning conversations • Include longer-term, career development activities in development plans • Make connections for employees with colleagues or mentors who can provide information and assistance	**Must** • Remind managers about career planning • Advise on career planning and development options • Make connections with external organizations or individuals in support of career development • Make sure career planning is discussed regularly in management meetings

Involving the employee

As stated earlier, the employee needs to take a leading role in discussing career interests, making career plans, and following these through.

Involving the whole organization

Similarly, many individuals in the organization can help an employee decide how to approach career planning.

Process

The career planning process is the same as the general development planning process, and career interests and development activities can be documented on the same form.

The only separate feature is asking explicitly what the employee's career interests are and then listening for any of the possible career paths described earlier. In other words, advancement, variety, and stability are all viable career options.

Tips

- Not all employees are interested in thinking about or planning for a 'career' at a given time.
- Some employees never take the initiative, or seem to be disinterested in having a career. This may be a legitimate choice for them.
- An employee's restlessness or boredom may be a symptom that it is time for the manager to ask about careers even if there is a bit of resistance.
- Respect and restraint are always appropriate. Enthusiastic support can also be appropriate.
- Beware of overly influencing a restrained employee or of trying to mould an employee who reminds you of yourself or for whom you have great hopes.

It can be difficult for some people to talk about career uncertainties or about ambitions with the person who rates them and influences their salary increase. If that might be the case, it may be appropriate for an HR professional or a mentor to discuss careers with those individuals.

Following up

As with other development activities, it is necessary to monitor and support the employee's follow-up. If the manager promises support, he or she must be sure to follow through:

- Review the copies of individual development plans that are submitted to the HR department after performance reviews and development planning are completed. Look for notes relating to career development activities that occurred in the previous period or that are planned for the upcoming period.
- Talk to members of the HR advisory council or its equivalent about what they and their colleagues are doing as far as career development is concerned and what steps their direct reports are taking.
- Check in with managers responsible for career planning individually, in meetings, and in informal situations.
- Survey employees periodically or include questions about career planning and development in employee satisfaction surveys.

Documenting

As stated above, it is important to document plans relating to career interests and development.

Template 7.2: Career plan

The career plan template is given here as a separate document. However, it may be combined with the development plan to avoid having too many meetings and to keep the documentation simple.

The template provides space and examples for three kinds of career goal. Depending on age, position, and experience level, the employee may not have goals in all timeframes. **At a minimum**, identify an immediate career goal. Having goals for all three timeframes is excellent but not required.

The 'development activities' area of this template may be omitted or left empty if a separate development plan form is already in use.

Name	
Current position	
Date	
Immediate career goal: 3–6 months *For example:* • Improve in current position • Expand responsibilities within current position • Learn more about alternatives in the organization	
Medium-term career goal: 6 months – 2 years *For example:* • Position in another area of the business or another location • Intensive education or training experience • Opportunities to train others • Expansion of responsibilities within current position • Promotion • Management position	
Long-term career goal: 2–5 years *For example:* Broad experience in several areas of the business Management level Training and consulting assignments Major educational experience Two or more promotions Middle (or possibly senior) management position	
Knowledge, skills, experiences, attitudes, or insights needed to achieve goals	**Development activities needed to advance the goals: work experience, on-the-job development, training or education, etc.**

Career development

Definitions

Just as career planning is a component of general development planning, career development is one component of the overall development programme. The career aspects of a development programme can include a variety of approaches:

- aptitude and interest assessments;
- training courses;
- on-the-job opportunities;
- individual coaching;
- mentoring.

To focus their career plans, employees may need to undertake assessments of their interests and aptitudes, or they may benefit from talking to senior colleagues.

To develop competencies for their next career steps, employees can attend training, take academic courses, or study online. They should also expect to learn on the job by shadowing others, doing short 'job swaps', or taking 'stretch' assignments.

Coaching and mentoring offer individual attention and focus on the individual employee's unique needs and questions.

Table 7.5: Responsibilities for career development

Business manager	*HR professional*
Must • Contribute to training courses • Look for on-the-job development opportunities, and help employees get into those activities • Act as a coach and mentor	**Must** • Make sure career development is a component of general development • Work with managers to identify on-the-job development opportunities and to find opportunities for employees • Act as a coach and mentor

Involving the whole organization

Since much career development occurs on the job, it is essential for the whole organization to have a commitment to supporting it, just as it supports general development. In fact, developing people needs to be an expectation of every manager in the business.

Role of the employee

On the other side of the picture, career development is very much the responsibility of the employee, both to initiate conversations and to follow through on plans. Taking charge of one's career growth can be an indicator of a high-potential employee.

Activity options

Development activities that are specifically useful for careers include the following:

- *Shadowing.* Regularly accompanying someone in the job of interest as the person performs his or her duties; for example, accompanying a loan officer at meetings with prospective borrowers, underwriters, and delinquent borrowers, to get a sense of the challenges of the position.
- *Job swaps.* Short periods of performing some or all of the tasks of a colleague's job in an area of career interest; this can be a true 'swap', in which individuals exchange positions, or it can be a substitution while someone is on holiday, on a special assignment, or on family leave.
- *Information interviews.* Conversations with individuals in positions of interest to find out what they do, what satisfies and challenges them, and how they were prepared for the position.
- *Presentations.* Hearing from people from different parts of the organization about what they do, what their group does, and what kind of competencies are required to work there.
- *Research.* Online or interview research outside the institution on types of positions, such as auditing or marketing.
- *Reading.* Newspaper and journal articles relating to a type of position, especially a head office function.
- *Professional organization meetings.* Attending organizational meetings for a position of interest, such as in HR or IT.
- *Conferences.* Accompanying a colleague to a conference related to management or to a functional area of interest.

Role of HR

HR makes sure career development activities take place in a variety of ways.

The HR department may offer or promote activities itself, for example:

- an external speaker programme or arrangements to visit other businesses, government agencies, or non-governmental organizations (NGOs);
- an internal speaker programme of senior leaders and specialists holding dialogues on their careers;
- event information for professional organizations and conferences;
- training and briefings for managers on what they can do to support career development among their direct reports.

HR can support managers by:

- encouraging managers and senior leaders to talk about their career paths and their professions;
- reminding managers to take junior staff with them to meetings, events, and conferences;

- training and briefing managers on career development options such as shadowing and job swapping.

HR can support employees by:

- briefing employees on the topic and what some of the options are, and reminding employees regularly that they are responsible for developing their careers;
- training and briefing employees on shadowing, job swapping, 'tagging along' to meetings and events, reading, attending conferences, and information interviewing;
- providing a library of career development tools such as information interview guidelines, industry and professional organization materials, online information sites, and career-oriented reading materials.

High-potential programmes and succession planning

Definitions

Succession planning is the process of identifying individuals who are currently ready or have potential to step into designated more senior positions. In younger organizations, succession planning may be relatively informal, limited to a few key positions at the executive level or in critical functions, and focused primarily on crisis response and leadership replacement. In more mature organizations, succession planning needs to become more formalized and applied to a wider range of positions.

'High potentials' are employees or younger managers who are considered to have the competencies and qualities needed to advance to senior levels, often more rapidly than is typical. Programmes for high potentials include identifying the individuals and then developing them. Both identification and development take place either informally or formally; the larger and more mature the organization, the better it is if the process is formalized.

Succession planning and identification of high-potential individuals are often linked, and the developmental work for high potentials is often directly connected to their future as successors in specific roles.

Importance and value

Succession planning and high-potential programmes address two significant business needs:

- avoiding the loss of a person from a key position with no ready replacement, which could result in confusion, loss of growth momentum, inefficiency, lower morale, concern among customers and investors, and quality problems;
- reducing turnover resulting from frustration or dissatisfaction among younger employees because of lack of advancement opportunities.

They address the organization's need to be prepared to fill vacancies, especially in critical positions, and they address individuals' needs to grow, be recognized, advance, and contribute at higher levels in the business.

Table 7.6: Responsibilities for succession planning and high-potential programmes

Business manager	*HR professional*
Must • Approve the design of processes for high-potential identification and development and succession planning • Participate in identifying and developing high-potential individuals • Participate in nominating successors, and in notifying and preparing successors	**Must** • Design processes and programmes for high-potential identification and development • Design a succession planning process • Coordinate and administer both programmes • Monitor development • Document both processes

Involving the whole organization

Designing and implementing the processes for identifying high-potential individuals and planning for succession needs to involve a fully representative cross-section of all areas of the institution, from mid-level managers to the CEO. Once processes are in place, the whole organization needs to support the development activities, as it would all other development. In a mature organization, when the identification process takes place, all managers and key technical staff participate in nominating and evaluating high potentials and possible successors. They also support the final choices.

Role of the employee

The individual employee has two roles in these processes. The first role is to be candid with the boss or a mentor regarding his or her interest in advancement. The second role is to follow through on the obligations of being nominated as a high potential or as a successor – developing, taking initiative, and showing leadership.

Policies

As early as possible in the growth of an organization, there needs to be a policy supporting the identification of successors for key positions, even if the process is informal at first and is limited to contingency planning and replacement designation.

Perspectives

For both succession planning and high-potential programmes, there will be different perspectives among different groups in the organization. The team that designs and takes the lead in implementing these processes needs to take these perspectives into account.

Employees' perspective. Employees who see themselves as candidates for high-potential development and succession to critical or senior-level positions are likely to be encouraged by the possibilities.

Employees who do not quite qualify – the 'solid citizens' – may need some reassurance about their importance to the organization to avoid resentment. For all employees, transparency and candour about the process, the criteria, and the choices are important.

Senior leaders' perspective. To undertake succession planning, senior leaders have to acknowledge that they may not be with the organization forever. This step can take a mature or philosophical mindset, which is not always present. The situation can be even more challenging when the organization is small or young, and the successors may have to come from outside.

Human resources' perspective. On one hand, HR professionals can be relieved that succession planning takes place and high-potential candidates are being developed. They see that the potential future stress of unexpectedly having to fill a key leadership or technical position is alleviated.

On the other hand, HR professionals are often the people required to coach the CEO, other senior leaders, critical mid-level managers, and key technical professionals into facing the possibility of no longer being in their jobs – not always an easy task! In addition, HR staff may be the ones to hear about the resentments of people who were not chosen as high potentials or possible successors.

High-potential programmes

A person with high potential is someone who has, to a greater extent than others, the characteristics and competencies, demonstrated through behaviour on the job, to become an effective leader in the organization.

To convert their potential into success requires them to have a desire for and commitment to success; to be able to balance individual success with organizational success; and to be willing and able to learn from experience.

For example, high-potential employees consistently exceed or far exceed performance expectations; they consistently participate in learning and development activities; and they focus on developing leadership competencies in general and those specific to the longer-term strategy of the organization.

Identifying people with high potential for leadership is a dynamic situation. An individual may start or stop demonstrating leadership potential at any point during the business cycle. The team responsible for overseeing the high-potential programme needs to be willing to work closely with these individuals as well as to move them into or out of the programme at each review cycle.

Did you know?

As described by Morgan McCall in *High Flyers*, people who learn from experience and fulfil their potential are good at getting the organization to pay attention to and invest in them. They are eager to take or create opportunities to learn, and they change as a result of their experiences.

Reasons for a high-potential programme. There are several reasons for having a formal high-potential programme:

- recognizing and rewarding strong performance without increasing payroll expenses;
- harnessing the potential of top-performing individuals early in their careers;
- focusing the attention of the organization on a key group of people whose talents, ability to produce results, and loyalty are critical;
- strengthening the retention strategy, giving the best and the brightest another reason to stay with the organization;
- reducing the extent to which bright, energetic, ambitious younger staff members feel frustrated or held back in their careers;
- creating a managerial talent pool for promotions, succession planning, and organizational growth.

Establishing the process for identifying people with high potential. With the support of senior leadership and the board, a cross-functional team or task group designs the process for identifying people with high leadership potential (the 'talent review') and proposes the criteria.

Once the appropriate groups of senior leaders and managers have contributed to and approved the design of the process and the list of criteria, the board gives its approval. Then the design team communicates information about the process – what it is, what it means, and how it will operate – throughout the organization.

Basic. In a newer, smaller organization, the executive management team, including the HR director, is likely to be the group that designs and implements the high-potential process.

Comprehensive. In maturing organizations, the high-potential design team is more likely to be a cross-functional group of senior managers from the branches and the functions. They design or upgrade the design of the programme, get the approval of the executive management team, and communicate information about it to the rest of the organization.

Once the high-potential programme is designed and approved, it is administered by the HR director. Executives and senior managers are involved in identifying candidates for high-potential status.

Criteria for high potentials. Standard criteria for individuals to qualify for a high-potential programme are listed here:

- performance ratings – exceed or far exceed expectations;
- developmental progress – participates in and shows outstanding progress or success in formal and informal development activities;
- leadership behaviour – includes creativity, taking initiative, being a spokesperson for a proposal, leading an initiative or team, and taking charge of a special assignment;
- foundations for senior leadership – include stamina, drive, strategic thinking, commitment to the business, concern for the team, providing direction, building relationships, authenticity, proactivity, and alignment with the organization's mission and culture;
- modelling the organization's values – one of the most important criteria because a future leader of the organization must be thoroughly aligned with the organization's values in ways that are visible to his or her superiors, peers, and direct reports;
- strong achievement or potential relating to more than half of the organization's specific criteria for leadership success in the future – means that the senior leadership team needs to think about the future of the business, the competitive market, the industry and economy, and the political situation, and identify four to 10 competencies that a leader will need in the future (five to 10 years from the present);
- enthusiasm for participating in the programme.

Did you know?

In the later years of his career, Jack Welch, CEO of General Electric, designed a model for deciding which up-and-coming managers to keep and develop and which to let go:

- Strong performance + strong alignment with corporate values = keep, promote – NO QUESTION!
- Less strong performance + strong alignment with corporate values = keep, train, coach, mentor, promote when ready.
- Strong performance + poor alignment with corporate values = dismiss.
- Poor performance + poor alignment with corporate values = dismiss.

What Jack Welch learned during his leadership tenure is that you can teach people to perform better and transfer them to positions that suit their skills, but you can rarely teach them to adopt different values or to care about values.

From the field

A central Asian MFI has identified high ethical standards, willingness to make tough choices with personal impact, strategic thinking discipline, willingness to take prudent business risks, and commitment to the business and social vision of the institution as keys to success in the future.

Who is involved. When the process begins to operate, the senior leadership team – the CEO and other chief executives, the division heads, and department heads – all participate in identifying and developing high-potential managers from the branches and from the functions.

Regional managers are involved in identifying branch-level high potentials.

The CEO, the president, and members of the board may be the appropriate people to conduct the talent review for other members of the senior leadership team.

While many organizations give the responsibility for coordinating and conducting the talent review to their HR professionals, it is better practice to have a small cross-functional (regions and functions), multi-level team, to encourage buy-in across the organization.

The process. Identifying high-potential individuals is an annual process.

1. The cycle begins with a review of the purpose, outcomes, and steps of the process. Individuals new to the process may need a briefing on their roles and the documentation. The leadership team or management committee may determine a maximum number of high potentials to allow in the 'pool' for the coming year.
2. All the designated managers identify individuals who meet the criteria for high potentials and submit their nominees, with appropriate credentials, to the coordinating team (or to HR).
3. The talent review is held between the twice-yearly performance review meetings. It is coordinated with a board meeting at which the pool of leadership talent is discussed and the list of proposed successors is also submitted for approval.

   During the talent review, everyone involved reviews the credentials of all nominees and uses a rating and ranking system. Then the ratings and rankings are discussed. A sample approach to rating and ranking is given at the end of the section.

   The critical role for the facilitator or coordinator of the high-potential programme is to help managers focus on the success of the organization more than on the success of specific groups or individuals. The process may work by consensus or by voting, depending on the organization's culture and the dynamics of the group.
4. The proposed talent pool of high potentials is submitted to the board or the committee for talent management for final review or approval.
5. When the list of high potentials is finalized, the senior leaders, the HR professionals, and the line managers are collectively responsible for meeting with each high-potential individual to discuss the implications of being in the 'pool'.

   The senior leaders may meet with some high-potentials in their role as manager or mentor to those individuals. They meet with the whole high-potential talent pool to reinforce the significance of their nomination to high-potential status. HR professionals meet with the high-potential talent pool to review the programme and the nominees' responsibilities. Each manager of a high-potential individual also meets with him or her to discuss development and support.

High-potential people need to understand the benefits – opportunities for visibility, development, and rapid advancement – and the obligations – higher expectations for leadership, commitment, and performance; increased scrutiny; and lower tolerance of ineffective behaviour. They will receive more coaching and counselling, but they may also be dropped from the high-potential programme during the year, depending on performance reviews.

6. Development planning and development activities for high-potential individuals may be intensified. The activities go on throughout the year.

Documentation. The input documents for the high-potential identification process include the following items:

- documentation of the individual's performance;
- development plans and records of developmental experiences;
- the manager's rating against the organization's criteria for high potentials.

The output documents from the process capture the key points of the talent review for each individual, including:

- the overall rating;
- summary of strengths and limitations;
- development and performance requirements for each individual to retain high-potential status;
- action steps to support each individual's ongoing development.

Template 7.3: High-potential identification package

Performance results summary

Summary of information from performance objectives and performance review forms.

Key performance areas (from twice-yearly performance objectives)	Performance ratings (from twice-yearly performance reviews)	Comments about exceptional aspects of performance

Development planning and progress summary

Summary of information from development plans (and possibly career plans).

Most important development goals	Major development activities	Achievements, progress, and accomplishments

Assessment based on organization-specific criteria for high-potentials

The criteria are established when the organization designs the high-potential programme.

Organization's criteria for the leadership competencies needed for future success	Rating: 1 = moderate potential to develop 2 = high potential to develop 3 = already demonstrated

Template 7.4: High-potential candidate's talent review – individual rating and ranking

Each individual nominated for the high-potential programme is rated by his or her own manager and by at least two other managers on each of the criteria. The rating is a score between 0 and 100.

High-potential candidate's name: ____________________

Criteria	*Rater 1*	*Rater 2*	*Rater 3*	*Average*
1. Models organization's values: • Integrity • Performance • Social responsibility • Teamwork				
2. Performance exceeds or far exceeds expectations				
3. Past or current leadership behaviour				
4. Foundations for senior leadership (stamina, strategic thinking, ease with different groups, business acumen)				
5. Achievement or potential for future leadership success: • Innovation • Global perspective • International standards of performance and ethical business • Flexibility and management of change				
6. Developmental progress in training and other development				
7. Enthusiasm for being a high potential				
Totals/overall average				

Template 7.5: High-potential candidate's talent review – individual rating and ranking

[To be completed during the talent review meeting on flip charts or whiteboards OR to be completed by HR and presented at the talent review meeting.]

In the appropriate columns, write the name of each person with the designated score.

NOTE: If all candidates have received scores above 95, change the ratings to smaller increments, such as 99/98/97/96/95.

Identify the qualifying candidates:

- individuals with all their ratings at the highest level;
- individuals with ratings in the highest level for criteria 1 to 5, and ratings in the second level for criteria 6 and 7.

If more candidates receive the highest ratings than can be included in the high-potential programme, discuss other criteria for choosing among them, and go through the rating and ranking process again for those additional criteria.

If fewer than expected candidates meet the ranking criteria, you have several possible courses:

- Discuss the advantages and disadvantages of having a smaller high-potential programme.
- Consider the option to have provisional high potentials – what that would mean in terms of development and performance expectations.
- Review candidates with slightly lower rankings and discuss whether any of them could be included in the programme and what the implications for development and performance would be.

Criteria	*Weighting*	*Score 95+*	*Score 90–95*	*Score 80–89*
1. Models organization's values: • Integrity • Performance • Social responsibility • Teamwork	20%			
2. Performance exceeds or far exceeds expectations	15%			
3. Past or current leadership behaviour	15%			
4. Foundations for senior leadership (stamina, strategic thinking, ease with different groups, business acumen)	15%			
5. Achievement or potential for future leadership success: • Innovation • Global perspective • International standards of performance and ethical business	15%			
6. Developmental progress in training and other development	10%			
7. Enthusiasm for being a high potential	10%			
Totals/overall average				

Succession planning

From the organizational point of view, succession planning is the process of planning how to fill designated positions in the event that the current holders retire, take positions elsewhere, are promoted, or can no longer serve for professional or personal reasons. The purpose of succession planning for the organization is to provide continuity of leadership and a smooth transition when leaders depart.

From the individual employee's point of view, succession planning is the process of identifying individuals who are currently ready or could be prepared in a relatively short time to step into key positions.

Along with identifying the successors, there needs to be development planning and developmental activities for these individuals. There are several types of succession planning, from contingency or emergency planning, to executive succession planning, to full succession planning. There are three categories of positions for which succession planning is most vital (and most frequently done):

- the CEO and other senior leaders;
- key technical specialists with critical and hard-to-replace expertise;
- positions that have significant influence on the business success of the institution, such as branch managers.

Possible successors may be internal to the organization, in which case they are informed of their status and participate actively in development for the position. However, sometimes the best or only succession candidates are outside the organization, in another business or institution. In those cases, the individual may not be contacted before the need arises, but his or her career progress should be monitored carefully. It is also possible, during succession planning for newer organizations or institutions in less developed financial industry environments, that one step in succession planning is to identify sources of or 'leads' to individuals who might be considered as possible successors.

Successors do not necessarily need to be identified on a one-for-one basis. In some cases, the members of the executive management team may readily fill in for one another and reallocate their duties. In another case, for an organization that has five regional directors and 25 branch managers, it may be sufficient to identify one regional director successor and three or four branch manager successors (assuming that the possible candidates are likely to be willing to relocate if they are needed to step into the positions).

It may also be appropriate to designate one individual as a successor to more than one position. For example, the executive vice-president for banking operations might be a suitable successor to the COO or the CEO.

Succession planning is closely tied to the high-potential programme. Successors for at least some leadership positions are usually high-potential individuals, and the criteria for being nominated as a high-potential employee include leadership capabilities and potential.

Succession planning is dynamic – not necessarily limited to one or two rounds of planning each year.

Successors may be promoted or transferred into their designated positions or, possibly, into other positions. In those cases, new successors need to be identified.

A designated successor may have performance or leadership problems or may struggle in or fail to complete development activities. In those cases, the successor may no longer be considered suitable, and a new successor needs to be identified.

Tiers of succession planning

BWDA has established three tiers of succession planning. Tier one consists of the five individuals who report to the MD – the leadership team. Tier two includes assistant general managers, senior branch managers, other senior managers, and key people in MIS and internal audit. The third tier comprises branch managers and assistant branch managers. The planning for and designation of successors is handled separately for each tier.

One advantage to this approach is that the succession planning process for each tier can be scheduled at a different time, so it is less time-consuming. Different groups have the primary responsibility for each tier's succession planning, which avoids placing a heavy burden on one group of managers.

Reasons for succession planning. The fundamental and most obvious reason for succession planning, from the organization's point of view, is that the organization may be put at risk if certain key positions are left vacant. Responding to an emergency or an unexpected departure is easier when successors have already been identified, and easier still if the successors have been preparing for the role.

Other reasons, from the individuals' point of view, are varied. The following are just a few examples:

- Founders sometimes want to move on to start up other enterprises.
- Successful entrepreneurial leaders may receive attractive offers from other organizations and may be tempted to move elsewhere.
- Founders, senior leaders, and key technical experts may expect to retire.
- Health and family difficulties can unexpectedly change leaders' or experts' career plans.

Succession planning, as with the high-potential programme, is another means of focusing organizational attention on promising younger or more junior individuals, which makes both programmes additional features of the retention strategy, as well as forms of non-payroll-based recognition and reward.

Types of succession planning

- *Contingency planning,* which can also be called disaster planning or emergency planning. Identifying short-term, emergency successors for positions critical to the ongoing operations of the business.
- *Replacement planning.* Naming either currently qualified or near-ready individuals to be longer-term successors for critical positions that might be vacated by the life or career transitions of incumbents.
- *Executive succession.* Focusing on near-ready or strong potential candidates for the senior leadership positions and actively preparing them for the succession.
- *Key position succession.* Identifying people who are ready now and others who could be prepared over one to three years to step into senior leadership and critical technical expert positions.
- *Full succession planning.* Planning for eventual succession in every leadership, management, and critical technical expert position in the organization, and considering levels of readiness and development needs, so that both contingencies and planned succession are accounted for.

Determining which level of succession planning is appropriate. Table 7.7 shows an approach to determining which level of succession planning is appropriate to a given institution, based on these criteria:

- age and development level of the organization;
- availability and sources of successor candidates – internal or external; interim or permanent; in-country, expatriate or consultant; fully prepared or partially prepared;
- capacity to provide development to designated successors.

An informal succession planning process

At the Reach Foundation, succession planning is handled by the Reach Discussion Group, which is made up of senior managers. The RDG regularly discusses fast-track performers – how to groom and prepare them to be the successors to the members of the group.

Who is involved in conducting succession planning. Succession planning is typically a process in which the HR leader has significant involvement:

- influencing senior leaders to develop and conduct the process;
- developing the forms;
- informing and training all participants;
- coordinating and facilitating the sessions;
- maintaining the documentation;
- monitoring the follow-up development of successors.

The other major players in succession planning are the executives and senior managers. They need to propose successors, finalize the choices, inform the candidates, and participate in the continued preparation and development

Table 7.7: Levels of succession planning

Type of organization	*Type of planning*
If your organization is: • New (operating for up to three years) • Small and simple (fewer than 200 people; fewer than 40 business locations concentrated in one to four geographic areas; not yet nationwide) • In a challenging, undersupplied job market for leadership talent and specialized expertise	**You must have:** • Contingency planning – to ensure relatively prompt, relatively smooth continuity of leadership **You should consider:** • Replacement planning – to prepare for the possibility that a founder leaves • Key position succession planning – in the event that a particular technical expertise is hard to find and, if absent, would severely disrupt operations (e.g. finance, treasury, internal audit)
If your organization is: • Maturing/approaching steady state (operating for three to 10 years) • Medium size and more complex OR large and simple (200–800 people; more than 40 business locations dispersed nationwide; not yet international; complex business structures, i.e. more than three lines of business (e.g. MFI, retail banking, insurance, commercial banking, investments) or holding company and subsidiaries)	**You must have:** • Contingency planning – to ensure relatively prompt, relatively smooth continuity of leadership • Replacement planning – to prepare for the likelihood that a founder or other leader will leave • Key position succession planning – to ensure continuity of all critical operations **You should consider:** • Executive succession planning – to provide motivation, career direction, development, and commitment to stay among high-potential leadership candidates
Also, if there is: • An internal pool of experienced managers **and** • A structured, reasonably well resourced management training and development programme	**You should have:** • Executive succession planning • A pilot or 'hybrid' full succession planning programme – to deepen the organization's commitment to management development; to expand the scope of career pathing and career development; and to strengthen talent retention
If your organization is: • Mature, steady state (operating for over 10 years) • Large and/or complex (over 800 people; national or international; multiple lines of business, holding company, complex partnerships)	**You must have:** • Contingency planning – to ensure relatively prompt, relatively smooth continuity of leadership • Full succession planning – to ensure a fully developed human capital strategy

of the successor candidates. The board of directors will sometimes be involved in helping to designate senior executive successors and in helping to locate appropriate individuals. In all cases, the board approves the proposed successors to executive positions. The successor candidates are involved in their own development, once they have been identified.

When succession planning takes place. The most important point on the timing of succession planning is to do it before the need for a successor becomes a crisis.

On a formal, organization-wide basis, succession planning should take place at least once a year, in conjunction with the annual formal development planning process. However, if promotions occur throughout the year, then succession planning conversations need to occur in conjunction with those decisions.

The process. The first step is to design the process. Four key elements must be defined:

1. the positions for which successors will be designated;
2. who proposes successor candidates for which positions;
3. what the criteria for selecting a successor are for each position;
4. when during the performance management cycle the successor identification will take place.

Once the leadership of the institution has agreed on the design of the system, the next step is to develop the procedures and forms needed for proposing successors, documenting succession choices, and outlining successor development plans.

Then the participants in the process need to be trained or briefed on what to do and when the process will occur. Participants propose candidates and forward the information to the HR leader. Proposals may or may not be circulated to all succession decision-makers in advance of their meeting.

The succession planning meeting is held to review proposed candidates and make final selections. The most important development needs for increasing each candidate's readiness to step into the designated position are discussed, including developmental activities and people responsible for providing and monitoring implementation and impact. Finally, the group agrees on who will discuss each successor's status with that person – his or her boss or a member of the senior leadership team. Successor candidates for executive or key specialist positions may be reviewed with the board of directors for its approval and support.

The successors are informed, and their development begins or continues.

Documentation. The most important documentation is the successor outline – specifying who the successor (or successors) is for each designated position. In addition, for each internal successor, there needs to be a written development plan.

Tips

- Set up the succession planning process early in the life of the organization. The first years of entrepreneurial activity are when the organization is most vulnerable if there are extended gaps in leadership or critical expertise.
- Involve the CEO in sponsoring the process and being a role model for following through. Succession planning is difficult, if not impossible, if it does not have top-level support.
- Keep the process transparent – when it is happening, how it works, and what the selection criteria are.
- Acknowledge that successors to certain positions are receiving more attention as 'highflyers' than other 'steady performers' do.
- Identification as a high-potential individual or as a successor to an important position is both an honour and a significant obligation to maintain the highest possible levels of performance and leadership.
- High-potential programmes and succession planning are rewards that motivate individuals, keep them engaged in the business, and promote their loyalty. These programmes are components of the institution's retention strategy.

Problems with high-potential programmes and succession planning

- *Poor organization* is demonstrated by failing to involve all the appropriate people, or, conversely, involving too many people. As a result, there is likely to be either confusion about what the programme is and how it works, or inefficiency or lack of progress while an overly large committee tries to meet, conduct business, and make decisions.
- *Lack of follow-through* occurs when high-potential individuals are identified and informed, but then no one takes any action to prepare, implement, and monitor their development plans. Or, even if the high potentials have development plans and developmental activities, their performance and continuing suitability to be high potentials are not monitored regularly.
- *Abuses* can take several forms. A high-potential programme can be abused by senior leaders who designate junior colleagues to the programme regardless of their qualifications or who exert influence to retain colleagues in the programme in spite of performance or behaviour that disqualifies them.
- *Perceived favouritism* can result from lack of transparency in the policies, the process and the decisions associated with a high-potential programme; in other words, insufficient or unclear communication on what the programme is, what the eligibility criteria are, how decision-making is done, when it happens, who is involved, what the outcomes are, and how the participants are monitored.

Any of the above problems can generate cynicism in the organization, undermining the programme and any others that HR proposes.

Problems with succession planning start with the failure to do it. Even if the process is done informally, it is absolutely essential that as early as possible in the life of an organization, senior leaders and HR explicitly discuss the contingency plans for handling an unexpected leadership vacancy. Some organizations avoid the issue because the founders are unwilling to face their mortality or the 'loss' of their role or the organization. Other organizations avoid it because it can be uncomfortable to consider an accident, ill health, death, or various personal difficulties that could cause a leadership position to be suddenly vacant.

Other problems with succession planning may occur as well. For example:

- *Conflict or ill will* among the members of the team or committee involved in selecting successors or among the potential successors themselves. This is particularly delicate if one senior leader is identified in preference to another as successor to the CEO. The CEO, board members, coaches, and consultants may all be appropriate resources for help if conflict arises.
- *Lack of involvement of the board of directors.* For selecting, supporting, developing, and backing successors to the senior leaders, the board needs to be involved, informed, and willing to work directly to address any problems that might arise, including the kind of conflict mentioned above. Failure of the board to be involved is likely to lead to confusion and chaos in the event that a sudden leadership vacancy does occur.
- *Lack of development for junior successors.* Successors who are not yet at the senior leadership level are high potentials and need to be developed as such so that they become increasingly ready to step in. Failure to develop them makes the planning pointless.

Success measures

Succession planning is successful when the following conditions apply:

- There is general agreement about which positions are most sensitive to sudden vacancies.
- There is a method to designate successors.
- There is an outline of successors.
- Written development plans for successors are prepared and implemented.

The ultimate success indicator for the succession planning process becomes apparent when a candidate steps smoothly into a suddenly vacant, sensitive position with the support of the board, the leadership, and the organization.

The success of a *high-potential programme* is linked to specific outcomes:

- its explicit use as part of the retention strategy;
- having regular selection and monitoring meetings by a cross-functional management team;
- ongoing development activities for the designated high-potential individuals.

There are three ultimate success indicators of the programme:

- High-potential individuals stay with the institution.
- They are available to take leadership roles as the business grows and as older leaders and managers retire or move on.
- They perform effectively in those roles.

Template 7.6: Successor planning package

Individual succession readiness rating

[To be completed for each person who is considered as a possible successor for a leadership or technical expert position.]

Name	
Position	
Time with organization	
Time in current position	

Overall performance rating: • Exceeds or far exceeds expectations in all aspects of job	
Potential rating • Highest – could move two levels above present position • High – could move at least one level above present position	
Readiness • Ready to succeed now • Ready to succeed in 6–12 months • Ready to succeed in 12–24 months	

Successor outline

[To be completed after each succession planning committee meeting.]

Position	Successor options	Names
CEO	1st choice: internal successor, ready now or in < 1 year	
	2nd choice: external successor, ready now	
	3rd choice: internal successor, ready in 1–2 years	

Position	Successor options	Names
	1st choice: internal successor, ready now or in < 1 year	
	2nd choice: external successor, ready now	
	3rd choice: internal successor, ready in 1–2 years	

Position	Successor options	Names
	1st choice: internal successor, ready now or in < 1 year	
	2nd choice: external successor, ready now	
	3rd choice: internal successor, ready in 1–2 years	

Position	Successor options	Names
	1st choice: internal successor, ready now or in < 1 year	
	2nd choice: external successor, ready now	
	3rd choice: internal successor, ready in 1–2 years	

Position	Successor options	Names
	1st choice: internal successor, ready now or in < 1 year	
	2nd choice: external successor, ready now	
	3rd choice: internal successor, ready in 1–2 years	

CHAPTER 8

Advancement

Advancement! Moving up! Promotion! Exciting words and exciting prospects for many employees, and an aspect of performance management that may not always receive the formal attention it warrants. Nonetheless, advancement has a key role to play in the organization at both the strategic level (helping the organization achieve its strategic goals) and the operational level (making sure everyone follows policies and procedures to get the right people in the right positions at the right time, doing the right work).

Advancements and promotions are ways an organization deploys its staff as it grows and as it specializes. They are motivators to encourage strong performance and rewards for those who hit the mark. Promotions are also a mandatory aspect of business continuity, succession planning, and succession management – preparing people to move into more senior positions. The selection of which people to promote and when to move them up shapes a maturing business's evolution from high growth to steadier state.

Given the significance of advancements, it is important that the HR strategy outlines how advancements and promotions will be used to support the organization's goals. At the operational level, it is equally important that there are well thought-out processes to make them happen. For both strategic and operational success, promotion decisions need to involve a number of people in the organization.

Definition

Advancement means giving an employee more responsibility, more authority, a new position, and changes in compensation and benefits. Advancement is the goal of employees on the upward or 'vertical' career path. It can take several forms.

Advancement within role and job grade

Within a given role and job grade, a person may advance by various means:

- taking on more complex assignments;
- having responsibilities with greater visibility to senior management, customers, or the public;
- stepping into informal leadership roles.

This type of advancement is a good first step for testing a person's readiness for greater responsibility. It can be a good reward when formal

http://dx.doi.org/10.3362/9781780447926.009

promotions and/or salary increases are constrained. And it is an excellent form of development.

This type of advancement is not usually referred to as a 'promotion'.

Advancement by moving up pay grades

In institutions that have pay grades within a designated job, advancement can be as simple as moving into the next pay grade. Pay grade advancement sometimes occurs purely as a result of time in the job; sometimes it is a reward for good performance. This type of advancement may or may not be called a promotion in any given organization.

Advancement by demonstrating increased competency

Some organizations have competency or responsibility bands within a position. For example, an IT developer position may contain bands designated 'novice developer', 'journeyman developer', and 'master developer'. In this kind of system, there are criteria for each band or level, and advancement is a recognition of increased competence and experience, and sometimes greater responsibility. There is typically a salary increase associated with moving up, and this type of advancement is often called a promotion.

Advancement to higher titles and greater responsibility

Other businesses have different titles for positions that require increasing levels of qualification and experience. Marketing associate may be the title for an entry-level marketing position, and market analyst may be the title for a position in which the individual leads market research initiatives and proposes and executes product marketing campaigns. Advancement to a higher level as described here is also usually referred to as a promotion.

Advancement to a manager role

A very significant form of advancement is the move from a 'doer', such as technician, specialist, associate, or individual practitioner, to a manager. This transition is always considered a 'promotion', and it requires consideration, preparation, and support, since competence and years of experience as a doer are not necessarily adequate preparation for managing doers.

Advancement to officer level

Another significant promotion in most organizations, and especially in financial ones, is to 'officer' or its equivalent in various business cultures. The term 'officer' or its equivalent designates someone who has broader levels of independent spending authority, can make and sign contracts that bind the business, and has both fiduciary responsibility and some form of legal liability.

Advancement to increased business responsibilities

One model for thinking about advancement focuses purely on financial responsibilities.

- *Cost centre.* The lowest level is to run a cost centre. Funds for expenses are allocated, and the discretion and control is over how and when those funds are spent. A function in the head office, such as treasury or HR, is likely to be a cost centre, and the director of one of those groups is called a cost centre manager.
- *Revenue centre.* The next level is a revenue centre, in which the manager is responsible for bringing in the funds for the unit's own use and for the business as a whole, usually through sales. A branch might be considered a revenue centre. It can be a significant jump for a manager to move from a cost centre to a revenue centre.
- *Profit centre.* The top level is to have responsibility for a profit centre. A profit centre is for all intents and purposes an independent business, even if it is within a larger business. It decides how to allocate its funds among various units; it brings in its own revenue; and it manages costs and revenue to make sure that there is a profit each year. Business people say that the manager of a profit centre has 'profit and loss' (P&L) responsibility.

In an MFI or SME, the business overall is initially the profit centre. If the institution develops other lines of business, such as business advising or insurance, then it may consist of several profit centres linked through a holding company. Moving to the level of managing a profit centre is another significant jump, as is becoming the leader of a holding company.

Advancement in levels of leadership

Finally, advancement should include moving into roles that require increasing levels of leadership, not just management:

1. Initially, there is personal leadership, the level of taking responsibility and initiative to lead one's own work life with vision and commitment.
2. Informal leadership may mean running a task force, being the contact person on a special assignment, or leading a committee.
3. Formal leadership – first-level managers who lead small groups of people within a function.
4. Formal leadership – middle managers who lead departmental groups or branches.
5. Formal leadership – regional and divisional heads who lead significant groups within a business, such as larger, more complex revenue or profit centres.
6. Formal leadership – general business leaders such as managing directors or CEOs with overall leadership responsibility for an entire organization.

Table 8.1: Alignment of people management responsibilities

Business manager – typical contributions	*People management responsibilities*	*HR professional – typical contributions*
Developing and preparing direct reports and others for greater responsibility, management, and leadership Collaborating in setting criteria for advancement of various kinds – within position or grade, within unit, and into management and leadership Contributing to the decisions to promote Discussing promotion prospects with employees Delivering news about promotions to employees Helping direct reports transition out and transition in	Give people increased responsibility, authority and leadership Provide leaders for the organization	Monitoring development and preparation of employees for advancement Collaborating in setting criteria for advancement and promotion decisions Ensuring managers discuss promotion prospects with direct reports Ensuring managers deliver news about promotions to direct reports Informing the organization of promotions awarded Coaching and advising managers on promotion-related transitions Possibly preparing press release information about higher-level promotions Maintaining and advising managers on pay scales and level-related benefits Monitoring compliance with pay scales and benefit plans Keeping advancement statistics, and analysing trends Performing payroll and other administrative tasks

Connections to other components of the performance management system

As indicated earlier, advancement and promotions are significant to several other components of the people management system.

Being able to point to strong trends in advancement and promotion opportunities is very helpful in *recruiting* top candidates.

Miniature versions of the *on-boarding process* need to be conducted, informally or formally, for newly promoted individuals, especially when they move into management, to review operational and organizational aspects of their new position.

Motivating outstanding performance from employees who are interested in moving up is grounded in there being advancement opportunities.

For 'upward-bound' employees, *performance review conversations* need to include how current performance levels will affect advancement prospects.

Setting goals and performance targets can also be linked to preparation for more advanced positions as well as to the criteria for promotion.

Development planning conversations are one of the primary venues for discussing an employee's interest in advancement – in which direction and to what level.

Career pathing and *career planning* focus directly on advancement options and ways to achieve them.

Training and development, formal and informal, internal and external, including on-the-job coaching, are essential to prepare employees for promotion and to support them once they have been promoted.

High-potential programmes are fast track promotion programmes for well-qualified and highly committed individuals.

Succession planning is the process of identifying who is most likely to be advanced into which senior positions and how soon that transition might occur.

Promotion has several purposes

Sonata promotes staff in conjunction with its expansion programme. Promotion also motivates and rewards strong performers. When talented employees are promoted, they also take on responsibility for managing and mentoring newer, less experienced staff.

At Sonata, a career path of regular promotions is outlined as early as the orientation programme, both as encouragement for good performance and to ensure that everyone is clear about the timing, criteria, and process for promotions.

When an employee reaches a promotion point, usually every six to 12 months at the lower levels of the organization, he or she is assessed in terms of competencies, experience, and recommendations. He or she must pass a written test and go through an interview. To qualify for promotion in the manager ranks, an employee is assessed on his or her ability to run a unit and train staff.

Responsibilities for advancement

Table 8.2 shows the business manager's and HR professional's responsibilities for advancement.

Perspectives on promotions

Several constituencies have an interest in or particular perspectives on advancement and promotions.

The board of directors. The board does not want or need to be involved in every advancement decision. Still, given the links between promotions and strategic goals as well as succession management, the board has an interest in certain aspects of advancement. For example, it needs to do the following:

- know the direction of the HR strategy linking business goals with promotions;
- review the promotion and advancement aspect of succession planning for senior-level positions;
- be involved in decisions about whom to promote into top executive positions such as CEO, CFO, or COO, as well as in planning its role in preparing candidates for promotion to executive positions;
- be encouraged to act as coaches and mentors for newly promoted executives, especially in regard to their relationships with the board.

Table 8.2: Responsibilities for advancement

Business manager	*HR professional*
Must • Hold development and career planning conversations with direct reports • Get direct reports into training programmes to prepare for or support promotions • Provide developmental experiences to test readiness and prepare for promotions • Identify individuals ready for promotion • Propose and advocate for advancement or promotions for appropriate direct reports • Make advancement and promotion decisions in collaboration with other managers and HR • Let direct reports know the status of promotion opportunities and promotion decisions • Prepare newly promoted direct reports to transition out • Receive newly promoted direct reports transitioning in, with 'mini' on-boarding, coaching, and training, as appropriate **May** • Work with other managers and HR to establish criteria for promotions to levels within the unit or function	**Must** • Ensure managers hold development and career planning conversations • Track 'promotable' individuals • Review managers' proposals of individuals to promote • Conduct promotion review meetings and document decisions • Ensure managers keep direct reports informed of the status of promotion opportunities and promotion decisions • Advise managers on transitions and on-boarding for newly promoted individuals transitioning in • Make all necessary changes to payroll and benefits administration to reflect employees' new levels • Track promotions, time at level in relation to retention, employee satisfaction, and organizational health **May** • Ensure that training is available to prepare employees for promotion and to support new promotions • Ensure that employees have developmental experiences • Work with managers to establish and apply the criteria for promotion • Notify marketing or corporate communications of significant promotions for press releases

Senior leaders/executives. People development and succession planning are among the most essential responsibilities of the senior leaders or executives of any business. They have the overall perspective on what kinds of leadership are needed in the present and what will be needed in the future – one year, three years and five years hence. Making sure the right people are in place at the right time is one of the senior leadership team's duties of care to the business.

Advancement and promotion are key to the development aspect of the high-potential programme and the preparation of succession candidates. The development plans for these people should specify what are the best promotion options for them – positions that would best develop new competencies and fulfil their aspirations. The development plans also need to estimate the timing for these promotions, balancing readiness and time to fully learn the ropes in a current position, with stimulation and challenge.

Senior leaders need to support and advocate for the advancement of successor candidates and other high potentials. However, there are some classic obstacles to executives giving the necessary level of attention to the issue of promotions and advancement (along with succession planning):

- *Time constraints.* In the earliest, most entrepreneurial phases, they may be overwhelmed by getting the business running and providing as much technical input as leadership perspective.
- *Lack of awareness.* Their experience or training has not made them aware of the need to pay attention to the issues, and they assume HR or middle managers will take care of whatever is needed.
- *Discomfort with transition.* They are uncomfortable thinking about the transitions in their own roles implied by promoting others into leadership roles.
- *Discomfort with having less control.* They find it difficult to think about giving up control, which would eventually be necessary as their successors are promoted into place.

HR professionals, mentors to the executives, board members, and even external coaches can assist with or intervene to address these obstacles.

Business manager and HR. One aspect of managing people's performance in which it is necessary for business managers and HR professionals to maintain alignment is in connection with advancement and promotions. There are several ways in which they can fall out of alignment, usually with positive intent on each side but ultimately acting at cross-purposes, often to the detriment of employees. In most cases, full, ongoing discussion is essential, along with shared information and agreement on criteria for decisions. Persuasion, tact, and negotiation may be required, as well as senior-level intervention.

An example could be that the manager pushes for advancement but HR holds back. Sometimes this misalignment occurs when the manager sees readiness or potential, and 'on-the-ground' experience makes him or her want to propose advancement earlier than others would consider it. These cases call for full and frank conversation and well-considered transition plans. In another case, the manager might favour a direct report or try overly hard to please a demanding employee, even though advancement is probably not a wise move. Handling this situation requires tactful counselling from HR and from senior managers.

When an organization is growing rapidly, or when an employee suddenly leaves, managers may push for promotion of individuals who do not seem ready to move up. Once again, these situations need full discussion, and any advancement that does occur needs to be well supported with coaching and training.

In other circumstances, a manager may advocate for the advancement of his or her direct report without knowing about candidates from other parts of the organization who are better suited to the promotion opportunity. HR and the appropriate management committee need to share information and fully discuss criteria for promotion decisions.

On the other hand, the manager may take little or no action for advancement, and HR might push for advancements to be given. This misalignment can also arise from a difference in perspectives on readiness or timing – the view in the field and the view from further away. Open discussion can help, along with persuasion and negotiation.

It can also occur when a manager is highly dependent on a strong performer and does not want to lose the employee to other commitments. Coaching interventions may be needed from HR and from senior managers.

Occasionally there are reasons relating to control or egotism, and HR may need to help address those obstacles on behalf of the manager's direct reports.

Finally, some managers fail to take action relating to their direct reports' advancement because the managers are overwhelmed or unsure what to do. In such cases, the HR professional is definitely in a position to assist.

A manager might resist advancement actions, whereas HR advocates for them. This kind of misalignment is likely to arise for all the reasons given above. However, the manager's position is a more active form of resistance. The HR professional will need to exercise every form of persuasion and influencing skill available. Beyond those tactics, it may become necessary for a management committee or members of the senior leadership team to get involved.

Direct reports. Keeping the direct reports' perspectives in mind in relation to advancement and promotion is another important aspect of this area of managing people's performance. Their perspective is respected when they are kept informed about promotion opportunities, criteria for being promoted, processes for applying for a higher-level position, and the process and timing of decisions.

It is imperative that decisions on advancement are seen to be fair; subjectivity or favouritism in promotions is one of the fastest ways to damage morale, heighten cynicism, and increase employee turnover.

Finally, no matter how busy and hectic the work environment, managers and HR professionals must take time to discuss promotion opportunities and decisions with interested employees. It is at least as important to talk at length with the employees who are not promoted as with those who are.

Here are some specific employee perspectives to pay attention to:

- *Employees considered promotable who have not expressed strong interest.* The HR professional needs to find out whether development and career planning conversations have taken place. If they have, the manager may need to explore more fully the employees' perspective on direction, level of drive and interest, and timing, in line with the three types of career paths (see Chapter 7).

- *Employees considered not yet ready who are pushing for immediate promotion.* The manager and the HR professional may need to explore the gap between the employees' perceptions and expectations and those of the organization. Do the employees understand the performance requirements? Do they know the promotion criteria? Have they had a full and candid performance review? Did they fully understand the review? Is something else driving their need?
- *Strong candidates who are not promoted.* The manager and the HR professional need to develop an approach to talking to these people that will give them realistic hope and encourage them to stay. It is also essential to give full, open information about numbers of openings and promotion decisions in advance, as well as to discuss how selected candidates were chosen. Having other options to offer can be helpful. Beware of making promises that cannot be kept, just to soothe upset feelings.
- *Demanding but unsuitable candidates who are not promoted.* This example calls for an approach similar to the preceding advice. In these cases, candid discussion of what needs to improve for the employee to be in line for a promotion can sometimes be most effective.
- *Employees put forward for promotion who had not expressed strong interest.* Sometimes a key vacancy needs to be filled immediately, and the best candidate is someone who has not expressed strong interest in a promotion. Nonetheless, the management committee that handles promotions nominates the individual. Both the manager and the HR professional need to advocate that the decision be provisional until it can be fully discussed and negotiated with the employee. Can the promotion be interim? Can it be given with special considerations (teleworking, perhaps) or special support (e.g. childcare arrangements)?

Involving the whole organization

The whole organization is involved in advancement and promotion in various ways. First, most organizational cultures have norms and expectations about who gets promoted, how quickly people are promoted, when promotions should be given, and so on. Senior leaders need to manage and address this cultural dimension to ensure that it aligns with what is appropriate for the business and its strategic goals.

When promotions occur, people may leave a group or location, moving into a new group or a new office. Not only is there a psychological impact on the person who is promoted, but there is a social impact on the group being left behind, and the group gaining a new person. All societies have customs and 'rituals' for these circumstances, which can be applied on the job too, and, over time, businesses develop traditions to use for these transitions. For example, the group losing a member may have a 'goodbye lunch' with him or her, and the group gaining a new person may have a 'hello coffee hour'.

Even just one promotion has ripple effects throughout an organization. There may be speculation about alliances or cliques that supported or opposed the promotion, or about changes to groups when the promoted person leaves or joins. The promoted person's position is now open, which is a promotion or hiring opportunity for someone else.

Sometimes a promotion occurs because the previous incumbent was terminated or left under circumstances that lead others to speculate. In cases where attachment to or support for the departing individual could interfere with the acceptance and success of the newly promoted person, senior leadership, immediate managers, and HR need to strategize ways to manage the situation in advance and then follow these up. For example, they could appeal to individuals' special experience or expertise to support the new manager, or they might rally the group around an important project or upcoming deadline.

Policies

Most policies relating to advancement and promotion will be linked to job levels, such as first-level supervisor, department manager, or branch manager, and they will primarily address criteria for promotion to the level and the position.

The general policies need to cover all relevant requirements:

- publishing opportunities for promotion within a specified time before the decision is made, and allowing a minimum window of time for submitting applications and going through the consideration process;
- a standard, consistent, and published process for the following activities: publicizing opportunities for promotion; taking applications from internal candidates for promotion; nominating a candidate for promotion; stating the criteria for promotion and the qualifications for the position; interviewing and evaluating candidates for promotion; making promotion decisions; informing all candidates of the decision; and announcing the decision to the organization;
- procedures to avoid favouritism or the appearance of favouritism; for example, promotion decisions cannot be made exclusively by close relatives, close friends, or people in any other relationship in which undue pressure or undue influence might occur; and the process for making promotion decisions for a manager's direct reports must include at least one decision-maker from outside the work group or business unit;
- compliance with all laws, regulations, and company policies relating to equity and non-discrimination;
- appeals process;

- specifications for what management level(s) must be involved in promotion decisions, above the manager advocating for the promotion or the manager to whom the promoted person will report;
- what level of senior promotion must involve the board of directors;
- what situations would result in a freeze on promotions that carry increased authority and responsibility, in general or of a specific nature, or on pay increases that are usually linked with increased authority and responsibility.

The promotion process

Structures

Several structures need to be in place to support the promotion process:

- organizational frameworks for work groups and business units – what the levels are and the reporting lines;
- strategic goals and metrics for work groups and business units – what the group or unit is required to accomplish and how its success will be measured;
- job descriptions for existing positions and for newly created positions, including general goals and performance metrics;
- pay scales and benefit plans;
- the following functions being conducted at least twice-yearly: performance review process, with feedback and ratings; goal setting and review of performance expectations (targets and metrics); development planning or a review of development progress, with documentation for each component;
- a management committee that monitors performance management activities, including needs for promotion and proposals to promote individuals.

These structures provide the context for promotions, the information needed to evaluate candidates for promotion, and the group that will oversee opportunities for promotion and the candidates who are put forward.

Two models

The process of approving a promotion can get started in two ways. One way is in response to a vacancy – someone leaves or the business expands or reorganizes. The other way is applicable when an individual is ready – either the manager thinks the person is ready, or the person seeks the promotion. Since individuals are rarely promoted to positions created simply for their own sake, the two streams eventually come together, as outlined below.

For *starting point A (a vacancy)*, the process is likely to follow these steps:

1. The vacancy is anticipated or occurs.
2. HR meets with the manager of the vacant position to review promotion criteria, the job description, the announcement of the opportunity, the timeline, and the individuals to be involved in interviewing and evaluating candidates. At the same time, they discuss whether to recruit externally as well as internally, and, if so, what the timing will be (in parallel with the internal process, or only if no suitable internal candidates can be found). See step 3 for senior-level promotions.
3. The HR professional meets with the performance management committee to inform it of the above decisions, unless the opening is at a senior enough level for the committee or the board to take on the role of hiring manager. In those cases, the HR professional works with one of those groups.
4. For most promotion openings, the announcement is made internally, with qualification requirements, job description, timeline, and application details. If external recruiting is to occur in parallel, recruitment activities start at this point (see Chapter 3). If the promotion is to a senior level, external recruitment may be through headhunting or networking, and those activities will start at this point.
5. Applications are received and reviewed.
   For all applicants. Applicants to be interviewed are informed, and interviews are scheduled.
   For internal applicants (to maintain morale and good will). An HR professional meets with each internal applicant who does not meet the qualifications, to explain the decision. If appropriate, the hiring manager may meet with unqualified internal applicants to give them feedback, coaching, and encouragement for the future.
6. Interviews are held, and each candidate is evaluated against a standard set of criteria for the position.
7. At a minimum, the HR director and the hiring manager review the evaluations and select the individual for promotion. Depending on the situation, it may be necessary to speak to the managers of the strongest internal candidates, to explore any transition issues.

   As with external hires, the hiring manager's boss may be involved in finalizing the selection. The performance management committee may either participate in making the decision (for more senior promotions) or be informed of the decision.
8. The hiring manager informs the accepted candidate. The hiring manager or the HR professional also talks to the manager of the person being promoted (whose vacant position is being filled). Transition issues and timelines are finalized. Pay and benefits are confirmed.

The hiring manager also informs each of the internal candidates who were interviewed, to explain how the decision was made and to offer encouragement for future promotions, if appropriate.

9. The HR professional may announce the promotion to the organization or may prepare an announcement for a manager or an executive to deliver.

   For a senior-level promotion, HR may prepare a press release and other announcements for external constituencies such as the board, the investors, the local business community, an industry publication, and professional organizations or publications.
10. The HR professional and the business manager discuss any needs for a 'mini' on-boarding (if the group, the location, and any aspects of the position are new to the person who has been promoted). They also review initial training and development needs and make plans to address them.
11. HR takes care of all payroll, benefits, and other contractual processes and documentation. HR or the manager will make arrangements for moving and setting up a work space – furniture, equipment, telephones, computers, etc.

If the process starts from *starting point B (the individual)*, then the following steps would be appropriate:

1. Either a manager determines that a direct report is ready for a promotion to more responsibility or to a management position, or a direct report requests consideration for a promotion and seems ready.
2. The manager discusses the possibilities with HR and with the performance management committee.

   In an expanding business, it may be possible to anticipate promotion opportunities and the manager and employee can be advised of the type of position and the timeframe. In a steady-state situation, the employee's readiness and interest are taken into consideration, to be followed up when a vacancy occurs. The employee is informed of the outcome of consideration of his or her promotion.

   In any case, once there is a vacancy, the organization goes through a process like the one outlined above.

Implementing a promotion

As outlined previously, there are several steps in implementing a promotion:

- communication about the promotion;
- publicity, if appropriate;
- transition management: if the person is promoted out of a group, discussions with that group's manager to ensure an orderly transition; if the person is promoted within a group, preparations for him or her

to discuss the change, plans, and expectations with the group; and if the person is joining a new group, discussions with the new group's manager about transition, expectations, roles, and responsibilities;
- logistical changes, such as work space, furniture, telephones, and computers;
- new business cards, and possibly new stationery;
- updates to company directories and organizational charts.

Mini on-boarding

When a person is promoted to a new group or to a new role and responsibilities, there needs to be a process like an on-boarding for him or her. The smaller the organization, the easier it is to assume that the newly promoted person already knows everything about the new position and group, just by virtue of being in the same organization. Experience indicates that this is an untrue and unwise assumption.

Actions in bringing someone into a new position include the following:

- review the tasks and duties of the new position;
- discuss the expectations of the new manager;
- establish goals and performance standards;
- introduce new people – both internal and external to the organization;
- tour any new locations;
- train on new equipment or software;
- review policies applicable to the new role and new level of responsibility, even if those policies are covered in the initial on-boarding;
- review how the new position interacts and is interdependent with other positions and what the flow of information, tasks, and documents is;
- convey information on routine meetings to be attended and committees to work on, including their purpose and the individual's expected role in them.

Managing advancements and promotions

- Keep all parts of the process as objective, fair, and transparent as possible.
- Communicate decisions and the reasons for them promptly.
- Maintain alignment among HR professionals, managers, and the leadership team. Once a decision has been discussed and made, individual views are put aside and everyone supports the decision.
- Do not disclose private and confidential information discovered or discussed during the promotion review process.
- Plan the process thoughtfully. Choose the timing carefully.

Template 8.1: Criteria for promotion to supervisor or first-level manager

Knowledge

The individual must demonstrate complete knowledge of the following aspects:

- operations of the work group;
- quality standards;
- safety and security standards, policies, and procedures;
- all general company policies;
- other *[complete as required]*.

Skills

The person must have shown at least a 4.0 rating (on a scale of 1 to 5, with 1 = novice, 5 = master level) on the basic skills of the operations work group. *[Basic skills to be listed below.]*

Aptitudes

The person must demonstrate either existing skill or aptitude for and readiness to learn the following activities:

- written and oral communication;
- team building and leadership;
- business management – planning, budgeting, monitoring, allocating resources, etc.;
- people management – explaining priorities, setting expectations, giving feedback, etc.
- other *[complete as required]*.

Attitudes

The individual must demonstrate through words and actions the following characteristics:

- commitment to the welfare of the organization and its employees;
- enthusiasm and support for the organization's vision and mission;
- support for the organization's values and ethical standards;
- alignment with the organization's culture;
- other *[complete as required]*.

Educational requirements

The individual must have:

- appropriate degree or certificate;
- relevant licence or professional certification relating to the position (driver's licence, certified public accountant, etc.);
- specialist training, if appropriate;
- languages, if appropriate.

Experience

The individual's experience must include:

- minimum time working for the organization;
- minimum length of experience in the specific work area;
- prerequisite experience (for example, minimum of three years of working experience or one year of customer service experience).

Other

[Complete as required for the position.]

Template 8.2: Rating comparison form for evaluating candidates for promotion

[For each position open for promotion, customize the form with the criteria in each category.]

Each person participating in the review and evaluation of candidates for promotion completes a rating for the individuals interviewed and evaluated.

If all reviewers/raters spoke to and reviewed the qualifications of all candidates, then HR can also compile average ratings for an overall view of how the candidates compare.

Ratings

1 = weak – missing significant factors (notes to be attached)
2 = satisfactory – meets the criteria to at least 85 per cent and can develop or acquire missing factors
3 = outstanding – meets the criteria 100 per cent or meets many criteria to at least 85 per cent and exceeds that percentage on some criteria

Category	Candidate name	Candidate name	Candidate name	Candidate name
Knowledge				
Skills				
Aptitudes				
Attitudes				
Education				
Experience				
Other				
Other				

CHAPTER 9

Managing performance problems

Managing performance problems – that is, handling the underperforming or misbehaving employee – is one of the hardest tasks that a manager has to tackle. Addressing performance problems requires a mix of professional detachment, empathy, and resolve.

Unsure of their abilities to handle such situations well, many managers put off addressing them altogether or handle them ineffectively. As a result, the employee never gets the coaching needed, performance does not improve, and the entire organization can be affected. This chapter of the Handbook is designed to provide effective strategies for coaching a staff member to improve his or her poor performance by approaching it with a non-judgemental, results-based focus.

Managers and their direct reports need to have a clear view of the organization's culture and values, and they need a complete understanding of a comprehensive performance management system that embodies the culture and values. Through the activities of the performance management system, employees need to know where they fit in, what is expected of them, and how the performance management system applies to them.

An oft-reported cause of poor workplace morale is that managers do not hold all employees accountable for their performance. Whether a performance issue is related to how the employee performs the job or is a behavioural problem that is disrupting the work of others, it needs to be handled effectively.

Many performance problems result not from the unwillingness of an employee to perform the job, but from a lack of knowledge or skill, from unclear or poorly communicated work expectations and priorities, or from misaligned incentive systems.

Most employees want to do a good job and succeed in their positions. For those cases, rather than traditional disciplinary measures such as warnings, suspensions, or pay cuts, progressive performance management is the most appropriate way to help someone recognize the problem and improve performance.

Avoiding performance problems, if possible

An Indian MFI works diligently to prevent performance problems or detect them at a very early stage. It provides intensive monitoring of individual and branch compliance with procedures and policies. Branch managers meet with delinquent borrowers, both to reinforce the need to repay and to discover whether any behaviour by the credit officer has contributed to the delinquency. In addition, senior managers from head office, up to and including the managing director, make surprise visits to branches to review compliance with policies and procedures for the processing and disbursement of loans and internal controls. In a rapidly expanding business with many very young staff, monitoring catches problems early and shores up any faltering knowledge or uncertainties.

http://dx.doi.org/10.3362/9781780447926.010

Table 9.1: Alignment of people management responsibilities

Business manager – typical contributions	*People management responsibilities*	*HR professional – typical contributions*
Collaborating on developing policies and procedures for responding to poor performance – penalties, discipline, performance improvement plans, redeployment, termination, etc. Monitoring performance Giving feedback and coaching on poor performance – results and behaviour Following policies and procedures to administer penalties and disciplinary measures Collaborating on developing a performance improvement plan Implementing the performance improvement plan and monitoring employee performance Collaborating on redeployment and termination decisions Communicating with the employee about redeployment and termination	Make sure employees learn to do the work Make sure they perform Make sure people get better at doing the work	Collaborating on developing policies and procedures for responding to poor performance – penalties, discipline, performance improvement plans, redeployment, termination, etc. Following up and advising on cases of poor performance Collaborating on developing a performance improvement plan Receiving and reviewing reports on implementation of the performance improvement plan and employee performance Collaborating on redeployment and termination decisions Ensuring compliance with laws, regulations, and policies Communicating with the employee and senior leaders about performance problems, disciplinary action, performance improvement plans, redeployment and termination Conducting exit interviews Maintaining documentation and compiling data

Connection to other components of the performance management system

Recruiting, interviewing, and selection form the first line of action to avoid performance problems by ensuring that the people who are hired are a good fit for the institution, the position, and the performance objectives.

During *on-boarding,* employees need to be informed about what constitutes poor performance and unacceptable behaviour and what the responses of their managers will be.

The manager's initial acts in *setting expectations* and *on-the-job coaching* are intended to prevent performance problems from the very beginning.

Ongoing *feedback and coaching* from the manager contributes to keeping performance on track.

Similarly, *training* and other *development activities* are intended to give employees the knowledge and skills needed to maintain good performance.

Motivational activities, rewards, and incentives should play their part in directing employees towards strong performance and away from poor results.

Involving the whole organization

There are two fundamental ways in which the whole organization is involved in managing performance problems. As already mentioned, the organization's culture and values indicate what is expected of all employees – what to focus on, how to behave, and what kind of mindset to have. To the extent that the majority of employees are strongly aligned with the culture and values, a component of managing performance problems is 'built in' to the system.

On the other hand, failure to uphold the organization's culture and values eats away at performance and corrodes organizational integrity – sometimes gradually, sometimes rapidly and dramatically. For example, in a branch of a professional services firm, the senior partner performed poorly, disrespected his direct reports, and worked his own hours. Retention became a significant problem – no one, from the most junior level to the most senior, wanted to work in that branch for that senior partner, and people did everything they could to be redeployed. In another branch of the same organization, the director hoarded information, took the best work projects for himself, and was stingy about sharing resources. Word got around that morale was low; people tended to work from home or at client sites more often. Then one day, when the director called for an 'all-hands meeting', all his senior direct reports refused to participate. An embarrassing and major intervention by HR and other senior leaders was required to get the branch back on track.

Role of senior leaders

Senior leaders have enormous power to influence performance by role modelling the work standards and professional behaviour they expect from everyone else. Seeing and hearing that the members of the executive team 'walk the walk' – perform their jobs competently, achieve good results consistently, follow policies and procedures, and behave professionally with customers and staff – has an outstanding impact on everyone else. Senior leaders show what is expected and set the tone of compliance.

They also have a role as managers of managers. They monitor their reporting managers' performance and address performance lapses promptly, equitably, and constructively. They also advise and support the middle managers in handling performance problems among those managers' direct reports.

Role of middle managers

Middle managers have a dual role in managing performance problems. They have a similar role to that of their superiors in modelling professional conduct, along with the responsibility to make sure everyone in the unit knows what's expected in terms of performing the work, achieving results, and behaving appropriately.

They also have the 'frontline' role of observing, monitoring, and intervening when a direct report does not perform as expected.

Role of direct reports

The employees who carry out the work – the largest group in the organization – have their part to play in managing performance problems. It is important that they are professional enough to align with the culture, values, performance standards, and behaviour expectations or discuss their concerns with their managers. It is equally important that they support one another in performing well, by coaching peers, giving informal feedback, and pointing out when something is out of line. One of the hardest tasks for staff members can be standing up for the official policies, procedural requirements, and other expectations in the face of one or more of their peers who question 'the rules' and propose or carry out omissions or violations.

> **A structure for addressing performance problems**
>
> As in most businesses, the first level at which performance problems are addressed at BWDA is with the employee and the manager. If a satisfactory resolution cannot be achieved, the problem is referred to a regional discipline committee for a higher-level, more cross-functional perspective. The final level is the head office discipline committee, which is the 'court of last resort'.

The three steps in effectively managing performance problems

Managing performance problems involves three steps:

1. *Identify the performance gap:* sometimes a performance problem will become clearly evident when an error occurs or negative feedback is reported by another team member or a client. Or it may arise through a regular performance management activity such as one-on-one meetings or performance appraisal sessions when the parties are comparing targets with actual performance.
2. Regardless of how the performance problem is brought to light, it is important to *analyse why the gap exists* through the use of the analytical flowchart.
3. *Address the performance problem* using progressive discipline and the performance improvement plan methodology.

Role of the HR department

The role of HR is advisory and supporting. HR makes sure that policies and procedures are developed and communicated. HR professionals help managers think through ways to address performance problems. They collaborate with managers on the steps to be taken to respond to poor performance. That said, the actual management of performance problems is done by managers, not by HR professionals.

This point is emphasized because, in newer organizations or for less experienced managers, it is tempting to try to get the HR department to 'handle' a performance problem, and HR professionals can be tempted to step in to play the manager's role. They must maintain their role as advisers and supporters of the managers but not become managers of the underperforming employees.

Policies

Managing performance problems is an area in which clear and comprehensive policies are much needed, to ensure objectivity and fairness as well as compliance with laws and regulations. Policies need to cover the following components:

- types of underperformance and behaviour problems – e.g. sales below targets or unexcused late arrivals at work;
- approved disciplinary actions, including guidance about appropriateness and proportionality;
- prohibited disciplinary actions;
- procedures for determining when to take disciplinary action, whom to notify, and how to document it;
- how to use redeployment to address performance problems;
- redeployment request procedures;
- when to use a performance improvement plan;
- how to set up the plan, whom to notify and report to, how to communicate with the employee, and how to implement the plan;
- when to consider termination, when termination is appropriate;
- procedures for documenting the need for termination, whom to notify, how to communicate with the employee, and steps to take.

The three stages of managing performance problems effectively

There are three stages in managing performance problems:

1. *Determining that there is a performance problem.* In this stage, it becomes apparent that there is a problem with the way work is being done, with the results, or with workplace behaviour.

2. *Analysing the reason for the performance problem.* It is essential to determine what is causing the performance problem in order to decide on the most effective way to respond.
3. *Addressing the performance problem.* Depending on the nature and cause of the performance problem, steps are taken to address the problem through progressive discipline and the use of performance improvement plans.

Identifying the existence of the performance problem

Definitions

A number of terms are used in discussing performance problems for which it is helpful to have clear definitions.

Mistake – doing a task incorrectly or behaving inappropriately to a relatively minor extent because of lack of specialized knowledge or skill. Examples include: counting change incorrectly; leaving the lights on in an office at the end of the day when they are supposed to be turned off for the night.

Non-performance – not performing some aspect of the job or not doing an expected workplace behaviour that affects productivity, security, revenue, and so on. Examples include: failing to make the prescribed number of sales calls; not filing loan applications; not doing follow-up monitoring with borrowers; failing to lock the cash drawer when leaving the teller station; failing to notify the supervisor when off sick.

Problem of commission – a problem resulting from someone actively doing something incorrectly or something prohibited. Examples include: entering incorrect amounts in the transaction log; bringing alcoholic beverages into the office.

Problem of omission – a problem resulting from someone not doing something he or she is assigned to do or has agreed to do. Examples include: failing to reconcile the cash drawer at the end of a day; failing to provide promised competitor research to a colleague.

Poor results – problems with the output of work, such as not enough deposit accounts opened, loan applications submitted, or job applications processed. May be easiest to identify, since results are usually quantifiable and subject to targets or quotas, and reported in numbers, money amounts, or percentages.

Underperformance – this usually refers to a problem reflected in results that are below expectations. Examples include: a teller is handling cash or transaction records in a way that results in the cash drawer not reconciling at the end of the day; an IT specialist is unable to diagnose frequently occurring problems with the LAN or unable to explain basic office IT functions or programs (email, Explorer, Word) to non-IT colleagues.

Performance problems

Performance problems encompass all of the following areas:

- problems with the way in which the work is done – too slowly or carelessly; using the wrong tools; disregarding prescribed procedures, policies, safety, or security;
- results that are below target;
- behaviour in the workplace that violates expectations, policies, or general social norms.

A range of undesirable or unexpected actions may be defined as 'problems', and it is essential for managers to define for themselves and their direct reports some simple 'degrees' of problems. For example:

- *Minor problems.* A single mistake by a new employee or someone doing a task for the first time is probably not a performance problem. Results below target for a short period or doing a task incorrectly before being corrected may be minor performance problems. If they are corrected when feedback is given, they are no longer considered performance problems and may become irrelevant fairly promptly.
- *Problems.* Making the same mistake repeatedly after being corrected or bringing in results below target for a more extended time is probably a clear performance problem.
- *Serious problems.* Continuing the unacceptable performance after it has been identified as a problem and efforts have been made to improve the situation is a serious performance problem. Resisting efforts to improve the situation is a serious performance problem, as is behaving inappropriately or performing a task incorrectly in a blatant or defiant way.
- *Grave problems.* Breaking the law or violating banking regulations is likely to be a grave performance problem leading to immediate termination and possible legal action.

Indicators of performance problems

How does a manager know if there is a performance problem? While the answer may seem obvious, one point needs to be made clear, repeatedly, in order for all types of performance management to be valid: **There must be data or evidence to support the designation of a 'performance problem'.**

The data or evidence can take several forms. Here are typical examples:

- direct observation by the manager of non-performance or incorrect performance;
- disclosure by the employee (asking for help or describing a problem);
- tasks not done or not done completely;
- incorrect or missing information or documents;
- lack of results (e.g. no sales) or results below target or quota.

Sometimes performance problems are reported by another party – a customer or another employee – and are not evident through observation or results. These second-hand indicators demand more objectivity, research skills, and maturity on the part of the manager to investigate, give feedback, and make judgement calls.

In most cases, if there is no evidence or data, the manager may not claim there is a performance problem and may not take disciplinary action. In cases where there is doubt or uncertainty, the manager should definitely consult with appropriate people to help decide what the indicators would be, discern the indicators, or get to the root of his or her concerns. The appropriate people to consult with include two in particular: the manager's manager and an HR professional.

A manager who listens to or spreads gossip regarding an employee's possible performance problem is acting unethically and irresponsibly. Discussing a possible performance problem with the employee's colleagues, with other managers who have no need to know, with customers, or with anyone else outside the scope of the situation is unprofessional.

When performance problems show up

For work activities that report results, performance problems are most likely to show up when the results are reported. Problems with cash transactions show up daily, when numbers are reconciled. Problems with signing up borrowers show up weekly, when loan applications are tallied and submitted.

Problems with the way the work is being done and with inappropriate or undesirable behaviour can be discovered by managers who spend time with their direct reports, observing them at work, working alongside them, and talking to them about their tasks. Consistent and supportive attention from managers is one of the first lines of defence against performance problems and one of the easiest and earliest opportunities for intervention: feedback, coaching, redirection, and reinforcement are all vital.

The obvious point at which performance problems can be detected is at the regular performance appraisal times, when managers compare actual results with targets. However, if the performance appraisal period is the first time at which the manager notices a performance problem, there has been a significant failure of performance management throughout the quarter or half-year. Performance appraisal conversations should be occasions for summarizing and reviewing performance problems that have already been identified, analysed, and addressed. There should be no surprises and no 'new news'.

Analysing performance problems

Examining performance problems

Once the manager or the employee has determined that there is a performance problem, the next stage of the process is to analyse the cause. The result of the analysis will indicate what types of action are most likely to resolve the problem.

Most performance problems are the result of one of four causes:

- Obstacles are preventing the desired behaviour – lack of equipment, insufficient time, or misaligned schedules.
- Performing the desired behaviour leads to negative consequences – missed meals, aching back, harsh replies from prospects, or disapproval from family or friends.
- Performing alternative or undesirable behaviour is rewarded – loan applications exceeding lending limits are always approved; reports turned in late receive warm thanks.
- It doesn't seem to matter whether the behaviour is performed – reports are not read by the manager or the committee; employees at all levels arrive and depart when they choose, without consequence.

Inexperienced managers may be tempted to conclude that an employee is underperforming because he or she chooses not to perform to expectations or 'just doesn't care'. This is the case sometimes, but not typically.

Another commonly assumed reason for poor performance is lack of skill or knowledge of how to do the task. However, other reasons are more common than one might believe, and therefore it is important to examine reasons for underperformance rather than making assumptions (see Table 9.2).

Thinking through the performance gap

What is the performance discrepancy?

- What is the employee actually doing? What evidence do I have?
- What is the difference between what the employee does and what should be done?

Is the gap important?

- Why am I dissatisfied?
- Why is the discrepancy important? What is its cost?
- What would happen if I left the discrepancy alone?
- Could doing something to resolve the discrepancy have any worthwhile result?

Is it a skill deficiency?

- Could the person do it if really required to do it?
- Could the person do it if his or her life depended on it?
- Are the person's present skills adequate for the desired performance?

Table 9.2: Performance problem analysis tool

Question 1	What is the performance 'gap' or problem? (See the questions below, under 'Thinking through the performance gap', for help with questions 1 to 3.)
Question 2	Is the gap or problem meaningful or important in the overall picture of results, in the way the work is performed, or in expected workplace behaviour? • If **no**, then ignore the situation. • If **yes**, then continue to question 3.
Question 3	Is there a lack of knowledge or skill? (This is determined by asking the employee, checking the training record, observing, or asking others.) • If **no**, then go to questions 6a to 6d. • If **yes**, then continue to question 4.
Question 4	Has the person done this task before? • If **no**, then arrange for formal training or other ways to gain experience. • If **yes**, then continue to question 5.
Question 5	Has the person done the task often or recently? • If **no**, then arrange for coaching, practice, observation, or shadowing. • If **yes**, provide feedback and consider questions 6a to 6d.
Question 6a	Is there a negative consequence or punishment associated with performing the task/behaviour? • If **no**, consider questions 6b to 6d. • If **yes**, remove the negative and provide a positive consequence.
Question 6b	Is alternative or undesirable performance rewarded? • If **no**, consider questions 6a, 6c, and 6d. • If **yes**, remove the reward for the wrong performance and institute negative consequences instead.
Question 6c	Does it seem as if performing the task/behaviour does not matter? • If **no**, consider questions 6a, 6b, and 6d. • If **yes**, establish follow-through and positive consequences for performing the task/behaviour.
Question 6d	Are there obstacles to performing the task/behaviour? • If **no**, consider questions 6a to 6c. • If **yes**, remove the obstacles and reward the performance.

Possible skill or knowledge deficiency

Does the person have the physical or mental capabilities to perform the task or behaviour?

Could the person do this task or behaviour in the past?

- Could he or she perform before and now cannot?
- Has the person forgotten what to do or how to do it?

Is the skill or knowledge used often enough that the person could remember what to do or how to do it?

- Is there an easily accessible source of information? Could there be a job aid, manual, or checklist? Would a review or a demonstration help?

- Is there ready feedback on performance? How does the person find out how well he or she is doing the task or behaviour?

Is the person overqualified and/or bored with this task?

Negative consequences for desired performance

What is the consequence of performing as desired? Is it perceived as a negative consequence to people doing the task or behaviour?

Would the person's environment or job be less satisfying if he or she did perform as desired?

Positive consequence for alternative or undesired performance

What is the consequence of doing the task or behaviour in the alternative or undesired way?

What does the person get out of doing things the other way – attention, status, reputation? Is there more attention for the alternative (poor performance) than for desired performance?

Is the alternative or undesired way of doing things less tiring, less worrying, or less stressful?

No consequence for not performing

What encourages performance by this person? What discourages it?

What consequences, feedback, reaction, or impact may result from performing the task or behaviour? Is doing the task or behaviour recognized in any way? How would the person know that performing the task or behaviour matters?

Is this task or behaviour satisfying? Can the person take pride in it?

Is it relevant? ... to the job? ... to the person? How would the person know it was relevant?

Obstacles to performing

What prevents this person from performing? For example:

- not knowing what is expected and when;
- conflicting demands on this person's time;
- lack of authority, time, or tools;
- restrictive policies, such as a 'right way of doing it', or a 'way we've always done it' that ought to be changed;
- work environment problems – lighting, discomfort, or noise;
- mixed messages, urgent items, or unclear priorities.

Addressing performance problems

Next steps

Many of the causes of performance problems suggest the reasonable ways to address them. Insufficient knowledge or outdated skills can be addressed with formal training or on-the-job coaching. Obstacles can often be removed. Unexpected consequences can usually be changed.

What follows is a checklist of questions to ensure that the most effective and comprehensive approach to addressing the performance problem has been selected. (It is taken from *Analyzing Performance Problems* by Robert Mager and Peter Pipe.)

The first part of the checklist should be used in most situations and can be applied quickly and easily. The second part of the checklist is valuable when the performance problem is complex, likely to be time-consuming to address, or for whatever reason is more significant.

Must do

- Does each aspect of the solution address one or more problems identified during the analysis (such as skill deficiency, absence of potential, incorrect rewards, punishing consequence, or distracting obstacles)?
- Is the cost (time, effort, attention, and money) of the solution reasonable?
- Is the approach practical and feasible?
- Will this approach give the most results for the least effort?

Refinements

- Have we considered a full range of potential solutions?
- Have the intangible (immeasurable) costs been assessed?
- Which solutions are we (individually, as a unit, or as a business) best equipped to try?
- Which remedy suits us most? (Or, on the other side of the coin, which remedy is most visible to those who must be pleased?)

Addressing performance problems using progressive discipline

Progressive discipline is a series of steps that a manager takes to help an employee turn around or improve poor performance.

There are several reasons for the progressive discipline approach. First, an employee has the right to know when he or she is performing poorly and be given an opportunity to improve. Second, a progressive and documented process provides a solid base from which to take further action, such as redeployment or termination. Most importantly, success in helping a poorly performing employee improve can lead to that same employee becoming committed and inspired. Furthermore, improving the performance of an experienced employee saves the organization the potential expense – financial, operational, and emotional – of a termination.

Steps in progressive discipline

A progressive discipline process generally follows four steps:

- step 1: counselling and/or spoken warning ;
- step 2: written warning;
- step 3: suspension;
- step 4: termination.

These four steps are typically taken for moderate performance problems when the manager believes that there is the potential to turn them around. Very serious violations may necessitate jumping to the more serious levels of discipline, such as suspension or immediate termination. If a relatively minor performance problem is repeated, the situation may warrant repeating one or both of the first two steps.

What is crucial, though, is consistency. The same level of performance discipline must be provided to all staff at all levels. To do otherwise is poor management; it can cause accusations of favouritism and ill-treatment among the staff, and it may expose the organization to legal risk.

Using a performance improvement plan

A key element of a progressive discipline system is the documented performance improvement plan (PIP). The process of developing a PIP creates a dialogue between an employee and his or her supervisor as they clarify the performance to be improved.

Developing a PIP and meeting with the employee should be fully coordinated between the manager and the HR department, to protect both the manager and the employee and to ensure that all procedures are followed correctly.

A PIP should not be confused with the annual or regular performance management review that all employees participate in. Rather, it is intended to be used as a tool to address performance issues and enable the supervisor and staff member to communicate clearly and openly about specific expectations.

The eight-part PIP

A PIP outlines in writing the following eight components:

1. The performance to be improved – specific, with examples.
2. The expected performance standard – level, frequency, and/or amount.

3. The actions required to achieve the expected performance – what exactly the employee will do (start doing, stop doing, do more, or do correctly).
4. The timeline for implementing the actions and achieving the desired performance level.
5. The support and resources the employee will receive – the kinds of help available and how to gain access to them.
6. The means of feedback to the employee – specific meeting times, with whom.
7. Measurements for determining success.
8. Possible consequences if performance standards are not met.

The PIP meeting

Holding a PIP meeting is similar to holding a performance review meeting, so many of the same guidelines are useful. The primary difference is that most of the conversation will be about what the employee is not doing well and what changes he or she needs to make to meet the expected performance. Of course, it is possible to bring in positive feedback – in many cases, the employee's strengths can help him or her improve the weak area.

Here are some reminders to ensure that performance discussions with an employee will be successful.

1. Come prepared – review the employee's file, make notes, and gather relevant data.
2. Meet in a private area where you will not be interrupted, and turn off mobile phones.
3. Put the staff member at ease as appropriate for the seriousness of the performance problem:
   - Set the tone by taking the time to make a personal connection.
   - The purpose of the PIP is to improve performance, and the meeting can be a positive experience if handled well.
4. Explain the purpose and agenda for the discussion:
   - Be open, frank, and respectful; listen carefully.
   - Outline the performance deficiencies and the impact they are having on the organization.
   - Support your statements with examples and explanations.
   - Deal with specific job tasks and objectives.
   - Avoid vague, general statements, such as 'I'm not happy with your performance'.
   - Ask the employee to appraise his or her performance.
   - Ask for his or her input throughout the discussion with open-ended questions.
   - Identify points of agreement between the two evaluations.
   - Pinpoint specific disagreements, and ask for specific evidence the employee has.

5. Show confidence in the employee's ability and willingness to solve the problem – discuss potential solutions to the problem or improvement actions to take.
6. Outline the PIP you have prepared:
   - Ask the employee for his or her reactions, and discuss.
   - Take his or her comments and suggestions, and amend the plan where feasible.
7. Come to an agreement – the PIP will work only when all parties are committed to it.

Termination

Definition

Termination refers to the act of ending the employment contract between the organization and a staff member.

There are two types of termination: *voluntary termination* refers to a decision by an employee to leave a job; and *involuntary termination* results from management's decision to end the person's employment with the organization. Involuntary termination can be the result of economic or business constraints, where an organization decides to reduce its workforce – a layoff or reduction in force. The other form of involuntary termination is for cause, where an organization decides to end a person's employment because of poor performance or misconduct.

Table 9.3: Responsibilities for termination

Business manager	*HR professional*
Documents the performance issues Provides evidence of progressive discipline, as outlined previously Leads the termination meeting	Provides advice on the form of termination Links with legal counsel and others Assists during the termination meeting

Policies

There must be a set of policies relating to termination. The primary policy is directed to ensuring that terminations adhere to the laws and regulations of the jurisdiction in which the organization operates. Unlawful or improper termination can expose the organization to significant penalties and sanctions.

Planned termination for non-performance or misconduct

Assuming that the manager has taken all possible steps to help an employee improve his or her work performance, and there is not sufficient change within a reasonable period, the time comes to fire the employee.

Even before that time arrives, the manager and an HR professional should be in regular communication. This collaboration helps ensure fair treatment for the employee as well as giving the manager backup and guidance about all procedures and documentation.

There are various legal and ethical considerations in employment termination. Handled improperly, a termination can expose the organization to significant legal risk and can reflect very poorly on the organization to other employees, customers, and the public.

Equally important is having a set of documents, starting with a job description, job targets and performance standards, and all the input from performance reviews.

Make sure performance standards are applied fairly, and treat any employee who is doing the same thing in the same way. All employees who are failing to follow your policies must be disciplined in the same way; never focus on only one person's performance.

Before the termination. To have a solid case for termination, and to lessen the risk to the organization of litigation, follow the progressive discipline steps carefully and thoroughly. Keep written records of evidence of the performance problem, the content of meetings, the PIP, and all feedback conversations. Also keep records of all other disciplinary actions, such as suspensions or pay cuts.

Consult legal counsel. Termination is an extreme measure, for both the terminated employee and the organization. Managers should consult with the HR department to determine what the organization is required to do regarding notice and severance pay. It is also recommended that the HR department consult with the organization's legal counsel to make sure there are no features of the situation that would require special treatment.

Termination meeting. Prepare for the meeting, using all the tips and guidelines provided for performance reviews and PIPs:

1. Hold the meeting in a private office, where there will be no disruptions.
2. The parties to the meeting are the employee, the manager, and an HR professional or the manager's manager.
3. Some experts recommend that the termination meeting takes place mid-afternoon and midweek, to ensure that HR has enough time to process the termination, and so that the employee is able to start a job search immediately.
4. Tell the employee the reason for the employment termination. Do not berate or argue, but be direct in explaining why his or her employment is being terminated.

5. Allow the employee to speak and to ask any questions he or she may have. Do not be reluctant to engage in discussion about what went wrong in the employment relationship.
6. If asked, tell the staff member your opinion of what kind of job he or she might succeed in, how to locate job search resources, and his or her strengths.

As difficult as such situations are, when they are handled with compassion and empathy, a termination meeting can help an employee to rebuild self-esteem.

Immediate termination

On rare occasions, a situation arises for which immediate termination is the only appropriate response. This is usually for a violation so serious that progressive discipline is not an option. It is the likely response when an employee does any of the following:

- threatens violence or commits a violent act;
- commits a criminal offence, including fraud, embezzlement, or theft of funds or property;
- engages in behaviour that is damaging to the organization.

In these circumstances, the manager and the HR department need to move quickly, to ensure the safety, security, and integrity of the organization.

If violent and/or criminal behaviour is involved:

1. Ensure that the employee is not a danger to himself or herself or other employees. (If the employee appears to be a danger, help other employees to safety, and call public authorities and security personnel immediately.)
2. If a crime has occurred, contact the police or other appropriate authority.
3. Remain polite and respectful. State the reason for the termination calmly and in the presence of a witness, and tell the staff member that his or her employment is terminated.
4. Have all company property returned, or make arrangements to have it returned.
5. Allow the employee to pack personal items from his or her work station, if circumstances allow this. If this is not possible, tell the employee how personal possessions will be returned.
6. Provide the employee with information on how to obtain further information on the termination.
7. Ensure that the terminated employee is escorted from the property.

Template 9.1: Sample written warning

To: *[employee's name]*

From: *[supervisor's name]*

Date:

Subject: Disciplinary action – written warning

This memo is a written warning for unsatisfactory job performance.

This written warning is issued because your work performance or workplace behaviour on *[insert date]* is below standard or in violation of company policy.

[Insert details of the incident or history of non-performance]

[Describe the impact that this behaviour has had on the rest of the organization/other team members]

[State what actions and/or previous discipline has been taken to correct the problem]

You were orally warned on *[insert dates]* about this performance problem.

A meeting is scheduled for *[insert date and time]* to review next steps.

You will be responsible for performing your work according to the performance improvement plans discussed and reviewed/amended at the scheduled meeting. If you do not make the required job performance improvements, it will be necessary to consider further disciplinary action, up to and including dismissal.

Employee:

______________	______________	______
Print name	Signature	Date

Manager:

______________	______________	______
Print name	Signature	Date

Template 9.2: Sample suspension notification warning

To: *[employee's name]*

From: *[supervisor's name]*

Re: *[subject]*

Date:

This letter is to inform you that effective ________________________, you are being suspended without pay for ____ work days.

[Insert details of the incident or history of non-performance]

This action is being taken as a result of *[list details of non-performance, or situation for which the suspension has been issued].*

[Summarize the impact that this has had on the rest of the organization/other team members]

[Summarize actions and previous disciplinary measures taken to address the problem]

On ___________, you were counselled for ____________________________.

On ___________, you received a written warning for ____________________.

On ___________, you were suspended for ____________________________.

You will be expected to return to work on ___________________________.

This suspension should serve as a strong warning that your performance will continue to be monitored and that another incident of this nature will result in more severe disciplinary action, up to and including termination.

Employee:

______________________	______________________	________
Print name	Signature	Date

Manager:

______________________	______________________	________
Print name	Signature	Date

Template 9.3: Sample notification of employee termination for non-performance

To: *[employee's name]*

From: *[supervisor's name]*

Date:

Further to our meeting of *[date]*, I confirm that your employment with *[company]* is terminated with effect from *[date]*.

As stated at our meeting on *[date]*, the reason for termination of your employment is as follows:

[Outline the reasons and previous disciplinary action taken]

[Clearly state individual requirements such as return of equipment, or submission of expense claims and any other administrative matters, details of notice period, holiday pay, general pay and pension or other benefits, plus severance if appropriate]

We wish you the best of luck in your future endeavours.

Yours truly,

Template 9.4: Sample performance improvement plan documentation form

Employee name:	
Date:	
Performance in need of improvement:	*[Be specific. List the standards to be obtained. Include skill development and changes needed to meet work performance expectations.]*
Expected results:	*[Be specific.]*
Actions to be taken to achieve results:	
Timeline:	
Support:	
Evaluation measures or indicators of progress or success:	
Interim checkpoints for feedback:	
Progress at review dates:	

CHAPTER 10

Promote diversity and the advancement of women in the workplace

With globalization of commerce and information, increasing levels of international trade and tourism, and in view of ongoing levels of migration into, out of, and within regions and countries, organizations need to continue their work to promote diversity.

'Diversity' is a term used to describe a more heterogeneous work force that gives equal representation to women and men, that fairly represents various age levels, racial, ethnic or tribal groups and regional or national origins, as well as including people of different lifestyles and people with disabilities. A more heterogeneous workforce is less dominated by people from the traditionally more dominant group or groups, which may have been male, and from certain social, ethnic, and educational backgrounds.

'Promoting diversity' refers to planned efforts to proactively address issues relating to having a diverse workforce, and to create a culture that values a more heterogeneous employee base and sees the business value of doing so. Promoting diversity is a process, not an end result; an ongoing feature of the culture, not a one-off programme.

Of particular importance in the discussion of diversity is the imperative to advance women into the workplace and up the ladder of leadership.

What is entailed in defining and achieving diversity in a given country, region, and financial institution must be considered within the context of the national and local culture. For example, opening all positions to women may be problematic in regions where women are frequently at risk of violence, and it is unthinkable to pursue a campaign of bringing people of alternative sexual orientation into the workplace in a country where such orientations are criminalized.

However, most opportunities for advancing women and creating a more fully diverse workforce are not constrained by such drastic limitations. Leaders may need to exercise courage and creativity to change mindsets and practices, but that is what is expected of leadership. They may need to adapt their vision, their communications, and their role modelling to most effectively influence their peers and employees, but that is indeed the work of leaders.

Managers and HR teams will be heavily involved in and accountable for the execution of their banks' strategy for diversity and women's advancement. Managers serve on the front lines, and HR is the support team in the campaign.

http://dx.doi.org/10.3362/9781780447926.011

Why promote diversity?

Social responsibility and strategic talent management agendas

Global bodies such as World Vision and the United Nations are promoting goals and campaigns to create more heterogeneous employee groups and advance women into and upwards in workplaces. From the perspective of social responsibility, research on many fronts has shown that the advancement of women in particular contributes to poverty reduction, family welfare, and better futures for communities. Family health improves and infant/child mortality declines. Women become more politically active in relation to infrastructure improvement, and they are better informed of their rights in legal, economic, and personal safety terms. When women earn more money, they spend more money – on their families' food, healthcare, and education.

On the talent management side, by including a more diverse set of employees and by advancing women in the business, institutions take advantage of the total available pool of talent. They also bring on board talent that mirrors the total customer pool. Given the trends in migration and immigration, banks have two choices when it comes to bringing in women and minority group employees: they can maintain a relatively small employee base consisting of the 'usual' people, and reduce their chances of reaching a wider customer base; or they can diversify their workforce and thereby increase their chances of broadening their customer base.

The impact of strategies promoting diversity and the advancement of women

Research on the impact of diversity and advancing women in the workplace gives sound business reasons for making those issues part of an institution's strategy.

Catalyst, a leading diversity training and advisory firm, conducted a study in the US that found that companies with the highest representation of women in top management positions also had a 35 per cent higher ROE (return on equity) and a 34 per cent higher return to shareholders (Lockheed, 2004a).

Studies conducted in the European Union found that achieving workplace diversity improved team effectiveness, led to greater cooperation among team members, improved productivity, and built up the businesses' standing with their customers.

McKinsey's research worldwide revealed that companies scoring in the top quartile of its gender diversity index also had 41 per cent higher ROE (22 per cent in the high-scoring businesses versus 15 per cent for lower-scoring ones) and 56 per cent higher operating results (17 per cent EBIT (earnings before interest and taxes) for higher-scoring firms versus 11 per cent EBIT for lower-scoring businesses) (Desvaux et al., 2009).

Other benefits of diversity and the advancement of women mentioned in a variety of sources include:

- access to a more diverse customer pool;
- access to a wider, more diverse talent pool;
- greater employee engagement and higher levels of retention;
- higher levels of innovation and openness to change;
- more trusting, open atmosphere and higher morale;
- an enhanced image with investors and customers as a forward-thinking institution focused on good returns and good service to customers.

Reasons for the positive impact of diversity and advancement of women

What is it about bringing women into the workforce and increasing diversity that generates these impacts?

Gaining necessary competencies. McKinsey found that women tend to demonstrate leadership competencies that are needed most when the business environment is dynamic, volatile, and complex (Desvaux and Devillard, 2008).

Attracting women decision-makers and customers. An institution with a strong representation of women among its employees is better positioned to compete in markets where women make or heavily influence purchasing and business decisions.

Strengthening employee morale and engagement. When employees feel valued and respected, they tend to feel more loyal and more inclined to remain with their current employer. When the workplace is more positive and welcoming, there are fewer employee grievances.

Promoting creativity and innovation. Creativity and innovation are fostered in a culture that explicitly welcomes people with varying points of view and diverse backgrounds. They contribute a wider range of ideas, and they also contribute solutions that are likely to appeal to a wider range of customer segments.

Overview

Who is responsible for diversity and advancing women?

A wide range of experts state unequivocally that leadership for strategies to increase workplace diversity and advance women's position in the institution must come from the CEO.

It is essential to have a CEO who is committed to the causes of diversity and women's advancement, who takes a visible role in addressing mindsets, behaviours, and workplace systems, and who speaks and writes to all the bank's stakeholders about the value and benefits of programmes for women and diverse employees. The specifics of what the CEO needs to do are given under the discussion of action area strategies.

With the leadership of the CEO, the rest of the management team, from the very top to the most junior frontline supervisor, must also be involved. Managers serve as examples to promote diversity and women's advancement action programmes to the employees.

The role of the HR team is to support leaders and managers, supplying technical and subject matter expertise, coordinating programmes, and developing tools and materials.

Table 10.1: Alignment of people management responsibilities

Business managers – critical contributions	*HR professionals – typical contributions*
Tone and attitude: respect and interest Character: ethical and inspiring Focus on results and performance-based metrics, not personal characteristics Setting challenging goals and giving challenging assignments to all team members equally Giving all team members equally constructive feedback regularly Delegating and empowering all employees Listening without bias or favouritism Motivating individuals based on their needs and interests Advocating for women employees	Educating and coaching executives and managers Becoming subject matter experts and staying current with the field, and with laws and regulations Checking in with executives to ensure that they are giving diversity and women's advancement their ongoing visible support Providing training to managers on skills and tools to improve their competence and confidence with diverse and women employees Embedding diversity and women's advancement requirements into all human capital management systems Role modelling advocacy and best practices in the HR department

Connections to other components of the performance management and human capital systems

Every single component of the performance management and human capital systems needs to reflect the institution's commitment to and practice of promoting diversity and women's advancement.

Leadership. The institution's leaders need to be champions for promoting diversity and advancing women in the workplace, role modelling, 'walking the walk', and holding everyone else accountable for playing their parts. A powerful leadership practice in this area is for executives to make a point of publicly communicating and connecting with women and diverse employees. It is also critical for the executives to show sustained commitment so that employees all understand that diversity and advancing women are not temporary flights of fancy.

Management of people. All managers need to fully and fairly provide management to women employees and employees of diverse backgrounds. As a foundation, managers need to build appropriate professional relationships with all members of their team, regardless of gender or background. They need to allocate work fairly and give women and diverse employees an equal opportunity to take stimulating and career-developing assignments. Similarly, all employees need to have equally challenging goals and receive equitable levels of support to meet them. This support includes the same level and quality of feedback and development, as well as fair and objective assessments of performance.

Culture. Promoting diversity and advancing women are most likely to happen when executives take care to ensure that the business culture is inclusive, welcoming to all employees, and respectful. Transparency and empowerment are also essential.

Engagement and retention. At the heart of being successful in advancing women employees and those of diverse backgrounds is helping them feel fully engaged and intent on staying with the business. To ensure that engagement and retention are addressed, institutions must evaluate and monitor engagement and retention among all employees, and especially among women and diverse employees. When deficits are found, they need to be addressed fully and promptly. In addition, the particular issues and obstacles that diverse employees and women may encounter must be given attention, such as flexibility for religious or dietary practices, for childcare, or for use of work technologies.

Job descriptions. To set the groundwork for fairness to women and diverse employees, it is critical that job descriptions are free of bias and that they contain no irrelevant criteria or constraints.

Recruitment, interviewing, and selection. An early step in promoting diversity and advancing women in the workplace is finding and hiring such employees. Recruitment needs to be extended to sources where women and minority recruits can be found. There need to be goals for finding and hiring an established percentage of qualified diverse and women job candidates. Recruiting materials must be free of bias and irrelevant qualifications or restrictions that would exclude women or diverse candidates. The panels that screen applications and conduct job interviews should include women and people of diverse backgrounds. Recruitment efforts must be evaluated for their success at meeting the goals for hiring diverse employees and women. Managers and the HR team need to be held accountable for meeting those goals.

On-boarding and induction. The people who present during on-boarding and the materials that are given to new hires need to be relevant and welcoming to women and diverse employees. Both pictures and examples need to be inclusive and show women and people of many backgrounds carrying out the tasks described in the training.

Goal setting. As stated above, all employees need to be given challenging work goals with objective metrics.

Feedback and coaching. Feedback and coaching must be given consistently, to all employees, without favouritism or bias. Managers should use objective data in these conversations, with all employees. It is also important for managers to show equitable levels of genuine interest in the success of their employees on the job, regardless of the employees' background or gender.

Performance appraisals. Performance appraisals are based on objective, data-based criteria; they cannot be subjective or personal. Senior managers and the HR department need to monitor the review process and employees' performance ratings to ensure that appraisals are indeed being conducted in a fair and unbiased way.

Non-financial rewards and recognition. Rewards and recognition must be available and delivered equally to diverse and women employees.

Addressing poor performance or unacceptable behaviour. As important as equitable recognition is equitable attention to problems with performance or behaviour. Such interactions must be carried out without bias, and the processes used need to be transparent. The criteria for defining poor performance or unacceptable behaviour will be objective and neutral. While performance problems may be met with a progressively stronger response, discriminatory behaviour cannot be tolerated. Unacceptable behaviour from any employee towards another, including men towards women or from any employee towards a diverse employee, must be addressed firmly and promptly from the outset.

Training and development. As with on-boarding, the content and materials for training courses and the conduct of trainers must be objective and respectful towards women and diverse trainees. Recommendations that employees attend training, and support given to them while they are attending training, need to be handled fairly and consistently across all team members. Senior managers and the HR department need to monitor the statistics on participation of women and diverse employees in training programmes, and both managers and HR need to be held accountable for achieving training goals relating to those employees.

Career development and promotions. To be inclusive for women and diverse employees, the definitions of career paths need to be broadened. Opportunities for career development must be inclusive, fair, and available to all employees. The institution must set goals for promoting a percentage of women and diverse employees to more senior positions, and promotions criteria and the promotion process need to be transparent and free of bias.

High-potential programmes, mentoring, and succession planning. As with career development and promotions, high-potential programmes, mentoring, and consideration for succession need to be open to all. There need to be goals for an increasing percentage of women and diverse employees to be included in these programmes. The criteria and selection processes must be transparent and unbiased, and managers monitored and held accountable for their support of diversity and women's advancement.

Compensation, benefits, and incentives. Compensation, benefits, and incentive schemes must be fair, equitable, and neutral as regards gender or other diversity characteristics. These schemes also need to incorporate flexibility where flexible work arrangements are needed or desired.

Manpower planning and HR strategy. When an institution prepares its manpower plan and HR strategy, it needs to incorporate goals for having diverse employees and increasing numbers of women at all levels in the organization. Progress in meeting those goals will be monitored, and managers held accountable. Moreover, senior managers and the HR team need to anticipate demographic trends so that hiring and promotion within the institution remain reflective of the demographic patterns in the workforce and the customer base.

Action strategies

Ensuring that the bank's workforce is as diverse as possible and that the bank does everything possible to advance women requires a strategic commitment – a big picture, long-term perspective. A long-term perspective is particularly important because mindsets and behaviours do not change overnight, and reconfiguring the demographics of the workforce is linked to natural attrition and the bank's ability to hire.

The strategy is translated into a phased plan and specific timeframes, and assigned a budget and a champion as well as an implementation leader and team. Leadership talents and change management techniques need to be utilized throughout the implementation of the strategy. Everyone – all stakeholders – needs to recognize that sustaining diversity and the advancement of women in the workplace is ongoing; it is not a 'campaign' or a 'programme' that ends at a given time.

Whether the focus is specifically on diversity or advancing women, there are many phases, steps, and action strategies common to both concerns. The work needs to include:

- a kick-off or 'grand opening';
- vision and goals;
- data gathering – a current status review and needs assessments;
- advisory groups or steering committees that include women and diverse employees;
- implementation planning;
- pilot activities;
- phased implementation of processes and tools;
- monitoring, feedback, and evaluation;
- course corrections;
- communication and publicity;
- celebration of successes and accomplishments.

Kick-off or grand opening. The CEO and the executive team have a kick-off event to announce the vision, goals, and plans for establishing specific action strategies. They discuss the advisory groups and the ways in which employees will be asked to input. Accountability is strongly emphasized. They give an overall outline of the planning and implementation processes. Pitfalls and challenges are mentioned to ensure that the strategy has credibility and that people's uncertainties and reservations are acknowledged.

Vision and goals. The vision relates to the kind of workplace the institution aspires to be, promoting equity for and acceptance of women and people from diverse backgrounds.

Goals will be both qualitative and quantitative. A qualitative goal might be the extent to which managers emphasize special contributions made by people of diverse backgrounds or the impact of managers' communication about the value of diversity.

Quantitative goals will be percentages or numbers, such as the percentage of women to be hired, women employees' pay levels, or the percentage of women to be promoted from supervisor to manager. Other goals typically include:

- rates of attrition;
- pay levels ;
- ratio of women and diverse employees promoted to all people eligible for promotion;
- women and diverse employees in all levels of management and leadership.

Data gathering. The organization should collect information about the current status of women and diverse employees:

- in the recruitment pipeline: contacts, interviews, and hires;
- in all positions and at all management levels;
- pay and incentives levels;
- promotion ratios;
- training participation;
- succession and high-potential pool profile;
- plus any other factors.

A culture audit that touches on trust, respect, team play, and inclusiveness provides insight about softer factors by asking for employees' input on:

- who is seen to get ahead/who is seen to fall behind;
- who seems to be involved in making big decisions;
- who gets 'the best' assignments, and who gets the boring or unpleasant ones;
- who is accepted or included, both for business purposes and for workplace socializing;
- who is held accountable and who is not;
- whether any group comes in for more unofficial penalties or negative treatment.

A needs assessment is also useful, and should be carried out among women and diverse employees to determine what programmes and services they consider most valuable. Make sure that you find out whether any programmes or services are needed urgently; for example, adaptations to work surfaces for a person in a wheelchair or facilities for washing and praying for Muslim employees.

Advisory groups or steering committees. An advisory group or steering committee can guide the data collection and planning, and serve as a source of people for subsequent employee councils. The group consists of a reasonable representation of women, people of diverse backgrounds, and other employees. It may give input to or review strategies and action plans. Employees are encouraged to use the group to have input and to get information. The group monitors the leadership commitment as well as the implementation of the action strategies and the progress towards goals. The best use of an advisory group is when it is empowered to ask for accountability and when it is seen as an honest advocate for the whole employee population.

Planning, pilots, and phased implementation. The designated implementation leader and the implementation team need to include business managers and HR professionals. They may be supported by consultants or interns, but the majority of the team needs to be internal to the institution. They take on the step-by-step work of developing plans for specific programmes, such as reviewing and revising job descriptions or upgrading the succession planning process. They receive input from the advisory group, from leadership, and from the employees, and they keep all those constituencies informed.

Just as the overall diversity or advancing women strategy specifies 'who, what, when and how', the next level of more detailed planning needs to do the same. Plans for each programme may include a pilot effort, and may be rolled out in phases. Success factors and metrics need to be defined, monitored, and reported on. Completion should be celebrated.

The implementation team's most important responsibility is to ensure that the diversity strategy or the strategy for advancing women is holistic. The strategy needs to encompass and integrate all aspects of human capital management. It needs to ensure that policies, procedures, practices, and systems for one component do not contradict those of another. For example, policies relating to sick leave or maternity leave must not be in conflict with recommendations to managers on offering flexible work arrangements.

Monitoring, feedback, and evaluation. As mentioned above, accountability is critical to the success, ongoing application, and credibility of all strategies to upgrade diversity and women's advancement.

The people who monitor progress must have, and must be seen to have, integrity, and they must be willing to speak up if a programme has not been started, has been abandoned, or is failing to meet its goals.

Feedback about progress needs to go to the implementation team as well as to senior management. It is most constructive if feedback can be delivered in a problem-solving manner rather than with blame or political posturing.

Evaluation of progress – whether goals have been met, exceeded, or not met – needs to be communicated widely.

Course corrections. Along with the feedback and evaluation, there need to be plans and support for galvanizing a flagging programme, and for adjusting and redirecting one that is only partially successful.

In a strategy as all-encompassing and long term as changing workplace culture and demographics, there are bound to be mistakes and delays. An attitude of problem solving and moving forward is most likely to produce the best outcome.

Communication and publicity. Because of the scope and potential impact of improving the institution's diversity profile or strengthening its advancement of women, communication is a must. As with all change management programmes, the communication needs to be regular, sent to all constituencies, and delivered in a variety of media and formats.

Celebration. Along the way, it is important for individuals, the implementation team, and the whole organization to acknowledge successes and celebrate people and their accomplishments. Celebrations build momentum and are a form of recognition and reward. They encourage employee engagement.

Addressing harassment and negative behaviour relating to diverse employees and women

Unfortunately, no matter how carefully announced, launched, and implemented the roll-out of policies and practices that promote diversity and advance women may be, there may still be employees who behave badly towards people in one group or another. In the case of women, unacceptable behaviour is usually characterized by sexual harassment or creating a hostile work environment. In relation to employees from diverse backgrounds, harassing behaviour may range from derogatory, disrespectful, or intimidating comments to bullying and perceived or actual physical threats.

What behaviour (action or speech) is considered harassment or discrimination may be defined by the laws and regulations of any given country, and the ways in which individuals and institutions can or must respond may also be determined externally. Unacceptable behaviours may include:

- making unwelcome sexual advances or requests for sexual favours, whether verbally or through touching or gestures;
- making employment, performance ratings, promotions, or continued employment contingent on compliance with sexual requests;
- commenting in the workplace in a sexual way about an employee or about her (or his) presumed sexual behaviour;
- discussing sexual matters in such a way that employees cannot avoid overhearing and are unable to remove themselves from the vicinity of the discussion, making their workplace hostile and demeaning;
- speaking in disrespectful, demeaning, or hostile terms, including crude and negative slang terms, about any employee, including women or people from a diverse background (ethnicity, region, tribe, religion, lifestyle, sexual orientation or disability);
- describing interest in doing harm or stating one's intent to harm any employee, including people from diverse groups or women, whether in career terms or in physical terms;
- physically intimidating or bullying, or actually doing physical harm (pushing, restraining, slapping, pinching, and so on).

Managers and HR teams must be fully informed of the laws and regulations and fully prepared to enforce them. All employees need to be informed as well, with consequences spelled out and the reporting and investigation processes outlined. In addition, each institution needs to have its own code of behaviour that covers harassment and discriminatory and threatening behaviour towards diverse employees and women. Enforcement is essential to maintain the credibility, safety, and attractiveness of the workplace.

There also need to be processes by which employees can report negative behaviour in confidential or anonymous ways. Complaints about harassment or discriminatory or threatening behaviour must be taken seriously and must be documented. The institution needs to develop procedures for investigating complaints. This is an area in which seeking the advice of a local specialist can be very helpful, so that not only are laws and regulations obeyed, but local custom is also considered.

Finally, the institution must be prepared to respond promptly and decisively to instances of harassment, discrimination, or threat. No matter who the employee is, action must be taken. At the very least, failure to act damages the institution's reputation and credibility; at worst, the institution becomes liable for retribution or legal action, depending on local practice.

Reaching beyond the institution

One of the most impactful ways of demonstrating the importance of diversity and the advancement of women is by seeking to include more women and more people of diverse backgrounds on the bank's board of directors. A board whose membership is 50 per cent female and reflects the general population's distribution of other important groups (e.g. ethnic, tribal, regional origin, or religion) would be an important goal.

As part of this process, the board itself can be involved in finding suitable candidates for membership. Diversity within the board contributes to the public image of the institution, enhances recruitment, and provides another source of mentors and role models.

Factors specific to women's advancement

Reasons for concern about advancing women in the workplace

There continues to be a number of concerns that drive the need to give ongoing attention to bringing women into the workplace and advancing them through the levels of leadership:

- Fewer women are economically active than men in many parts of the world; for example, only 33 per cent of women are economically active in India (Gap, n.d.).
- Women do not move as readily as men into middle and senior management positions where they would develop their competencies and earn more (Gap, n.d.). For example, a McKinsey article drawing on work by Sylvia Hewlett and Catalyst came up with the following figures: an average of 53 per cent of new hires are women, but that percentage drops to 37 per cent of first-level managers, 26 per cent of vice-presidents and senior executives, and 14 per cent of executive committee members (Barsh and Yee, 2011).

The Center for Women's and Gender Studies lists the five most common reasons why women leave the workforce (Rudrappa, 2005). These reasons are also a cause for concern:

1. need to take care of personal and family obligations;
2. excessive, inflexible, non-negotiable work hours that interfere with meeting personal and family obligations;
3. personal choice to stay home as a wife or mother;
4. inadequate compensation;
5. forced choice to stay home full time (forced by husband or extended family).

From the field

The CEO, CFO and COO of an African microfinance bank were standing in the hallway, shaking their heads and looking gloomy. The COO had just received a phone call from the husband of one of the highest performing and highest potential women on the staff. In fact, this woman had been considered for development as a future COO. The husband had called to tell the manager of his wife's boss that he had recently come to the conclusion that her continued work violated his religious principles and the wishes of her family. She would be allowed to continue working until the end of the month so as not to jeopardize her pay packet, but from the first of the following month, she would no longer report for her position. The tone and volume of the husband's statement allowed for no discussion and no negotiation. An institution committed to raising the economic status of women in the country had lost a valued woman employee.

Issues and obstacles

The issues and obstacles involved in advancing women in the workplace exist at the level of society and the community, within the organization itself, and for individual women. The issues and obstacles at one level are likely to set up and reinforce issues and obstacles at other levels. Each individual institution is well positioned to address the organizational and individual obstacles and limitations, and can take on a societal leadership role if its executive team has the courage and resolve to do so.

At the socio-political level, there are the following obstacles:

- societal and familial expectations that women will stay at home and care for their husbands and children;
- stereotypes of women's intellectual or work-related capabilities and of the kinds of work they should or are able to do;
- lack of technical education to prepare women to work in business;
- the 'double burden' of expectations that women should work full time and take care of their home and family full time.

At the organizational level, the following could limit women's advancement:

- the 'anytime, anywhere' mindset that puts employees at odds with work–life balance;
- the assumption that the pathway to leadership success is linear and uninterrupted;

- lack of sponsors within the business to recruit, encourage, mentor, and advocate for women employees;
- untested assumptions that women don't want 'tough' assignments, won't move away from home, won't travel frequently, or cannot be away overnight;
- a lack of high-ranking female role models;
- negative perceptions of women's commitment to careers or perceptions of a 'family first' orientation.

There can also be limitations at the individual level:

- concern about the extra pressure of higher-level positions adding to the 'double burden' of work plus home and family;
- the tendency for women to take staff jobs rather than 'line' ones because of work pressure and role models;
- the tendency for women to be more risk averse than men in relation to career advancement, refusing difficult assignments or promotions until they feel 100 per cent confident that they are qualified and prepared;
- attributing greater value to having an adequate work–life balance than men do.

What attracts and retains women

The factors that attract women to work at a business are not uniquely attractive to women. In fact, many of them attract all kinds of employees and constitute critical employee engagement factors. However, the factors found by research to be critical for retaining women appear to be the result of focused attention and explicit programmes intended to recruit and advance women employees.

According to Rudrappa (2005), the factors that attract women to a business are:

- good compensation and benefits;
- the business's strong market position (performance and reputation);
- opportunities for challenging work;
- opportunities for advancement;
- identification with company values.

The factors that have the most influence in retaining women are (Rudrappa, 2005):

- supportive managers;
- supportive networks **outside** work to help with personal and family obligations;
- flexible work hours, part-time work options, job-sharing options, and the ability to work from home;
- the business's commitment to diversity and a welcoming culture;
- opportunities for challenging assignments for women employees.

Policies to promote the advancement of women in the workplace

To advance women, policies relating to equity and fairness are essential. Job descriptions are gender-neutral, with requirements and criteria that are strictly relevant to the work and the results. Compensation, benefits, and incentive schemes provide the same pay and benefits for the same work and for the same performance against goals, regardless of gender. Recruiting, interviewing and hiring are open equally to all and include women from the institution in the process, to ensure equity. Performance goals are specific and performance-based. Appraisal feedback and ratings are also performance-based, not political or based on personality. Promotions are transparent and open to all eligible employees.

To promote the inclusion and advancement of women, some of the most important policies relate to work–life balance, including part-time work, flexible work hours, job sharing, and the option to work from home.

On the other side of the picture, it is also important to have policies that forbid management practices and individual behaviours that are discriminatory, disrespectful, or hostile to women. In some environments, it is necessary to be explicit about what exactly constitutes discrimination, disrespect, sexual harassment, inappropriate behaviour, and hostility.

Programmes

In addition to flexible working arrangements, other programmes and facilities can help to attract and retain women employees:

- childcare or sick baby services in or near the institution;
- school holiday childcare support;
- flexible benefits packages that can include childcare or elder-care support;
- support for relocating husbands, if promoting a woman requires her to move to a new area;
- transition programmes to support parental leave.

Other programmes that support women in the workplace include the availability of coaches, mentors, or advisers, and skill development (see below for more on this).

To make it possible for women to report and seek help with discriminatory, disrespectful, or hostile behaviour or sexual harassment, there needs to be a combination of services. These services do not necessarily have to be staffed by new people, but they do need to be handled by staff with the appropriate mindsets and preparation:

- a hotline or other reporting channel;
- an adviser or counsellor;
- an advocate or ombudsman who acts on the woman's behalf to address a problem, with the individual and within the institution, if necessary.

Networking and affinity groups

One type of programme used in many organizations is the women employees' network or affinity group. Such groups can be useful as forums to bring women employees together, give them opportunities to celebrate successes and discuss challenges, and provide some of the other women's programming.

However, networks and affinity groups are not sufficient on their own; they can actually lead to frustration if there is no way for women to address effectively the work-related challenges they might discuss with other women. However, in combination with other mechanisms, networks, and affinity groups, they add strength to the strategy to advance women.

Goals

As discussed earlier, there need to be goals for the number or percentage of women at all levels:

- new hires and at various lengths of employment;
- levels of non-managers, from entry level to professional staff;
- levels of management, from first-level supervisor to the most senior levels;
- executive level.

Goals need to be translated from the institutional level to the level of each manager. That means that there need to be goals for numbers of women at the head office, in the regions, and at each branch. Function and operations managers need to have targets for the number of women on their teams.

Accountability

Senior managers must be held to account for advancing women and must have goals and measures set for their departments and divisions. Senior managers' promotions and bonuses should be linked to meeting their goals for advancing women, and there should be regular reports to the board on the overall advancement of women and on the success of the senior managers. All managers need to be accountable for retaining and advancing women employees.

The organization needs to address discriminatory or hostile behaviour promptly and firmly, using the full range of penalties and consequences and making sure that employees are aware of penalties.

Recruitment

The organization must actively and explicitly recruit women, and therefore it should extend recruiting activities to locations and groups where women can be found. To support success in recruiting women, policies that attract and retain women need to be in place. Women recruits must also be given the opportunity to meet women already working at the institution.

Development

There needs to be a leadership development pipeline to bring women up through the levels of management. Managers should set goals to achieve certain percentages of women in development programmes and women ready for promotion, and set goals for how many women participate in high-potential programmes and are on succession plans.

The institution must include women in strategy planning meetings, bringing them along until those groups contain 50 per cent women. Strategic thinking will benefit from the perspectives and competencies contributed by women, and participating in these meetings will help develop women managers.

Women can be challenged to take on riskier, higher-stakes assignments or promotions, and supported through objective measures of success (not personal or political) as well as coaching and development. It is essential for women to have experience in diverse roles so that they are prepared to be well-rounded business leaders.

Skill building for managers

Managers are likely to need tools, strategies, training, and coaching to develop their competencies, confidence, and comfort in managing a larger number of women employees. Among those resources, there needs to be:

- sensitivity training to attune managers to requirements for a women-welcoming workplace, motivating women workers, and interacting appropriately;
- information and reinforcement about the reasons for and components of the bank's strategy, goals, policies, and programmes for promoting women in the workplace;
- skill building, to include: motivating women workers; delegation and empowerment; communication and use of language with women workers; collaboration and conflict resolution; educating the team and reinforcing the bank's goals and policies with them.

Skill building for women

As indicated above, there are constraints and limitations for women imposed by societies, institutions, and women themselves. Some of these barriers can be reduced or eliminated by building women's competencies in:

- developing 'executive presence' in meetings, individual interactions, and public occasions;

- strategic thinking, influencing and persuasion, analytical thinking (if needed), business acumen, and other critical leadership competencies;
- taking ownership of accomplishments and making sure that peers and superiors are aware of them;
- asking for what they want, negotiating, and using appropriate and effective forms of assertiveness in working with men;
- stepping up for promotions and riskier assignments;
- requiring that objective, performance-based metrics be set for their work;
- asking for feedback at designated intervals and on an informal basis;
- building relationships with significant peers who know and can support their work;
- building relationships with senior leaders who can mentor and advocate for them;
- learning the 'dominant code' (language or behaviour) used by men at work and needed for success and promotion to higher levels;
- learning how to communicate with male peers and senior leaders, using business language that is meaningful to men, interrupting effectively, holding one's ground, and standing up for one's own ideas.

Senior-level sponsorship

Senior managers should be encouraged to nominate women to the high-potential talent pool, to leadership development programmes, and to visible roles and assignments. A senior leadership sponsorship programme for women allows senior leaders to act as advisers to and advocates for women and to provide mentoring. In particular, as many senior-level women as possible should be encouraged to sponsor and mentor younger and more junior women. McKinsey's research found this factor to be one of the most important for recruiting, retaining, and promoting women into leadership.

Tips

- Make it acceptable for both women and men employees to discuss, in an appropriate forum, their discomfort with the strategy to advance women and the problems and challenges they face.
- Encourage an attitude of charity and generosity, so that people who make mistakes in the midst of a well-intentioned effort to implement the strategy receive feedback and support rather than blame and criticism.
- Cultivate the art of making an apology, since people will make mistakes and will misunderstand one another.

Cautions and pitfalls

A new focus on women is likely to generate concern, anxiety, and resistance among some or all male employees. The champions for the advancement of women strategy need to be prepared to address these reactions with sensitivity, empathy, and support.

As much as possible, policies and programmes associated with the advancement of women need to support men as well and portray them in a positive light. In particular, work–life balance programmes need to be open equally to men, whether they are single fathers, fathers with wives at home, fathers in two-working-adult relationships, or men who are unmarried and childless. Similarly, if there are skill-building modules for women employees that are of interest to male employees, every effort should be made to offer the same skill building to all.

Where it is necessary to talk about what is inappropriate or unacceptable in the environment or in interactions, the wording must try to focus on behaviour, not gender. Equity and fairness must be paramount so that male employees can be reassured that their compensation, performance appraisals, development, and promotions will not be undercut by less qualified women. Senior leaders, both men and women, need to speak and behave impeccably as the strategy for the advancement of women is being rolled out. Stories, jokes, comments, or body language that is not aligned with the strategy will be broadcast widely among both men and women employees, and the credibility of the strategy and the leadership team will be seriously damaged.

Factors specific to promoting diversity

What is diversity?

As mentioned earlier, creating a more diverse workforce means bringing on and retaining employees from a wider range of:

- ethnic, tribal, regional, or national origins;
- age groups;
- language groups;
- physical abilities or limitations;
- lifestyles or sexual orientations.

Having a strategy to diversify the employee group requires dealing with mindsets – assumptions and prejudices everyone has about people different from themselves. This is especially important in relation to people who are not members of the dominant culture group or groups.

It also involves changing long-standing policies, systems, and management practices.

Reasons for promoting greater diversity in the workplace

Many of the same reasons given for promoting the advancement of women in the workplace apply to creating a more diverse employee base. People of diverse backgrounds are increasingly part of the institution's customer base and are more likely to want to do business with an institution whose employees look, speak, or act like them. Many studies show that a more diverse employee group can come up with more creative, innovative, and diverse ideas for products and services as well as solutions to problems.

On the down side, there are still barriers in societies and in business to bringing people of diverse backgrounds and capabilities into the workplace. Experience around the world has shown that, by and large, those concerns are not as problematic as they are thought to be, and/or there are many ways to address them.

From the field

A highly successful Asian MFI moved much of its HR information to an internal website, in the hope of making it more easily accessible and reducing the cost of distributing paper documents whose content changes frequently. To their chagrin, the HR and IT teams received two pieces of critical feedback: as a result of expanding its services to more remote and rural regions, there was an increasing number of bank branches and sub-branches with very limited internet access. Below manager level, employees did not have access to a computer. Furthermore, the HR information was in English, but more and more of the loan officers and branch managers were in regions where local languages predominate and where fewer people learn English. Until these issues were pointed out, senior management had not recognized that, while the employee base had become more diverse, the institution had not adjusted to serve them.

Action strategy considerations for diversity

In addition to the action strategy material mentioned earlier in this chapter, there are some considerations that apply in particular to strategies to promote diversity. The process of developing a diversity strategy and then planning the actions to roll it out requires inclusiveness and the involvement of as diverse a group as possible.

Conducting a climate survey focused on diversity concerns is essential. Because people from the predominant cultural group or groups may be unaware of some facets of diversity, it may be helpful to work with a specialist resource to design or provide the climate survey.

It is also important to carry out a needs assessment among representatives of the diverse groups to find out what changes in mindset, behaviour, policy, and practice they believe are needed to create a climate that welcomes diversity. If some members of diverse groups are not yet on the workforce (for example, when a bank is planning to enter a new regional market), then research among diversity-oriented businesses with those employee groups already on board can be helpful.

Policies

Policy changes will reflect the constraints that have prevented diversity as well as the needs reported by employees from diverse groups. Policies to address the negative issues arising from increased diversity will most likely be similar to those outlined for policies relating to advancing women in the workplace.

Programmes

Some programmes similar to those described for promoting women in the workplace can be implemented to promote and support a more diverse workforce.

With input from employee councils (see below), develop programmes including:

- flexible benefits that respond to diverse groups' needs;
- flexible holiday or time-off policies and practices to allow for religious or medical needs;
- providing space and other facilities if needed by diverse employee groups.

Recruiting

There need to be explicit attempts to attract a diverse workforce, including recruitment activities among new sources of employees. Recruitment materials need to be written in local languages, with photographs and images that show a diverse culture in the organization.

In situations where people from a particular group may not be sufficiently prepared for employment at the institution, develop pre-employment programmes:

- partner with schools and training centres;
- establish internships;
- work with other employers who could serve as 'feeders' and training grounds for the bank, with bank employment as a 'next step up' for people in the other employer's workforce, whose career ambitions are limited by that organization's structure.

Affinity groups

The organization could set up employee councils that can be both affinity groups and a means of representation for key groups of diverse employees.

Language

Any language barriers should be removed by translating materials into the local languages used by employees. Managers can be provided with training in local languages and rewarded for language proficiency; while employees can be offered language training in the official business language, the dominant language of the bank's head office, and/or other local languages, and rewarded for language proficiency. Employees with language proficiency should have the opportunity to be translators (if they wish), for visibility and career development.

Career development

As with advancing women in the workforce, there need to be explicit goals, metrics, programmes, and monitoring to ensure that:

- employees from diverse groups receive the training, development, coaching, and mentoring to advance in the organization;
- each career development programme, from initial training to succession planning, incorporates goals for increasing diversity among managers and leadership.

Skill building for managers

Many of the competencies managers need to be effective in managing women employees are relevant to managing a more diverse group of employees. In addition, there may be some unique requirements relating to appropriate terminology, customs, and etiquette.

Skill building for employees

Similarly, many of the competencies that women need for advancement in the workplace may be appropriate for employees from other diverse groups. This is particularly the case for employees coming from traditionally non-dominant cultural groups.

Troubleshooting diversity problems

Certain problems commonly arise as a business works on promoting diversity, and, in those cases, a number of 'classic' interventions have been defined.

Table 10.2: Problems encountered when promoting diversity and suggested interventions

Problem	*Probable source(s)*	*Suggested interventions*
Glass ceiling – employees seem not to be able to advance beyond a given level of management	Training and development programmes Career development programmes Promotion system High-potential programme Succession planning	Set and enforce goals for putting diverse employees into all programmes and ensuring that they reach senior management levels Make selection criteria and processes transparent and unbiased Post openings widely
Unwritten 'rules' trip up employees who aren't aware of them and exclude those employees from activities and relationships important for success in the institution	Policies and the ways in which they are administered Tolerance of lack of diversity Lack of opportunities for interaction	Update policies and monitor how they are administered Provide refresher sessions on policies and administration Adopt a zero-tolerance position on bias or exclusion Provide training on the unwritten rules Set up mentoring arrangements
Dominance of the 'old guard' – older, more senior employees dominate groups, conversations, policymaking and decision-making	Management development and training Leadership of the diversity strategy Lack of movement or turnover in the organization The way in which meetings are managed	Promotions and succession planning – bring along new faces Training and formal mentoring with diverse mentors and participants Create more movement in the leadership pipeline, e.g. 'golden handshake' early retirement options and/or career advancement plus outplacement Manage meetings explicitly to allow newer voices to be heard and newer ideas to be considered
Uncomfortable environment – exclusionary, stereotyping and disrespectful	Roots and values Policies not made, not known, and not enforced Poor role modelling by senior leaders Tacit or explicit acceptance of exclusionary behaviour	'Translate' older values to promote a newer, more diverse culture Refresher sessions on values and policies Prompt enforcement of diversity policy violations Recommitment to diversity leadership Explicit condemnation of exclusionary or disrespectful behaviour

CHAPTER 11

Tracking success – is the performance management system working?

The performance management system has value to the organization only to the extent that it provides tools, processes, and support that help managers and staff do a better job of serving customers, achieving their goals, and finding satisfaction in their work and their environment. Ultimately, the performance management system must function to help the business be successful with its strategy, embody its values, and align with its culture.

To be sure that the system is providing full value and serving its function, its effectiveness needs to be evaluated from time to time. There are several questions to answer in the evaluation process:

- Is the performance management system providing the data, tools, processes, and advice that everyone needs to deliver and manage optimal performance?
- Are the tools and processes used widely, appropriately, and effectively?
- Do the people using the tools and involved in the processes know what to do, how to do it, why they need to do it, and how what they are doing contributes to delivering or managing performance?
- Is it possible to make direct connections from the activities of the performance management system to the business strategy and the business results?

Some of the reasons for evaluating the system are to accomplish the following goals:

- make sure that it is delivering value;
- find out whether everyone is using the components of the system and using them appropriately so adjustments can be made if needed;
- upgrade the system as the organization changes;
- fill in gaps and remove redundancies, inefficiencies, or unnecessary components;
- ensure alignment with the organization's mission, strategy, and culture.

http://dx.doi.org/10.3362/9781780447926.012

Table 11.1: Alignment of people management responsibilities

Business manager – typical contributions	*People management responsibilities*	*HR professional – typical contributions*
Defining needs – data, tools, processes, and advice Implementing the processes and use of tools Providing feedback and suggestions for enrichment or improvement Demonstrating commitment, responsibility, and accountability for his or her role in managing performance	Making sure the systems for managing people's performance are effective	Requesting input on performance management tools, processes and data needs Facilitating, supporting, and training on its use Tracking compliance and following up on non-compliance Collecting and analysing data Collecting feedback and evaluating the performance management components and overall system

Dimensions of effectiveness

Providing data, tools, processes, and advice

Does the organization have enough and the right kind of resources?

- *Data* that informs the organization about the kinds of people it employs, their skills and knowledge, their interests and aspirations, and their performance improvements and professional growth over the period of their employment.
- *Tools* that allow managers and staff to be clear and consistent about goals, specific performance targets, achievements, and shortfalls; tools and methods to address problems, grow in the job, and advance to the next job.
- *Processes* for finding and hiring the right people; for getting them started in their jobs; for feedback and coaching every day; for training and professional development; for advancement or termination.
- *Advice and counsel* to help all employees use the tools and processes of the performance management system effectively.

Tools and processes used widely, appropriately, and effectively

Do all managers and all staff maximize potential benefits?

- Use the tools and processes to manage people's performance – their own and others.
- Use the tools in the right ways, at the appropriate times, for appropriate reasons; avoid using them in sloppy, haphazard, inaccurate, or abusive ways.

- Get the results they need from the performance management tools and processes, for themselves and for the organization.

Knowledgeable and skilful use of the system

Do all managers and staff have sufficient knowledge?

- What to do to implement the components of the performance management system.
- How to manage people's performance skilfully.
- Why it is important to the individuals, the business units, and the overall business to use the performance management system.
- How using the performance management system contributes to being successful and delivering results.

Contributing to business performance and results

Do the components of the system support the business in meaningful ways?

- Performing the work.
- Achieving the target results.

Linked to vision, mission, strategy, values, and culture

Are the dynamics clear to everyone?

- How the design of the performance management system and the way it is implemented supports and contributes to the purpose and future direction of the business.
- How the priorities of the performance management system are directly linked to helping the business execute its strategy.
- How the design of the system and the way in which each person implements it is aligned with the organization's values and culture.

How to evaluate the performance management system

Evaluation of the effectiveness of the performance management system can come about in two ways. In the first case, the HR department and the leadership team might decide to evaluate the system, for one or more reasons. In the paragraphs below, an approach to evaluating the system is laid out.

In the second case, there may be new challenges, changes, or problems that are linked to components of the performance management system and that may require changes in those components. At the end of the chapter is a troubleshooting template to help identify which components of the system may need attention, given a particular business challenge.

Overview of steps

The steps to take to conduct an evaluation are listed here:

1. Determine the goal or goals of the evaluation – what you want to find out, for what purpose, and what you will do with the findings.
2. Decide on methods – how you will collect data, who you will report to, and how you will report.
3. Plan the process – how much time, which people, when to start, key milestone points, when to finish, and what resources and funds are needed.
4. Communicate to the organization and stakeholders – identify who to notify, how often, on what topics, and in what form.
5. Prepare materials – survey questions, interview questions, and focus group topics.
6. Schedule activities.
7. Implement the plan – survey, interview, meet, and monitor progress.
8. Collate and analyse findings – numbers, trends, interpretation, and assumptions associated with the interpretation.
9. Prepare to report on findings, give recommendations, and answer questions.
10. Issue the report.

Details about setting goals and selecting methods are given below.

Setting goals

The evaluation could be conducted to find out about one or a combination of the following issues:

- level of compliance with policies and procedures;
- appropriate and skilful implementation of steps and processes;
- need to upgrade or adjust the system to align with organizational changes or evolution;
- finding out about new needs, redundancies, or inefficiencies;
- confirming or strengthening alignment of the system with the company mission, strategy, and culture.

Methods

The system can be evaluated by means of surveys, interviews, observation, and focus group sessions.

Surveys ensure dissemination of a consistent set of questions or topics. The results are easiest to report in quantitative form. Likewise, surveys are easy to re-administer for follow-up, to look for improvement or trends. They are also open to individual interpretation, however, with no opportunities for probing or follow-up. They need to be carefully written, and the responses should not be over-interpreted.

Interviews can combine standardized questions with the flexibility of individual reporting, examples and anecdotes, and follow-up questions. The responses provide more depth and nuance than survey answers. Interviewing, of course, is more time-consuming, and it needs to be done skilfully and professionally to give valid results.

Interviews can have a powerful impact on the organization, so this should be considered and planned for. They open up discussion of topics that may not have been discussed before, and they may raise expectations that problems will be addressed or changes are going to happen.

People who are interviewed feel more engaged with the evaluation, so it is important to be sure that they see or hear what comes out of their interviews.

The chief drawbacks of interviews are that some interview subjects are intimidated by being interviewed, and some will be inclined to say what they think are the 'right' answers.

Observation is a powerful way to find out whether processes and procedures are being conducted as expected. It gets away from the subjectivity of self-reporting. However, the presence of an observer can sometimes inhibit people, and it often puts them on their best behaviour rather than their typical behaviour. Observing also takes some skill and professionalism to avoid intrusiveness and to maintain confidentiality. It is a good method to combine with at least one of the other methods.

Focus groups are group interviews. They can save some of the time required for individual interviews, and the interchange among participants sometimes brings out more insights and ideas than would come from one-to-one conversation. It takes planning, skill, and thought to run an effective focus group.

Also, moderators need to be aware of the risk of 'group think', where everyone agrees with the opinions expressed by one or two highly vocal participants. Quieter or more reserved individuals may not speak up or may be reluctant to give full opinions in a group, especially in a group that sets a strong trend and is less tolerant of diverse points of view.

Evaluating the system for completeness and compliance

Two reasons for evaluating the performance management system are to determine whether all the right components are in place and whether everyone is using them at the expected times and in the expected ways.

Are the *tools* in place? Are they the right tools? Are they being used by the right people at the right time for the right purpose?

Are the *processes* in place? Has everyone been trained or briefed on the processes and related policies? Do all people know how to implement the processes? Is everyone implementing the appropriate processes and using them correctly – dates met, forms completed correctly, etc.?

Have the *skills* needed to implement the performance management system been identified? Does everyone have the skills, through either prior experience, training, or briefings? Is there regular follow-up with advice, counselling, and coaching?

The template that follows – the compliance and completeness checklist – is a resource to help managers evaluate whether the tools, processes, and skills are up to the required standards.

Addressing compliance issues

Getting everyone to implement the performance management system on time and as expected can become a significant challenge for managers and for the HR department. The best solution is to avoid it becoming a challenge in the first place; some ideas about how to do that are given below. In addition, there are some tips for what to do if compliance problems do occur.

Building in performance management compliance

Performance management needs to be seen by everyone in a business as part of the job. In short, employees know they come to work to do their jobs, do them as well as they can, and help the organization be successful in achieving its mission and making enough profit to keep going.

Clear, shared commitment. Make sure that everyone in the organization, from drivers and cleaning crew to credit officers and tellers to the chief executive officer, has the same basic understanding: we come to work to do our jobs, do them well, and make sure the organization achieves its mission profitably. If there are any gaps in this understanding, **everyone** needs to pull together to change the situation. This is not an HR responsibility; this is a leadership responsibility.

Management responsibility for managing people's performance. Make sure people who manage others know they are responsible for explaining the job, checking on how well it is being done, and helping their direct reports do a better job. Again, this is not an HR responsibility; it is a management responsibility, to be communicated and reinforced by every level of management.

Accountability for managing people's performance. Since everyone who manages someone is expected to manage performance, that responsibility needs to be in the managers' job descriptions. It also needs to be covered in their performance appraisals, by their managers. If a manager is not following through on people management expectations, he or she needs to receive feedback, coaching, training, and consequences from his or her manager.

Communication and feedback. The expectation of participation in performance management activities needs to be communicated throughout the levels of management, by the managers and leaders of the business. The HR department's responsibilities are to explain the processes and the tools, coordinate the schedules, track compliance, and keep files on components such as training needs, course attendance, and disciplinary actions. In addition, HR needs to collect feedback on whether the performance management system is serving managers well or how it needs to be adjusted.

Alliances and involvement. If the HR department builds alliances with managers from the early months of the business, it will be in a good position to find out what help they need to manage people's performance. One way to build these alliances is to have either a formal HR council or an informal but regularly occurring series of ad hoc meetings with managers. Through these mechanisms, HR professionals can solicit input on how to set up performance management systems and tools, share data, hear about problems, and cultivate champions for changes or additions to the systems.

Methods for addressing compliance gaps

The least effective response to lack of compliance with the performance management system is for someone from HR to scold, lecture, or take a 'policing' role with managers. Some combination of the following tactics is more effective:

Inquiry. While maintaining an objective, neutral tone, find out what is preventing the person from completing the performance management task.

Involvement. Consider the possibility that the component needs adjustment, and make a forthright attempt to engage the non-complier(s) in redesigning it.

Business case. Every component of performance management should have been presented to managers and staff in terms of the business reason(s) for using it. For example, job descriptions exist so that there is a common and consistent statement about what the jobholders are supposed to do and so that the business can be sure to address changes in jobs when there are changes in the way business is done. Consider reviewing the business reason, in a business-like way, when requesting compliance.

NOTE: The HR professional should be discussing the business reason with the manager(s) of anyone who is non-compliant, with the goal of encouraging those people to fulfil their responsibilities and thereby help make sure that their managers meet all their own responsibilities. In any case, it is generally ineffective to ask managers to complete performance management tasks because 'it's the right thing to do' or because 'HR needs you to do it'; managers are better motivated by their own interests and by the need to get business results.

Business consequences. Related to making the business case is pointing out the business consequences of failing to follow through on some aspect of performance management.

For example, if performance appraisals are not completed, there are several possible business consequences. One is a lack of data on the ways in which business results are (or are not) being achieved – the growth or lack of growth in opening deposit accounts may be obvious, but why the growth has or has not occurred will not be known.

A second consequence is that, without information about how business results are or are not being achieved, trying to improve the results will be more time-consuming, expensive, and inefficient than it needs to be.

Third, under such circumstances it is impossible to give out incentives, pay increases, or promotions in a fair way. Morale will drop and eventually staff turnover will increase if rewards are either not given or given in ways that seem unfair.

Fourth, young, energetic, qualified workers often have many options for where to work. Having their managers give them attention in the form of feedback, praise, coaching, and a sense of future possibilities is a major factor in sustaining their loyalty. Lack of attention, feedback, praise, coaching, and prospects leads to turnover among the best and brightest.

Finally, if the right performance management activities have not been implemented, it becomes very difficult or impossible to fire an employee who behaves inappropriately or fails to perform. Employment law usually requires that reasons for involuntary termination be documented, and the performance management system provides the processes and the forms to meet that requirement.

Template 11.1: Compliance and completeness checklist

Performance management system components	**Performance management tools** In place? In use? At the right time? For the right purposes?	**Performance management processes** In place? Training or briefing on process and policies and how to implement them? Being implemented? Completely? Correctly? On time?	**Skills managers need to implement performance management** Identified? Everyone has them? Follow-up or support provided?
Job descriptions	✓ Job specifications ✓ Qualifications ✓ Skills, knowledge, characteristics, and attributes ✓ Special demands of the position	✓ Job analysis ✓ Skill and knowledge analysis OR training needs analysis	✓ Writing
Recruitment	✓ Application form ✓ Form letters of acknowledgement, acceptance, and rejection ✓ Information packs ✓ Interview guides ✓ Candidate evaluation forms ✓ Salary or compensation guide ✓ Benefits guide	✓ Publicity and information ✓ Recruiting events ✓ Application processing ✓ Screening interviews ✓ Assessment ✓ Selection interviews ✓ Negotiating terms and conditions ✓ Making the offer ✓ Preparing contractual documents ✓ Setting up and maintaining records	✓ Communication ✓ Interviewing ✓ Assessment and analysis ✓ Negotiation
On-boarding, induction, or orientation	✓ New employee manual ✓ Programme checklist ✓ Programme materials ✓ Probation requirements	✓ Manager briefing ✓ Orientations to company basics ✓ In-class sessions ✓ Tours and introductions ✓ On-the-job sessions ✓ Mentor or peer coaching system ✓ HR check-ins	✓ Writing ✓ Presentation ✓ Social relations ✓ Setting expectations and goals ✓ On-the-job coaching ✓ On-the-job feedback

		✓ Review of job tasks, performance goals, and work expectations ✓ Probation status review	
Performance monitoring	✓ Performance targets ✓ Reward and incentive policies ✓ Reward tools: cards, cash, gift vouchers, etc. ✓ Disciplinary policies	✓ Monitoring performance ✓ On-the-job feedback ✓ On-the-job coaching ✓ Motivating and rewarding ✓ Disciplining and penalizing	✓ Observation and data collection ✓ Giving feedback ✓ On-the-job coaching ✓ Motivating ✓ Conducting difficult conversations
Training and development	✓ Training and development needs analysis ✓ Training curriculum ✓ Development options ✓ Training policies ✓ Training courses ✓ Online materials ✓ External training information ✓ Books and journals ✓ Training registration forms ✓ Training evaluation forms ✓ Application for training forms	✓ Job skills and knowledge assessment ✓ Researching training options ✓ Designing and developing training activities ✓ Notifying managers and staff of training and development options ✓ Approving and registering for training ✓ Getting all employees into appropriate, timely training and development activities ✓ Evaluating satisfaction with and impact of training and development activities	✓ Interviewing ✓ Surveying ✓ Analysis ✓ Research ✓ Communication ✓ Commitment to employee learning

Performance appraisal	✓ Performance review form ✓ Performance review guide or checklist ✓ Performance rating guide ✓ Development planning form ✓ Development planning guide or checklist	✓ Performance review process ✓ Performance review training or briefing ✓ Performance review compliance analysis ✓ Performance review results analysis ✓ Development discussions ✓ Development planning training or briefing ✓ Development planning compliance analysis ✓ Development needs report	✓ Observation and data collection ✓ Giving feedback ✓ Setting expectations ✓ Conducting difficult conversations
Career planning	✓ Career path outline ✓ Career planning forms	✓ Career path analysis ✓ Career planning training or briefing ✓ Career plan discussions ✓ Career interests report ✓ Mentoring programme	✓ Conversation ✓ Mentoring
Succession planning	✓ Succession planning policies ✓ Succession planning guide ✓ Succession strategy ✓ Succession documents ✓ Successor development plan	✓ Succession planning preparation ✓ Succession planning meetings	✓ Analysis of readiness, potential, and development needs
High-potential programme	✓ Guide for identifying high-potential staff and managers ✓ High-potential review form ✓ High-potential expectations and criteria ✓ File for current high potentials under development	✓ Preparation for nominating high potentials ✓ High-potential nomination and follow-up/review meetings ✓ High-potential development planning sessions	✓ Analysis of readiness and potential ✓ Identification of development needs

Advancement	✓ Job descriptions ✓ Promotion criteria	✓ Promotion proposal and review meetings ✓ Promotion preparation and follow-up activities	✓ Analysis of readiness, potential, and development needs
Discipline and termination	✓ Policies ✓ Guidelines ✓ Performance improvement plan (PIP) forms ✓ Exit interview forms ✓ Warning notice forms ✓ Files	✓ Exit interviews for voluntary departures ✓ PIP meetings ✓ Disciplinary review meetings ✓ Termination review meetings ✓ Disciplinary discussions with employees ✓ Termination discussions with employees ✓ Documenting reasons for and steps taken for disciplinary action or termination	✓ Self-control ✓ Communication ✓ Conducting difficult conversations ✓ Courage and integrity ✓ Factual reporting
Compensation and incentives	✓ Policies ✓ Salary and incentives guides ✓ Procedure manuals ✓ Files	✓ Salary review discussions ✓ Salary/incentive discussions with employees ✓ Documenting changes in salary ✓ Documenting awarding of incentives	✓ Objectivity ✓ Communication ✓ Conducting difficult conversations

Evaluating the system for utility

The section on compliance touched on whether the performance management system is complete, fully utilized, and implemented appropriately. Utility refers to the system's capacity to generate data that can be used to recognize and explain trends and results and that correlates to business performance indicators.

For example, the HR department maintains demographic information about employees. In one financial institution, analysis of the age range and average age information dramatically highlighted how young the staff and managers were. Recognition of that factor was linked to the widespread lack of work experience, which then explained issues of general work behaviours and professionalism that needed to be covered during induction and reviewed regularly by line managers.

In another organization, staff turnover became a concern. Data from exit interviews combined with a review of the educational levels of the average employee showed that approximately one-third of people leaving were going on to higher education. Based on this information, the business developed schemes to support employees seeking additional education, including educational leave policies and tuition loans and reimbursement plans. With those new schemes in place, departures to pursue education decreased, and employees whose educational efforts were supported became more loyal and more likely to stay longer.

The list that follows is not comprehensive for all the types of data relating to people and their performance, nor is it necessarily the right list for every organization. Each business needs to decide for itself what data about people and performance it needs to collect, analyse, and report in order to be able to achieve its results, improve its processes, maintain its culture, and realize its mission.

Useful data from the performance management system would include:

- demographics;
- educational profiles;
- experience profiles;
- attendance;
- use of medical leave;
- use of vacation or other leave (or lack of use);
- training needs;
- training attendance (or lack of attendance);
- length of service;
- time in position;
- salary – number of employees at each level;
- incentives – amount and reasons (or lack of use);
- pay rises – who, how much, why, and when (or lack of use);
- development plans – what's planned and what has been implemented;
- job growth and promotion interests;
- performance ratings;
- disciplinary issues – what, and how they were handled;
- termination – reasons;
- voluntary departures – reasons and next steps (other employment, school, etc.);
- high potentials – who, development plans, and status;
- succession – successors, status, and development plans.

Evaluating the system for effectiveness

Finally, it is important to assess whether the performance management system is contributing to the organization's ability to produce results, achieve its strategic goals, fulfil its mission, and maintain its culture. The troubleshooting template that follows points to ways in which the performance management system can be used to address particular business problems.

Template 11.2: Troubleshooting performance management activities associated with business issues

If the business issue is ...	Consider performance management activities such as ...
Appropriate, qualified people to fill jobs are hard to find	• Get the mission, the culture, the values, and the excitement of working in the organization to be more widely known • Reach a different kind of recruit – e.g. foreign nationals, 'young' retirees, or ex-pats • Prepare potential job candidates in advance of employment decisions – e.g. internships or 'pre-training' programmes • Strengthen connections with people in appropriate training or educational institutions within the country or abroad
Competing against higher salaries and better benefits to attract or retain employees is difficult	• Excite and motivate people with the mission, the culture, the values, and the accomplishments of the organization • Connect employees more directly with clients and the ways in which the business's services are helping them • Reward and acknowledge employees with methods that are non-financial, lower cost, or deferred – e.g. learning opportunities, higher levels of responsibility, ownership, networking, contacts with well-placed people, or participation in exciting or challenging events
People are tired, discouraged, or overwhelmed	• Publicize the vision, the reason for the vision, and reports of progress, both quantitative and qualitative • Provide physical activities – e.g. sports, dancing, hiking, or swimming • Organize short, fun activities • Find ways to include family members or close friends • Teach ways to prioritize work and manage stress • Enforce the taking of holidays, and maintaining healthy work hours
Actions do not produce results Revenues or loan portfolios are not growing as quickly as planned Quality or productivity problems are excessive	HR professionals and managers need to work together to resolve the problem by: • verifying that job descriptions are complete and accurate • making sure that performance targets are in place and are broken down to daily, weekly, or monthly levels as appropriate • ensuring that work expectations such as arriving on time, participating in meetings, or cleaning up work areas are reviewed regularly

	• ensuring that there is sufficient direction, on-the-job training, and coaching for employees to know the work processes or steps • making sure that training is available and comprehensive, so workers have the skills, knowledge, equipment, information, and environment to do the work • ensuring that there is feedback and on-the-job coaching for ongoing performance, with correction as needed • reinforcing all employees' understanding of what the overall performance goals are and how they contribute to the success of the business • ensuring that problems with productivity, attitude, attendance, teamwork, 'freeloading', etc. are addressed promptly • confirming that staff are being rewarded – tangibly or intangibly – for the right things and being penalized – tangibly or intangibly – only for undesired behaviour or performance
Morale is down	Check several of the above performance-related issues. In addition, HR supports managers and leaders to accomplish relevant goals by: • addressing issues of mistrust or suspicion • enforcing fairness in both rewards and discipline • enforcing respectful behaviour from bosses and among employees • keeping everyone informed if there are business challenges or organizational changes • allowing people to express views and ask questions • taking prompt action in response to any behaviour by leaders or bosses that violates policies, regulations, values, or cultural norms
Staff turnover has increased	Find out why people have left, and use the tips above to address some issues. In addition, HR can consider how to respond, for example by: • strengthening managers' communication, interpersonal, and people management competencies • enhancing feedback and on-the-job development activities • reminding managers to look for reasonable opportunities for expanded or special responsibilities, promotion, and exposure to new challenges or senior-level activities • paying attention to 'fit' issues, such as employees fitting job requirements or demands; bosses fitting groups; and employee expectations fitting the reality in the office

Nobody is prepared to step into higher management or leadership positions	• Do succession planning, making sure the process is appropriate for the age, size, and environment of the business • Think creatively about identifying and building connections with external successors, such as nationals working abroad, professionals from consulting or investor organizations, 'young' retirees, and new graduates from overseas universities • Confront and courageously eliminate obstacles to development or promotion • Look for even one or two internal high-potential individuals, and focus on their development
Locations are not growing as rapidly as planned	• Make sure foundations for all performance management systems, especially recruiting, induction, and training, are well established and prepared to scale up • See the previous suggestions regarding problems with business results and with lack of successors

CHAPTER 12

Maintaining the strategic position of performance management

Managing the performance of people is one of the fundamental activities people in business organizations need to do constantly and effectively. However, the technical focus of leaders and managers in financial institutions does not always encompass that aspect of leadership and management. In addition, start-up businesses and microfinance and SME banking institutions are often so busy taking care of daily operations and navigating the whirlpools of economic and competitive pressures that they have little energy for other aspects of the work. As a result, HR professionals need to work constantly at showing busy managers the ways in which performance management helps them get the work done and achieve the results they want.

The HR function typically starts as a transactional and administrative group. It finds new employees, monitors attendance, deals with sick leave, sets up the payroll, and books rooms for induction meetings. It is generally only after the organization grows to 40 or more employees and starts operations in locations outside the head office that more attention is given to the need for a fully developed HR department. At that point, the HR staff may feel that they have already been cast in a back-office, tactical, operational set of roles, and they recognize that there will be real challenges in evolving into new roles, new status, and new relationships.

The direction of the evolution of HR needs to be towards leadership, partnership with other leaders and managers, consultation and collaboration, thinking like business people, and becoming strategic players. The positioning, design, and deployment of the performance management system can both shape that evolution and reflect its progress.

The HR strategy, also known as the human capital or talent management strategy, has to be tightly linked to the overall business strategy. The demands and constraints on implementing the HR side of the business strategy must be considered fully when strategic plans are laid out.

HR professionals take the lead in establishing effective processes for managing the performance of people, and they should expect to function as peers among the leaders and managers of their organization. Since the tools and processes of managing performance need to suit the business and its managers, HR professionals can be most effective when they work closely with their manager colleagues to learn about and respond to their requirements. In addition, HR professionals must be able to position each component of the performance management system in terms of business operations and results

http://dx.doi.org/10.3362/9781780447926.013

– i.e. how the performance management system will support operations, contribute to results, maintain or improve quality, facilitate expansion, strengthen product knowledge, and so forth.

Relevant terms and concepts

Strategic refers to seeing the longer term and bigger picture for the future direction of the business, including the customer segments; the markets; the competitors; the social, economic, and political environment; and the financial requirements. It involves setting goals and planning the steps to reach them. Strategic thinking requires asking 'what if?' questions, anticipating the reactions of other players in the industry, and planning in advance how to respond to or how to delay competitors' success.

The term 'strategic' may also refer to activities that are linked to helping the business accomplish its strategic goals. For example, if the HR department develops a 'recruiter-in-a-box' kit for regional managers to use during an intensive expansion period, that would be strategic – in support of the organization's growth strategy.

Transactional describes interactions that are limited, focused on accomplishing a specific task, and often prescribed by a policy or a regulation. Tracking the use of sick days and managing the payroll are some of the transactional activities of the HR department. Most HR activities need to be strategic and consultative.

Consultative describes a collaborative, service-oriented approach to providing tools, processes, and advice to one's colleagues. As the HR department matures, its responsibilities grow beyond the transactional ones of setting up personnel files, tracking absence and attendance, and handing out pay cheques. Its new responsibilities require HR staff to work side by side with managers to provide what the managers need to monitor performance, give feedback, develop employees, promote them, and so forth. Consultation relationships include conducting dialogues, asking for input, and designing tools and processes that help managers. Consultation also involves communication, influencing skills, and change management to achieve goals, rather than acting like an enforcer.

Leadership is not limited to a title or an official position. It is a willingness to have a point of view, to propose initiatives, and to advocate for something the leader believes in. Leadership also requires the ability to think about the whole group or organization, not just oneself. Finally, leadership is about deciding what the right thing to do is.

Partnership means working as peers, regardless of title and position. It is sometimes challenging for HR professionals to be seen as business partners when there are business managers who are dismissive of any part of the organization that doesn't bring in revenue or whose expertise is in areas very different from their own. It can take stamina and commitment for HR staff to maintain a partnership attitude with their line manager colleagues.

Business approach requires thinking and talking in terms of revenue, profitability, costs, budgets, market share, operations, efficiency, productivity, and competitors. It means thinking about how performance management policies, processes, and tools can help line managers achieve business results, as well as present HR resources in business terms. Ultimately, business managers will be persuaded to take action if they see the business reason for it and it benefits them; they are usually not interested in HR activities for their own sake.

Performance is usually a synonym for 'results' – the number of sales calls, the size of the loan portfolio, the quality of the loans, or the value of assets under management. Business is all about performance – producing the results it needs to survive and succeed.

Management is the collection of activities that makes sure that the steps that help achieve the strategy are carried out by the right people at the right time, within budget and to the desired level of quality. Management is about doing things the right way.

Maintaining the link between HR and business strategy

Every major activity of the HR department needs to be directly linked to the strategic goals of the business, and HR professionals need to be able to talk about performance management activities in terms of how they make the institution successful against its goals. Each year, the HR department sets annual goals and outlines the initiatives it plans to take on, based directly on the business strategy. If the business's primary strategic direction is growth, then HR activities need to focus on solidifying the foundations of performance management to tolerate change and growth, along with leveraging key parts of the performance management system to make that growth possible. Those key parts are likely to be recruitment, induction, and training.

Outlined here is a process for linking HR activities to the business strategy.

Step one – study the overall direction of the business strategy for insights into its human capital impact

The business's overall strategic direction is likely to be either growth or consolidation. Growth takes various forms: expansion into rural areas, moving into a new region, rolling out new products, forming partnerships with other types of business, or competing for a larger market share. Consolidation can be focused on efficiency and productivity, quality improvement, talent development, refining execution capabilities, or strengthening customer service. From the overview perspective of the business strategy, it becomes clear what the overall emphasis in the human capital area will be. Those insights take shape as HR initiatives.

Growth means:

- more recruiting and hiring;
- more on-boarding and employee orientation;
- more technical and basic business training;
- opportunities to promote high-potential employees;
- greater risk of putting people into positions they are not quite ready for;
- heavy demand for frequent coaching by managers.

A consolidation strategy puts the emphasis on:

- refining individual objectives or key performance indicators (KPIs);
- more carefully implemented performance reviews to ensure that performance standards for efficiency, productivity, quality, execution, or service are met;
- increased focus on management training and succession planning – activities that may not be put in place during an intensive period of growth.

Step two – dig deeper for numbers and timelines

Find out the specific targets within the overall strategy:

- How many branches, co-locations, or mini-outlets will be established, and over what period of time?
- How many new products will there be? Will they be introduced in sequence? Or as a bundle? Who will promote, sell, and administer them?
- How many people, and in which positions, will be involved in a partnership? How soon will the partners begin working together?
- What measures of efficiency, productivity, or quality will be the focus of improvement and what will the goals be?

Step three – make the specific connections between business activities and HR activities

Brainstorm all the activities involved in those future business activities, and highlight the HR connections. Then go into more detail about those activities.

For example, if the strategic plan focuses on growth, and the specific goal is to establish four new locations in the capital city and 12 new locations in the provinces where no branches currently exist, a 'to do' list of HR activities might include some of the following:

- job descriptions for urban and rural locations, to be developed or refined;
- sources of talent to be identified, especially for people willing to relocate;
- new elements in the incentive scheme to encourage existing and new staff to take rural assignments;

- methods for reaching the appropriate talent – advertising in urban areas, community gatherings in rural areas – to be researched;
- the content and focus of the induction programme needed in each new territory to be planned;
- staffing for inductions and the involvement of the CEO, given distant rural locations, to be worked out.

The list goes on – setting up performance management systems, training of all kinds, deploying experienced and inexperienced managers, ensuring that good performance is rewarded and problems receive appropriate discipline, and much more.

Step four – detail what is required to carry out all the HR activities associated with the business strategy as well as with ongoing operations

In step three, all the HR requirements were identified. The next step is to plan in concrete terms what will be needed to carry out those activities: people's time, materials and documents, HR staff involvement, new or expanded processes, use of space, and the funding to support it all.

For example, to meet the location expansion outlined above, one of the HR activities will be to prepare job descriptions for all positions, with careful thought about the ones for the new rural locations. Preparing job descriptions probably requires input from senior managers who oversee branch operations and from experienced branch managers. The HR department provides the format for new descriptions and facilitates the review and modification of processes. This whole process is fairly simple, but an HR professional needs to align everyone for consistency's sake. The time required of senior managers may be an hour or two, but several hours are needed from the branch managers and the HR professionals. Materials and equipment are minimal – maybe a meeting room and a flip chart – but everyone needs a copy of the HR manual as a guide.

Finally, the HR professional needs to calculate the funding support needed for the HR side of the business strategy initiatives:

- If the business uses the business case methodology for evaluating the requirements and impacts of its activities, that would be the most appropriate approach for analysing the funding support needed for strategic HR activities.
- If not, the most straightforward approach is to calculate the total number of hours per week over the estimated period of time for the people involved. Actual cash expenditures, such as for travel or meeting spaces, are also required.

For the expansion to four urban and 12 rural locations, the funding support needs for the HR activities alone (separate from finding office space or buying computers) might be:

- half-day per week of three head office branch operations managers for 12 months;
- half-day per week of two experienced branch managers for 12 months;
- two to four days per week of one HR professional for 12 months;
- travel to each location by head office managers, branch managers, and HR professionals at least twice over eight months.

Step four is the beginning of implementation planning and the time spent thinking it through as early as possible saves confusion, disappointment, overtime, and delay later on.

Step five – assess the impact of executing the HR strategic initiatives

With the detailed planning in hand, it is possible to assess the feasibility and the impact of the human capital aspects of the business strategy as it was originally formulated. Part of being a good strategic partner to top management is helping members see the concrete implications of their conceptual plans and then helping them decide whether it is reasonable to proceed.

Sometimes the full scope of a concrete implementation plan allows a high-level business leader to re-evaluate a strategic goal. The goal might be feasible but also risky because of the level of resources required to execute it. Or it might turn out to be more cautious than necessary, and a more expansive effort would be feasible with moderate risk.

In the expansion story, each new location would require hiring one manager and three staff members: a total of 16 managers and 48 staff members. To hire 48 qualified staff members would probably mean interviewing 100 to 150 people. If each interview took 30 minutes, and at least 60 people had second interviews, the time consumed just by interviewing would be 80 to more than 100 hours. Given these numbers, it is possible to make a sensible estimate of how many weeks the recruitment process might require and the time commitment the organization is asking of its managers and its HR staff. So, just from the analysis of the recruitment demands of the expansion strategy, the HR leader can help the leadership team quantify the level of focus, effort, and commitment required to execute a strategic initiative, as well as make explicit what activities cannot be carried out in parallel.

Putting performance management in business terms

What are the business reasons for having a performance management system? The high-level answer is that the system is a set of tools and processes to help manage what people do at work so that they achieve the desired results in the intended way. For example:

- job descriptions serve two key purposes: they help make sure all the responsibilities of a business unit are assigned to someone, and they make it possible to assign the right people to do the work;

- training provides what employees need to be able to do their work and do it to the expected standard of quality;
- succession planning ensures that the organization will not be left without qualified leadership.

Another way to consider performance management in business terms is to look at some of the key types of 'performance' and what parts of the system address them.

Table 12.1: Business performance and supporting performance management activities

Business performance	*Performance management activities to support achievement*
Make the target number of loans	Recruit people with the right background for selling loan products Train on products, sales, and so on Give feedback on interim progress on reaching the target Reward success and motivate greater achievement
Expand the number of branches	Develop recruitment strategies for new locations Provide pre-employment training to raise the skill levels of new hires Prepare more people to be managers Give leadership assignments to high-potential managers
Improve customer service	Set performance expectations during annual goal-setting meetings Train staff on customer service behaviours Address underperformance promptly, with structured tools and processes Transfer or terminate persistent non-performers

With these two approaches the HR professional can, first, make sure that all HR activities serve business needs; and second, explain the importance of HR processes to business managers in terms that make sense to them.

Building the business case for a performance management initiative

A business case presents the benefits and value to the organization of taking an initiative as well as the risks or negative consequences of not taking the initiative.

- Benefits may be related to sales and revenue, to quality or efficiency, or to attracting top-quality job candidates.
- Risks or negative consequences can include costly inefficiencies, lost time, increased costs of replacing people, or reduced productivity.

A business case can be formal or informal, as appropriate to the idea proposed and the nature of the organization. However, in all circumstances it needs to be put in business terms, addressing business needs and business results.

A typical, formally written business case includes the following components:

- short description of the need or the situation that has led to the proposed initiative;
- summary statement of what the initiative is;
- impact – how implementing the initiative will benefit the organization and how failing to do so may harm the institution;
- start time, end time, and the point when the impact will first be felt;
- resource requirements – people, money, technology, and so on;
- if necessary, the one or more decisions to be made to put the initiative in place.

These key points may then be followed by more detail on each one, allowing busy executives to get the 'headlines' in a quick read while others can go into greater depth.

As an example, the HR department may need to propose a new component of the incentive scheme:

- *Situation.* Two new, highly profitable credit products have been introduced in the last six months, but loan officers continue to focus on the old, familiar products. The old products are less profitable and are at risk of becoming commodities, sold by every financial institution in the region. Product training and coaching in the field have been provided. The current incentive scheme rewards loan officers for staying with what they consider a 'safe bet' rather than offering products they are less familiar with and for which they receive exactly the same commissions.
- *Proposed initiative.* A step-down process for the incentive scheme associated with the older products – the commissions decrease gradually over six months – combined with an immediate increase in the commission for the newer products. There will also be gradual increases in sales targets, with bonuses for exceeding the target in any given month.
- *Impact.* Implementing the incentive scheme will increase sales of the newer product by 25 per cent to 35 per cent, which will increase profitability on the credit product line by at least 50 per cent. Failure to implement the scheme will result in declining profitability in the credit product line of up to 47 per cent in the next 12 months.
- *Timing.* Communication can begin within two weeks of the decision being made. The new scheme takes effect two to four weeks later. A shift towards greater profitability should be felt by the end of the next quarter.
- *Resource requirements.* These will include: input from credit managers to refine the scheme and the communication strategy; IT services to set up the new commission-tracking tools; HR time to change specifications for the payroll service, to brief managers, and to address concerns and

complaints; finance tracking to ensure that the scheme is having the desired impact.
- *Decisions needed.* These will include: approval for the scheme; positioning the message; pilot or total roll-out of the scheme; allocation of IT, HR, and finance time.

Alliances and organizational support

For all business activities to be successful, managers need to work collaboratively with their colleagues. No manager works for long in isolation. Branch managers need data from the treasurer, technical support from IT, and logistics help from the operations department.

Since HR touches everyone in the organization, it is important for HR leaders to build relationships with as many of their colleagues as possible. HR needs to participate fully in general management and leadership committees, specialized committees, short-term project teams, and retreats and internal conferences. Through these activities, they keep in touch with business activities, make visible contributions to decisions and operations, hear managers' needs and concerns, and get involved in information and support networks.

A formal mechanism for creating organizational support for performance management activities is the HR council. It may also be known as the HR advisory board, the talent team, or the human capital committee. Regardless of its name, it has a few simple and important functions:

- point of input from the organization to HR about performance management needs and problems;
- sounding board for HR's proposals and ideas;
- championing by mid-level managers of performance management innovations such as in-house mentoring, changes in incentive schemes, or creative approaches to management development;
- additional resources for designing and implementing initiatives that relate to performance management, such as succession planning or retention.

Ideally, an HR council is commissioned by a senior business leader, who may also act as its nominal head. Day-to-day leadership needs to come jointly from a business manager and an HR professional. The agenda can be based on current strategic needs and people problems, or on a standing list of performance management topics, but in all cases it needs to be established jointly between the business and HR members of the group.

Communication with leaders and other constituencies

An organization is a political place. There are opportunities to have power, to gain status, and to achieve recognition. An HR leader cannot make the performance management system work effectively without finding ways to work within the existing political system. Therefore, while not resorting to becoming a scheming manipulator, an HR leader is wise to pursue the following course:

- Pay attention to what matters to your boss, to his or her boss, to the CEO, and to the leadership team. Link performance management needs to their goals. Use performance management activities to make their strategies successful.
- Get coaching from reliable sources on how to communicate and work with senior leaders whose support is needed to allow performance management to function, to succeed, and to evolve.
- Learn how to communicate with the people who have power and influence in ways that are understandable to them. Do not force them to learn HR jargon.
- Pick your battles. Be clear about which performance management principles and system components should not be compromised and which can be adapted, delayed, or put 'on the back burner'.

Communicate regularly in the formats, media, and language of the various constituencies to which HR is linked – the board, senior management, consultants, vendors, sources of recruits, media, and so on. Think carefully about the desired impact, from the point of view of the audience, the point of view of the CEO, and the point of view of the employees. Get help with shaping communications if that is not a natural gift.

Promote the institution's vision, mission, and values. Tie as much of the performance management system as possible to them, and use the appropriate language when you communicate.

Making changes

Every update, improvement, or new initiative in the performance management system is a change for the people using it – the managers and their staff – so following the principles of change management is essential for success. Sometimes it seems to members of the HR department that the improvement they have made or the new component of the system is so simple and so easy that it is almost foolish to make a fuss about it. This is an issue on which the HR council members can provide perspective – if they see it as a definite change, then it needs to be managed like a change.

The principles of change management, as discussed in John Kotter's book *Leading Change*, are as follows:

1. *Establish a sense of urgency or priority.* People become more willing to change what they do or how they think if the new tool or process will solve a problem that is important to them and/or will address a source of pain and difficulty they experience – an urgent or high-priority

situation. Sometimes it is necessary to conduct a public relations or sales campaign to help people see that there is a problem or source of pain.

2. *Create an alliance to guide and lead the change.* The group needs to include the right people – people who have credibility, positions of authority, and leadership skills. There needs to be time for this group to develop as a team and define a shared goal or vision for the change.
3. *Craft a vision for the change.* The vision needs to reflect a positive and compelling idea for the future.
4. *Communicate the vision for change.* It is not enough to make one announcement or have one discussion in a meeting. Changes, even simple changes, need to be communicated frequently, regularly, and in many different forums and media. They need to be outlined by senior executives; announced in the company newsletter; mentioned in every team, unit, and department meeting; brought up at almost every occasion for a talk or public appearance; and reviewed in dozens of individual conversations. As busy as most people are, it can take many times of hearing about something before they absorb the reality of the change, the reason for it, and their part in it.
5. *Make it possible for people to actually carry out the change.* The vision needs to be communicated to all affected employees, and it needs to make sense to them. Structures such as performance targets and reward schemes need to be aligned with the new direction. Train everybody. Communicate with and eventually confront managers who interfere with a necessary and agreed-upon change.
6. *Make sure there are short-term wins.* The sooner that people see some sign of success or beneficial impact, the faster momentum supporting the new initiative builds. Reward change agents, i.e. the people who took to the change promptly. Keep senior management informed and updated.
7. *Use the momentum and credibility of one initiative to promote the next one.*

Putting the principles into practice

Consider the introduction of a formal succession-planning process. With the help of senior leadership, possibly including board members, construct a 'story' about the dire business impact of losing a key person without any plan for a replacement. The key person might be a senior leader such as the CEO or the CFO, or it might be a technical expert upon whom many parts of the organization depend, such as a highly skilled IT person or a brilliant marketer. Starting with the HR council, talk up this story and get people thinking about what needs to be done to avoid the risk.

Work with the council, if it is seen as a group of credible, authoritative leaders, or create a succession task force just for this initiative. Give that group time to think through the issue and the possible approaches; this also allows the body to build trust and create a vision. Then come up with messages about the value of succession planning and how it relates to all the different groups in the organization.

Then, every member of the task force contributes to outlining the ways in which and the times when they are going to communicate about succession planning – what it is, how it is done, who does it, and why it is needed. The members of the task force need to stay in touch with each other to make sure the communication occurs, and they report when they start to hear others bringing up the topic on their own.

While the communication campaign is under way, the task force also examines the performance management system to make sure that all the necessary components are in place to support succession planning – the high-quality performance reports, the complete development planning, the training and development options, as well as a supply of internal and external people to be coaches and mentors to designated successors. They make sure that the people for whom successors will be identified are on-board with the idea and will not undermine it. If resources or incentives are needed to motivate managers to get involved in succession planning and develop identified successors, those schemes need to be formulated and put in place.

Pilot the succession-planning process with just one or two positions, both to work out the kinks in the process and to be able to communicate about its success and value. Consider starting with a position whose incumbent is likely to be highly cooperative and enthusiastic about having an identified successor. Then communicate, communicate, communicate – about what has happened, how it is unfolding, and the benefits experienced.

Conclusion

To be successful in managing business performance by effectively managing people's performance, an institution and all of its managers and human resource professionals need to balance day-to-day operational execution with an overall strategic perspective. Each routine performance management activity is ultimately in service to a strategic business objective, and each strategic initiative can only be successfully implemented if the full complement of performance management activities is in play. Managers and HR teams need to collaborate and exercise leadership to sustain the strategic relevance of ongoing performance management activities. For these reasons, the Handbook opens and closes with chapters on the strategic perspective.

That said, performance management also requires daily attention to high-quality execution and application of best practices, and the heart of the Handbook covers those domains in detail. Each organization's performance management system will be unique to its culture and environment, and must be suitable for its stage of development in the business life cycle, so the material in the operations chapters can be adapted as appropriate. Whatever shape the system takes, everyone involved, from employees to managers, will benefit to the extent that it is run with professionalism, commitment, and concern for the well-being of the business and of the people who work there.

Bibliography and further resources

Bibliography

Asia-Pacific Human Development Reports (2010) 'New report: Asia-Pacific has one of the world's worst gender gaps' [website], New York, NY, USA: United Nations Development Programme, <http://content.undp.org/go/newsroom/2010/march/asia-pacific-has-one-of-the-worlds-worst-gender-gaps.en> [accessed 4 January 2013].

Bagati, Deepali (2011) *2010 India Benchmarking Report*, New York, NY, USA: Catalyst.

Barsh, Joanna and Yee, Lareina (2011) 'Unlocking the full potential of women in the US Economy' [website], New York, NY, and San Francisco, CA, USA: McKinsey & Company, <www.mckinsey.com/client_service/organization/latest_thinking/unlocking_the_full_potential> [accessed 4 January 2013].

Center for Women and Business (2012) 'Center for Women & Business Forum on: Moving from conversation to action' [website], Waltham, MA, USA: Bentley University, <www.bentley.edu/events/cwb/conference-recap> [accessed 4 January 2013].

Chu, Kathy, and Ramstad, Evan (2012) 'Report: Women in Asia face barriers to top jobs' [website], *The Wall Street Journal*, <http://online.wsj.com/article/SB10001424052702303649504577499781983988886.html> [accessed 4 January 2013].

Commission for Gender Equality (no date) *Strategic Plan 2008–2013*, Johannesburg, South Africa: Commission for Gender Equality.

Damiano, Paula (2009) 'Advancing women in India' [website], Workingmother.com, <www.workingmother.com/advancement-of-women/2009/11/incredible-india> [accessed 4 January 2013].

Deblieux, Mike (2003) *Performance Appraisal Source Book: A collection of practical samples*, Alexandria, VA, USA: Society for Human Resource Management.

Department for International Development (2009) *Gender Equality Action Plan: Africa Division 2009–2012*, London, UK: Department for International Development, <http://collections.europarchive.org/tna/20100423085705/dfid.gov.uk/documents/publications/africa-gender-equality-action-plan.pdf> [accessed 4 January 2013].

Desvaux, Georges, Devillard-Hoellinger, Sandrine and Baumgarten, Pascal (2007) *Women Matter: Gender diversity, a corporate performance driver*, Paris, France: McKinsey & Company.

Desvaux, Georges and Devillard, Sandrine (2008) *Women Matter 2: Female leadership, a competitive edge for the future*, Paris, France: McKinsey & Company.

Desvaux, Georges, Devillard, Sandrine and Sancier-Sultan, Sandra (2010) *Women Matter 3: Women leaders, a competitive edge in and after the crisis*, Paris, France: McKinsey & Company.

http://dx.doi.org/10.3362/9781780447926.014

Desvaux, Georges, Devillard, Sandrine and Sancier-Sultan, Sandra (2010) *Women Matter 2010: Women at the top of corporations: Making it happen*, Paris, France: McKinsey & Company.

Doumbia, Saliha and Meurs, Dominique (2003) 'Gender equality at work in sub-Saharan Africa: a case study of Mali's modern sector', *International Labour Review* 142(3): 295–316.

Dziatkowiec, Paul (2012) 'East Africa: Gender equality is still lacking' [website], *AllAfrica.com* <http://allafrica.com/stories/201203110234.html> [accessed 4 January 2013].

Ernst & Young (no date) 'Unleashing the power of women entrepreneurs: Women in the workplace' [website], London, UK: Ernst & Young, <www.ey.com/GL/en/Industries/Government---Public-Sector/Women-in-the-workplace---Unleashing-the-power-of-women-entrepreneurs> [accessed 4 January 2013].

European Institute for Gender Equality (no date) 'Gender equality index' in 'Frequently asked questions' [website], Vilnius, Lithuania: EIGE, <www.eige.europa.eu/content/frequently-asked-questions> [accessed 17–20 July 2012].

European Institute for Gender Equality (2011) 'Good practices in gender mainstreaming. towards effective gender training – mainstreaming gender into the policies and the programmes of the institutions of European Union and EU member states' [website], Vilnius, Lithuania: EIGE, <http://eige.europa.eu/content/document/good-practices-in-gender-mainstreaming-towards-effective-gender-training>.

Gap, Inc. (no date) 'Social responsibility: Advancing women' [website], San Francisco, CA, USA: Gap Inc., <www.gapinc.com/content/csr/html/Goals/communityinvestment/advancing_women.html> [accessed 4 January 2013].

Gibson, Madge (no date) 'Women lagging in the workplace' [website], HR Future, <www.hrfuture.net/career-development/women-lagging-in-the-workplace.php?Itemid=157> [accessed 4 January 2013].

Grensing-Pophal, Lin (2010) *Human Resource Essentials: Your guide to starting and running the HR function*, 2nd edn, Alexandria, VA, USA: Society for Human Resource Management.

Grobler, Pieter A., Warnich, Surette, Carrell, Michael R., Elbert, Norbert F. and Hatfield, Robert D. (2010) *Human Resource Management in South Africa*, 4th edn, Andover, UK: Cengage Learning EMEA.

Johnson, Lauren Keller (ed.) (2006) *HR Magazine Guide to Managing People*, Alexandria, VA, USA: Society for Human Resource Management.

Kamoche, Ken, Yaw, Debrah, Horwitz, Frank, and Nkombo Muuka, Gerry (eds) (2003) *Managing Human Resources in Africa*, New York, NY, USA: Routledge.

Klasen, Stephan and Lamanna, Francesca (2008) *The Impact of Gender Inequality in Education and Employment on Economic Growth in Developing Countries: Updates and extensions*, EUDN/WP 2008–10, Namur, Belgium: European Development Research Network.

Lockwood, Nancy R. (2004a) *The Bottom Line: Connecting corporate performance and gender diversity*, New York, NY, USA: Catalyst.

Lockwood, Nancy R. (2004b) *Diversity Practices that Work: The American worker speaks*, New York, NY, USA: National Urban League.

Lockwood, Nancy R. (2005a) '2005 Research Quarterly – Workplace diversity: Leveraging the power of difference for competitive advantage' [website], Society for Human Resource Management, <www.shrm.org/research/articles/articles/pages/0605rquart_essay.aspx> [accessed 4 January 2013].

Lockwood, Nancy R. (2005b) 'Workplace diversity: Leveraging the power of difference for competitive advantage', in Society for Human Resource Management, *Human Resources in Research and Practice: The RQ reader,* pp. 53–61, Alexandria, VA, USA: Society for Human Resource Management.

McCall, Morgan W. (1998) *High Flyers: Developing the Next Generation of Leaders,* Boston, MA, Harvard Business School Press.

Messmer, Max (2007) *Human Resources Kit for Dummies,* Hoboken, NJ, USA: John Wiley & Sons, Inc.

Okali, Christine (2011) *Searching for new pathways towards achieving gender equity: Beyond Boserup and 'Women's role in economic development',* ESA Working Paper No. 11-09, New York, NY, USA: Agricultural Development Economics Division, Food and Agriculture Organization of the United Nations.

O'Mara, Julie (1994) 'Managing diversity', in William R. Tracey (ed.) *Human Resources Management & Development Handbook,* pp. 103–26, New York, NY, USA: AMACOM.

Omari, Kulthoum (2012) *Closing the Gender Equality Gap in Southern Africa,* Cape Town, South Africa: Heinrich Böll Foundation.

Rollo, James (2009) *Performance Management: A pocket guide for employee development,* 2nd edn, Salem, NH, USA: Goal/QPC.

Rudrappa, Sharmila (2005) *Women in a Global Workforce,* Austin, TX, USA: Center for Women's and Gender Studies, University of Texas at Austin.

Sabattini, Laura and Carter, Nancy M. (2012) 'Expanding work–life perspectives: Talent management in Asia' [website], New York, NY, USA: Catalyst. <www.catalyst.org/knowledge/expanding-work-life-perspectives-talent-management-asia-0> [accessed 4 January 2013].

Shellenbarger, Sue (2012) 'The XX factor: What's holding women back?' [website], *The Wall Street Journal,* <http://online.wsj.com/article/SB10001424052702304746604577381953238775784.html> [accessed 4 January 2013].

Society for Human Resource Management (2007) *HR Magazine Guide to Managing People,* Alexandria, VA, USA: Society for Human Resource Management.

Society for Human Resource Management (2011) *Human Resources in Research and Practice: The RQ reader,* Alexandria, VA, USA: Society for Human Resource Management.

Texas Wall Street Women (no date) 'Board Brief: Why gender diversity matters' [website], Texas Wall Street Women, <www.txwsw.com/pdf/board_brief.pdf> [accessed 4 January 2013].

United Nations Department of Public Information (2010) 'Goal 3: Promote gender equality and empower women', 2015 Millennium Development Goals Fact Sheet – DPI/2650 C, New York, NY, USA: UN Department of Public Information, <www.docstoc.com/docs/93937488/Promote-Gender-Equality-and-Empower-Women> [accessed 4 January 2013].

United Nations Development Programme (no date) 'UNDP and gender in Africa', Fast Facts fact sheet, New York, NY, USA: UN Development Programme, <www.sl.undp.org/1_doc/fast_fact_genderafrica.pdf> [accessed 4 January 2013].

United Nations Economic and Social Council (no date) 'Gender equality and empower women: MDG 3' [website], New York, NY, USA: United Nations, <www.un.org/en/ecosoc/about/mdg3> [accessed 4 January 2013].

Verité (2009) *Advancing Women's Rights and Social Responsibility: Capacity building in Mexico*, Amherst, MA, USA: Verité.

Wikipedia (no date) 'Gender inequality' [website], <http://en.wikipedia.org/wiki/Gender_inequality> [accessed 4 January 2013].

World Vision (no date) 'Gender' [website], Federal Way, WA, USA: World Vision, Inc., <www.worldvision.org/content.nsf/learn/ways-we-help-gender?Open&lpos=bot_txt_Gender> [accessed 4 January 2013].

Additional online resources

Websites/communities

Africa Human Resources – online resource, newsletter, membership organization, postings on conferences and training: http://africahr.ning.com/

CiteHR – online HR professionals resource: www.citehr.com

Human Resources IQ – www.humanresourcesiq.com

Professional groups – on social media and websites such as LinkedIn, Facebook, and Twitter

Society for Human Resource Management – www.shrm.org

World Federation of People Management Associations – www.wfpma.com

Digital journals

HR Future: Human Strategy For Business – www.hrfuture.net

Human Resources Management the Journal – www.hrmthejournal.com

The SA Journal of Human Resource Management – www.sajhrm.co.za

Online newsletters

Workforce – online newsletter: www.workforce.com

Workinfo.com: Human Resources for Today's Workplace – www.workinfo.com

About Small Business Banking Network

Small Business Banking Network (SBBN), a CapitalPlus Exchange initiative, is a global industry-building initiative and community platform that exists to expand the capacity, competency, and willingness of financial institutions to serve small and growing businesses – *the* engine of income and job creation in developing economies. SBBN works to accelerate the success of financial institutions that target underserved entrepreneurs by providing high-quality operational and strategic services, peer learning opportunities, and access to best practices and industry initiatives. This powerful combination of reinforcing services dramatically increases the scale, profitability, and development impact of the financial institutions that we serve.

This publication is part of a partnership between The MasterCard Foundation and CapitalPlus Exchange.

The MasterCard Foundation